P9-DMI-403

RELIGIOUS FREEDOM

AND THE CONSTITUTION

RELIGIOUS FREEDOM
AND THE CONSTITUTION

Christopher L. Eisgruber

Lawrence G. Sager

HARVARD UNIVERSITY PRESS

Cambridge, Massachusetts, and London, England

8/24/10
Lan
$18.95

Copyright © 2007 by the President and Fellows of Harvard College

All rights reserved

Printed in the United States of America

First Harvard University Press paperback edition, 2010

Library of Congress Cataloging-in-Publication Data

Eisgruber, Christopher L.
Religious freedom and the constitution /
by Christopher L. Eisgruber and Lawrence G. Sager.
p. cm.
Includes bibliographical references and index.
ISBN 978-0-674-02305-5 (cloth : alk. paper)
ISBN 978-0-674-04582-8 (pbk.)
1. Freedom of religion—United States. 2. Church and state—United States.
3. United States. Constitution. 1st Amendment. I. Sager, Lawrence G. II. Title.
KF4783.E355 2007
342.7308'52—dc22
2007043487

For our children,

Danny

and

Jessica, Emily, Matthew, Jemma, and Mariah

Contents

Acknowledgments

This book is the culmination of a collaboration that began more than a decade ago when we were colleagues at the New York University School of Law. We wrote the book while serving on the faculties of NYU, the University of Texas School of Law, and Princeton University's Woodrow Wilson School and University Center for Human Values. Those institutions provided us with intellectual environments as welcoming and generative as any scholar could desire; we are grateful to the many colleagues who read drafts and supplied comments. We also benefited from our membership in a broader academic community, one that extends not only beyond the gates of our home institutions but beyond this country's borders. The suggestions we received from friends and critics far and wide improved the manuscript immeasurably, and we thank them. We owe more specific debts to four people who helped shepherd the manuscript to completion: our editor, Michael Aronson; Sachin Panda, who provided extensive comments on the entire manuscript; and two readers for the Press, Michael Dorf and Andrew Koppelman. Finally, we wish to express our appreciation to our families, who patiently allowed us the precious hours needed to bring this long project to completion.

RELIGIOUS FREEDOM

AND THE CONSTITUTION

Introduction

MEMBERS OF THE HUMAN species have a poor record of living together in peace and an even worse record of treating one another fairly. Religious differences have often been the cause or at least the excuse for our most egregious failures. Even today, religious disagreement underwrites violence, disfavor, and discord in many parts of the world.

America's founders knew the perils of religious difference all too well. The Europe that the early settlers left behind was racked with religious conflict and persecution; indeed, many who came to America were victims of it. The colonists had a deep awareness of questions concerning religious liberty, and they self-consciously pursued the appropriate resolution of those questions. Before Thomas Jefferson and James Madison turned their hands to the Declaration of Independence and the Constitution, for example, they worked together to defend religious freedom in Virginia.[1]

The framers of the Constitution set themselves—and we as their heirs—against religious persecution and intolerance. The Constitution and Bill of Rights are remarkable twice over in this respect. First, they conspicuously avoid a single reference to God.[2] And second, spare as these founding documents are, they make room for three separate commitments to religious freedom: prohibitions on the free exercise of religion are declared unconstitutional; so too are laws respecting the establishment of religion and laws requiring religious oaths as a condition of public office.[3] No other element of justice receives such lavish treatment in the Constitution.

We have not always lived up to the ideal of religious freedom that is so firmly embedded in the Constitution. Americans at various times and in various places have found themselves excluded from jobs, schools, and neighborhoods because of their religious beliefs. While we have avoided religious wars like those that plagued Europe, there have been ugly episodes of religiously inspired violence. Turmoil over Mormon polygamy in the late 1800s sometimes turned vicious and bloody.[4] The Ku Klux Klan's campaign of hate and violence was directed against Jews and Catholics as well as African-Americans. Jehovah's Witnesses, including children, were beaten because they refused to salute the flag.

Over time, we have made considerable progress. In many settings, religious hatred has given way to distaste, distaste to acceptance, and acceptance to welcome. Americans appear to have transcended the worst of their religious prejudices. The nation that could not forget or forgive the fact that Al Smith was Catholic loved John Fitzgerald Kennedy; and the nation that once tolerated quotas for Jews in its most distinguished medical schools nearly elected Al Gore president on the strength of his energetically Jewish running mate, Joseph Lieberman. Remarkably, even in the wake of the 9/11 attacks by Islamic terrorists, few American politicians expressed intolerance toward Muslims; on the contrary, President George W. Bush went to a mosque to embrace an imam and praised citizens who had aided American "women of cover."[5]

The law has done its part. A web of state and federal statutes prohibits schools, employers, and public officials from discriminating on the basis of religion. Obscure and vulnerable faiths have enjoyed the protection of the Constitution. In 1993, for example, a unanimous Supreme Court—acting at the behest of members of the Santerian faith—struck down a ban on the ritual sacrifice of animals.[6] It would have been difficult to imagine such a ruling on behalf of so widely reviled a practice even two decades earlier, but the Court's decision passed without prominent notice or objection.

If we stop just here, there seems good reason to celebrate the success of America's great constitutional experiment with religious freedom: we are a remarkably religious country; we are home to an astonishing range of diverse faiths; our laws, policies, and dispositions are highly solicitous of minority religious viewpoints. If we look no further, there is a good case to be made that we are a religiously diverse people who have set ourselves to the task of finding fair terms of cooperation and have achieved a salutary degree of success.

But few if any are inclined to celebrate. Americans find themselves in angry confrontations over a growing number of issues involving matters of religious faith. They clash about faith-based social services and public financing of religious schools; they fight over holiday displays, Ten Commandments monuments, the use of the word "God" in the Pledge of Allegiance, and school-sponsored prayers at football games. Disputes about the teaching of evolution, creationism, and "intelligent design" have grown more and more intense. Religious divisions are vividly present in controversies over abortion, gay rights, euthanasia, and stem-cell research.

Americans are in troubled disagreement more generally about the interplay of religion, politics, and law. Some worry that America is in danger of becoming, in law professor Stephen Carter's words, a "culture of disbelief,"[7] and they lay at least part of the blame at the feet of the Supreme Court. Others contend that America is experiencing a new and dangerous mixture of religion and politics. Thus journalist Ron Suskind, writing about George W. Bush in the *New York Times*

Sunday Magazine, opined that Bush has created a "faith-based presidency." Suskind accused Bush of departing from the vision of America's founders, who, "smarting still from the punitive pieties of Europe's state religions, were adamant about erecting a wall between organized religion and political authority."[8]

Disagreement over complex questions about which people care deeply is inevitable and, in many cases, healthy. But the mood in American public life just now with regard to those questions that lie at the intersection of religion, politics, and law does not bespeak wholesome disagreement.

In all, there is a growing sense that, despite our remarkable success in pursuing religious freedom, we are giving up on the project that lies at the heart of that success. We seem on the brink of abandoning our commitment to find and follow fair terms of cooperation for a religiously diverse people. Religion has become a charged token in a politics of division, and America's commitment to religious freedom is in danger of being submerged beneath angry contestation.

Our foremost goal in this book is to return to the project of religious freedom, the project of finding fair terms of cooperation for a religiously diverse people. We do so by offering what we believe is an attractive, fair, and workable framework for approaching and resolving contemporary disagreements about how government should treat religious practices and institutions. Our approach is guided by two basic principles. First, no members of our political community ought to be devalued on account of the spiritual foundations of their important commitments and projects. And second, all members of our political community ought to enjoy rights of free speech, personal autonomy, associative freedom, and private property that, while neither uniquely relevant to religion nor defined in terms of religion, will allow a broad range of religious beliefs and practices to flourish. Like the framers of the Constitution, we are concerned with both liberty and equality, and we call the approach that results from these joined concerns "Equal Liberty."

These guiding principles should seem both familiar and immediately attractive, for equality and liberty are bedrock principles of American constitutional law. Though our argument is ethical rather than historical, we believe that Equal Liberty can claim a venerable constitutional pedigree. Moreover, we often find these principles at work in landmark judicial opinions, though sometimes veiled by tangled doctrinal tests and obscure theoretical formulations.

Equal Liberty may strike some as not only familiar but banal—after all, who could object to equality and liberty? But many popular views of religious freedom are pointedly at odds with the dictates of equality. Some people contend that religion has distinctive virtues that entitle it to special constitutional status. They say, for example, that religious obligations are more important or valuable to individuals than any others, or that God's commands (and God's commands alone) must trump the law, or that religion is uniquely generative of civic virtue. People who hold views of this sort often go on to argue that churches and religious practices should enjoy a unique immunity from otherwise valid laws, including tax and land use regulations. On the other hand, some people regard religion as especially threatening to the civic order; they claim, for example, that religion is uniquely divisive, or that religious conduct may be especially difficult for individuals and governments to control. People who see religion in this light often want to protect the public order by subjecting religion to special disabilities. A prominent version of this tendency is the view that it is unconstitutional for government funds to flow to religious institutions, even when comparably situated secular institutions are receiving identical forms of public support.

Remarkably, the dominant way of thinking about religious freedom in the United States insists *both* that the Constitution should confer special benefits like regulatory immunity on religious practice *and* that the Constitution should impose special disabilities on that practice, like starving it of any public support. The dominant approach centers on a single metaphor, "the separation of church and state,"[9] and from that metaphor extrapolates principles that alternately direct that religion be treated much better or much worse than other important human projects.

Equal Liberty, in contrast, denies that religion is a constitutional anomaly, a category of human experience that demands special benefits and/or necessitates special restrictions. It insists that, aside from our deep concern with equality, we have no reason to confer special constitutional privileges or to impose special constitutional disabilities upon religion. This puts Equal Liberty in sharp disagreement with the separation-based approach to religious freedom.

Though the word "separation" appears nowhere in the Constitution's religion clauses, most Americans seem to accept "separation of church and state" as shorthand for the appropriate constitutional treatment of religion, and that phrase is almost certainly known to more Americans than is the constitutional text itself. The phrase is so familiar that it is easy to overlook just how odd and puzzling the idea of separation is.

The notion of literally separating the modern state and the modern church is implausible in the extreme. Churches buy and sell property, build buildings, run schools, maintain staffs of paid employees, need roads for access, and are vulnerable to the same risks of fire and theft as every other entity. Church members drive cars, pay taxes, interact in countless ways with their fellow citizens, and vote in public elections. The state, for its part, maintains the regime of private law upon which contract and property rights depend, promulgates building codes, regulates the use of land, protects its citizens from unfair and discriminatory employment practices, builds roads, and acts as the default provider of police and fire protection.

This is only a partial list, merely suggestive of the numerous ways in which the enterprises of the state and the enterprises of the church are bound to intersect with and affect each other. But the point should be clear. Church and state are not separate in the United States, and they cannot possibly be separate. The question is not *whether* the state should be permitted to affect religion or religion permitted to affect the state; the question is *how* they should be permitted to affect each other. The metaphor of separation is of no help in addressing the numerous modern controversies that fall under that question. Indeed, as we shall see, the metaphor has, if anything, deflected Americans from the core project of religious freedom, the project of finding fair terms of cooperation for ourselves as a religiously diverse people. The same is true of the more general idea that religion is a constitutional anomaly requiring special and distinctive treatment.

To be sure, a commitment to "separation" includes one unambiguous and constructive proposition: unlike some countries—England is an example—we have no national church. But no one believes that we should have an official "Church of the United States" or, for that matter, a "Church of Texas" or a "Church of New Jersey." At its best, the separation metaphor has also served as a marker for a related but more general and more useful principle—namely the idea that no particular denomination or sect ought to be the special favorite of the state. That is an equality-based premise, consistent with the principles of Equal Liberty. For much of American history, the problems of religious freedom grew out of battles among denominations seeking to exercise power over one another. We believe that the staying power of the separation metaphor within American constitutional discourse resulted partly from its ability to serve as a proxy for the basic idea that the government ought not to play favorites in these denominational and sectarian competitions.

In recent decades, however, denominational rivalries have diminished, and religious interest groups have increasingly transcended sectarian boundaries. Public controversies over religion have tended to occur both within and across denominations, reflecting splits between believers who are (the terminology itself is controversial, so take your pick) more orthodox and less orthodox, more fundamentalist and less fundamentalist, conservative and liberal, or more secular and less secular.[10] (Pundits like to characterize the divisions as pitting religious persons against secular ones, but we think that is a misleading description; the vast majority of Americans regard themselves as religious, and most American disputes over religious freedom feature competition between different forms of religiosity, not a simple conflict between those who are religious and those who are not.)

As religious boundaries and alliances have changed, so too has the nature of the conflicts that involve religious freedom. Increasingly, modern controversies involving church and state have exposed the deficiencies of the separation metaphor. And they have proven to be severe.

Consider the diverse controversies that have arisen around faith-based social services. Some issues relate to claims for exemptions from regulations that would apply to secular providers. For example, churches in Washington, D.C., Richmond, Virginia, and Daytona, Florida, have claimed immunity from land use regulations that prohibit the operation of soup kitchens in residential neighborhoods. Another set of questions has to do with whether and when the government may subsidize church-run charities. Such questions have been lightning rods of political controversy during the presidency of George W. Bush, who created a White House office to promote partnerships between the government and faith-based social service organizations.[11] Many commentators—on both sides of the issue—reacted as though the president's proposal were entirely novel, a new chink in the "wall of separation between church and state." In fact, though, the government has long been the primary funding agency for church-run charities in the United States.[12]

Political and legal debate about faith-based social services has been dominated by the questions of whether and how we should treat religion as a constitutional anomaly. When exemptions are at issue, the claim for special treatment has been that faith-based enterprises should be constitutionally immune from laws that others must observe. When subsidies are at issue, the claim for special treatment has been that faith-based charities and other religious programs should be constitutionally ineligible to share in public funds that are available to their secular counterparts. Some people endorse both of these views, some endorse only one, and others endorse neither. This matrix of positions has created a strange landscape of disagreement in which all the available options are unsatisfactory: either we must treat religion far better and/or far worse than other important human enterprises, or we must treat it as a constitutional orphan. Missing from public discussion has been the idea that the Constitution expresses special concern for religion because and to the extent that religious difference inspires inequality in stature and reward, and accordingly, that the Constitution's fundamental religion-specific goal is that of opposing discrimination. The result has been, we think, an unappealing mixture of instability, confusion, and discord, producing tumultuous argument everywhere—in newspapers and on television, in courtrooms, and in legislative chambers at the national, state, and municipal levels.

In Richmond, Virginia, for example, a brouhaha erupted when a consortium of six churches wanted to operate a Sunday afternoon meal program for homeless people at the First English Evangelical Lutheran Church. The church was located in a historically significant and restrictively zoned residential neighborhood known as the Fan District,[13] and the meal program was inconsistent with applicable zoning restrictions. The consortium's members took the position that they had a religiously mandated mission to feed the poor, and that restrictions on the place, manner, or time of their efforts to discharge that mission were unconstitutional infringements on religious freedom. (We served as legal consultants to the city during part of this dispute, and so watched events unfold.)

What ensued was a political battle that lasted more than a year. The *Richmond Times Dispatch* ran a series of editorials criticizing the consortium. "No one quarrels with the church performing its God-given mission to minister to those in need," wrote the editors. "The issue is whether it should perform its good deeds in a location more convenient to the homeless, amenable to local ordinances, and agreeable to the church's neighbors—to whom it also has a responsibility to show charity."[14] City officials tried to shape a compromise that would allow the consortium to host some meals, subject to restrictions on the frequency of service and the number of persons served. But the offer of compromise seemed, if anything, only to fuel the fire. According to the *Times Dispatch,* "members of the . . . City Council were threatened with everything from hellfire to lawsuits" at the meeting when they passed the compromise arrangement.[15] Eventually the city relented and gave the churches more or less unfettered freedom to feed the hungry.[16]

Stories like Richmond's are becoming increasingly common. In the past decade, several such controversies have made their way into the courts, with the churches prevailing on some occasions and losing on others. In 2000 Congress tried to tilt the playing field on behalf of churches. The Religious Land Use and Institutionalized Persons Act (RLUIPA) enables churches to challenge in state or federal court any zoning regulation that substantially burdens their religious conduct. Under George W. Bush, the Justice Department has named a "special counsel for religious discrimination"; and the counsel, Eric Treene, has made RLUIPA a priority of the department.[17]

People will have different reactions to the events in Richmond. Some will sympathize with First English, others with the church's neighbors in the Fan District; most, whatever their view of the dispute, will probably admire the church's passion for aiding the poor. For present purposes, our interest is in the moral and constitutional character of the claim made by the church. The church contended that the state's power to regulate religiously motivated conduct is drastically limited. Only when the state has an extraordinary need is it entitled to get in the way of persons responding to the calls of their religion; such persons, in effect, have a presumptive constitutional right to disobey the laws that everyone else is required to follow. Claims of this kind are commonly made by litigants (and sometimes, though much more rarely, upheld by judges) in cases about the Constitution's Free Exercise Clause, which articulates the right of believers to practice their faith unimpeded by inappropriate legal requirements or burdens.

There are good reasons to be wary of the claim that the Free Exercise Clause should be read to give religiously motivated persons a presumptive right to disobey the law. Prominent among these is that it seems at war with the very idea of religious freedom. To see how, consider a favorite hypothetical of ours, one that plays off of the facts of the Richmond dispute. Suppose that two women live across the street from each other in the Fan District, that both happen to have the surname "Campbell," and that both Ms. Campbells want to open soup kitchens to feed the homeless. As we know, zoning restrictions applicable to the Fan District ban both of these parallel projects. Now, suppose that one of our Ms. Campbells is responding to her understanding of the demands of her religious faith; the other is merely responding to her great abhorrence of human suffering. If religiously motivated persons enjoy a unique prerogative to disobey the law, the first Ms. Campbell has a constitutional right to ignore the zoning ordinance while the second Ms. Campbell must obey the ordinance. The rights of the two Ms. Campbells, in other words, would vary according to the spiritual foundations of their beliefs. This result seems unjust on its face, and it also seems at odds with the essence of religious freedom in that it imposes a test of religious orthodoxy as a condition of constitutional entitlement.

There are other, blunter problems with the idea that religiously motivated conduct should be presumptively immune from regulation. For example, such immunity will usually come at the expense of other legitimate public values and purposes. Thus the *Richmond Times Dispatch* pointed out that the freedom of the churches to serve the homeless population in whatever way they chose might compromise the freedom of neighboring homeowners to pursue their own life projects, such as raising children in quiet and safe surroundings.[18] The variety of possible conflicts is as vast as the variety of religious obligations in America—which is to say, about as vast as one can imagine. Even mainstream religious beliefs may be at loggerheads with core constitutional values. For example, some religious service providers have contended that their religious convictions require them to engage in otherwise unlawful discrimination when hiring employees, and that they should enjoy a special immunity from antidiscrimination regulations even if they accept large amounts of taxpayer money to provide public services. An ongoing dispute of this kind involves the Salvation Army. Several employees and former employees of the Army have sued it; for example, Margaret Geissman, a former human resources manager at the New York division of the Army, alleged that it sought information about the religious convictions and sexual orientation of employees so that it could discriminate against them.[19] The Bush administration intervened in the case on the Army's behalf, claiming that religious organizations should have the right to discriminate in their hiring practices, even when they are disbursing public funds.[20]

Because the idea of a special immunity from laws that everyone is obliged to obey is so anomalous, and so potentially disruptive of legitimate public purposes, most people who have been tempted to embrace it—and, especially, most judges—have been anxious to limit its application to relatively innocuous cases in which the harm to third parties is minor. Many would not, for example, extend this immunity from valid legal restraints so far as to countenance exemptions from antidiscrimination laws. As a result, the claimed immunity for religiously motivated conduct, which in principle sounds arrestingly bold, often turns out to be remarkably timid in practice. One might regard this as merely a problem with the scope of the immunity—and people have tried to explain it that way—but we believe that it is best understood as a consequence of fundamental problems that beset the entire idea of a special immunity for religiously motivated conduct. We have already glimpsed those problems, and we will have more to say about them in the pages ahead; we regard them as decisive reasons for rejecting the idea in its entirety.

But to deny that religious projects are entitled to a unique constitutional immunity from otherwise valid laws is not to deny that such endeavors are entitled to robust constitutional protection. To the contrary, Equal Liberty depends on the proposition that religiously motivated conduct deserves meaningful constitutional protection, and it provides an equality-based test to effectuate that protection. The idea, in brief, is that minority religious practices, needs, and interests must be as well and as favorably accommodated by government as are more familiar and mainstream interests.

So, obviously, Equal Liberty entails that if Richmond accommodates a secularly motivated Ms. Campbell, then it is constitutionally obliged to accommodate her religiously motivated neighbor, too. But Equal Liberty demands considerably more than this. If, for example, Richmond specified exemptions to its zoning laws to accommodate other kinds of personal needs and commitments—such as physical handicaps, special financial hardships, educational interests, or expressive needs—then judges and other officials would have a constitutional responsibility to ensure that religious commitments were receiving equal regard. If Richmond's zoning scheme provided for individualized exemptions procedures—as it in fact does, and as every other land use plan in America likewise does—then courts would have a constitutional responsibility to devise review mechanisms to limit the risk that the zoning board might treat religious needs badly when deciding upon applications for variances and so forth. In the absence of a convincing equality-based claim, however, churches would have no constitutional entitlement to an exemption from valid land use regulations.

Once we realize that religious enterprises are entitled to robust constitutional protection against discrimination but not to the improbable privilege of disobeying otherwise valid laws, we have a sound and attractive approach to questions like those that arose in Richmond. We also have an explanation for why a pale form of the idea of such a special privilege has sometimes seemed appealing: privileges that may appear special are appealing and justifiable when and only when they function as proxies for the requirement of equal treatment.

Consider, for example, the first case in which the Supreme Court pursued the idea of a unique constitutional privilege for religiously motivated conduct. That 1963 case involved Adell Sherbert, a Seventh-Day Adventist who lived in South Carolina and was fired from her job because she refused to work on Saturday, which was her Sabbath day. When she applied for unemployment insurance benefits, a South Carolina board found that she lacked "good cause" for her refusal to work on Saturdays and therefore was not entitled to unemployment benefits. The Supreme Court held the denial of benefits to Ms. Sherbert to be a violation of the Free Exercise Clause. At one point in its opinion, the Court endorsed the broad principle that, absent extreme circumstances, the state had to accommodate Adell Sherbert's desire to engage in religiously motivated conduct.[21] Hence Sherbert's case became precedent for the idea that religious conduct is uniquely and specially entitled to a constitutional exemption from generally applicable laws.

But the Court also underscored a much more compelling feature of the case. Adell Sherbert and other Saturday observers were the victims of drastically unequal treatment. South Carolina law prevented employers from ever insisting that their employees work on Sundays; so only Saturday observers could be denied unemployment benefits because of their insistence on respecting the Sabbath as dictated by their faith.[22] This inequality moved Justice Brennan to bring his opinion for the Court to a ringing conclusion: "This holding but reaffirms a principle that we announced a decade and a half ago, namely that no State may 'exclude individual Catholics, Lutherans, Mohammedans, Baptists, Jews, Methodists, Non-believers, Presbyterians, or the members of any other faith, because of their faith, or lack of it, from receiving the benefits of public welfare legislation.'"[23] In our view, equality was what was really at stake in Adell Sherbert's case, and equality was what lent appeal to the proposition that religion enjoyed some sort of unique presumption of immunity to otherwise applicable regulation.

We will have much more to say about the question of exemptions from otherwise valid laws, but the spine of our argument should now be visible. In free exercise cases, the idea of a unique immunity for religious conduct offers polar outcomes and seems to insist that the Constitution choose between being "for" or "against" religion itself. Either religiously motivated persons get an extraordinary privilege to disobey laws that everyone else is obliged to follow, or they get no help from the Constitution at all. As a practical matter, the idea of separation has deflected attention from the project of finding fair terms of cooperation for a religiously diverse people, and encouraged a confrontational and extreme political discourse for which the facts on the ground offer no warrant.

Equal Liberty, in contrast, sees concerns of fairness as lying at the very heart of free exercise exemption controversies. What is critical from the vantage of Equal Liberty is that no members of our political community be disadvantaged in the pursuit of their important commitments and projects on account of the spiritual foundations of those commitments and projects. Part of our project in the pages that follow will be to see how this approach to free exercise cases works in practice.

We believe that an equality-based approach to free exercise is fair and workable, and is likely in the end to protect religious believers more effectively than the awkward idea that religiously motivated conduct should be presumptively exempt from legal regulation. Defending that belief is the burden of the chapters that follow. For now, we emphasize that Equal Liberty encourages reflection of the right sort about our common project of religious freedom—reflection, that is, about arrangements that are fair to us all, in the face of our acknowledged and prized religious diversity.

We have similar ambitions for Equal Liberty with regard to disputes about the Establishment Clause, which deals with government support for religion. As we noted earlier, the state has been in the business of funding religious charities for longer than most people realize, and state-funded religious charities exhibit varying levels of religiosity. Some are avowedly secular in content. For example, the Grace Church Community Center in White Plains, New York, is one of Westchester County's largest nonprofit social service centers. It has received grants from the county, state, and federal governments. In 2003 the Reverend Janet Vincent, who chaired the center's board of directors, characterized its mission this way: "We are certainly nonsectarian when it comes to offering services and we don't do any proselytizing, but the impetuses for offering the services came out of this congregation."[24] Michele Peavey, the manager of the state-financed Lutheran Home for Children in Jersey City, New Jersey, described the relationship between the secular and religious elements of her charity rather differently. "We want these children to understand that this is a religious program," she told a reporter. The children must attend church or Mass or mosque on the Sabbath, and they are taught to recite a nondenominational grace before meals.[25]

Other publicly financed programs have prompted lawsuits and allegations of discrimination. Iowa, Kansas, Minnesota, and Texas have contracted with InnerChange, a prison program run by Charles Colson that uses strong Christian religious content in an effort to rehabilitate prisoners. Participation is voluntary, but, according to a suit filed by Americans United for Separation of Church and State, prisoners who agree to participate receive privileges not available to others.[26]

Public debate about these cases characteristically has been framed by the idea that religion is a special category requiring unique constitutional treatment. That idea tends to minimize the important differences among the Grace Church Community Center, the Lutheran Home for Children, Iowa's Prisoner Rehabilitation Program, and the Salvation Army program. On one view—the "strict separation" view—all these programs involve unconstitutional public subsidies of religious activity. Another view—the "accommodationist" view—maintains that the separationists exaggerate the dangers of church-state partnerships and that churches should be allowed to share in public programs with as few strings attached as possible, so that the public square can benefit from the virtues of religiously motivated teaching and charity.

The conflict between the separationist and accommodationist views is abstract and sweeping—too abstract and too sweeping. Indeed, each of these two views promises to resolve not only every controversy about faith-based social services, but a host of others that involve (depending on your perspective) government "support" for religion or government "accommodation" of religion within the public realm—controversies about, for example, tuition vouchers for private religious education, crèche displays in the town square, prayers at public school football games, and the reference to God in the Pledge of Allegiance. In popular constitutional argument today, these practices are usually assumed to stand or fall together, along with the Grace Church Community Center and the Lutheran Home for Children—the single question in all the cases being, in colloquial terms, "how high the wall of separation should be."

This separation-inspired approach to Establishment Clause questions is the mirror image of the separation-inspired approach to the Free Exercise Clause questions about special exemptions for religiously motivated conduct. They form an odd couple. Both insist that religion is an anomaly, requiring exotic constitutional treatment different from anything else. Yet in free exercise cases, the idea of special immunities demands that religious believers be given an extraordinary benefit enjoyed by no one else; in Establishment Clause cases, the idea of separation insists that religion and religion alone be starved of public benefits available to everyone else. A surprising number of people embrace both ideas. The result is a curious position that requires government both to grant religion special privileges and to impose upon it special restrictions—so that, for example, the government must provide wealthy property-owning churches with exemptions not enjoyed by other landholders, but the government cannot allow poor churches to share in nondiscriminatory subsidy programs that benefit other charitable providers.

Arguments about "how high the wall of separation should be," in Establishment Clause social services cases, like arguments about the scope of special privileges for religious conduct, have generated a predictably unsatisfactory rubric for discussing religious freedom. Questions about the "height of the wall" inevitably push public debate in grand, speculative, and ideological directions. After all, how are citizens supposed to decide how much separation is constitutionally obligatory? They might appeal to history and argue about how Jefferson, Madison, and other framers conceived of church-state relations. But the historical record is notoriously indeterminate and unclear about such questions, and the historical debate inevitably becomes a proxy for, or simply gives way to, the argument that is now so familiar in the United States: an argument about how much public religion is good for society. And that question is both profoundly speculative and intensely divisive.

Equal Liberty recommends a different inquiry—in fact several different inquiries. Equal Liberty insists that no member of the community ought to be devalued on account of the spiritual foundations of his or her basic commitments. This equality principle applies to the government's treatment of both the recipients and the providers of social services. It, unlike the abstract question about whether government support for religion is a good thing, pushes us to review the details of the various programs we have described. One might take various approaches to reviewing those details. One might demand only that the text of the relevant statutes and regulations be formally neutral, neither preferring nor dispreferring religion. Alternatively, one might pay a great deal of attention to how the programs work in practice. For example, did Iowa's prisoners have an opportunity to choose among multiple rehabilitation programs, some of which were secular? Does it matter that the children arriving at the Lutheran Home had no real choice about where they were sent? Do the programs that fund the Home for Children, the Grace Church Community Center, and other church-run charities benefit religious providers disproportionately? These are the sorts of questions that Equal Liberty directs us to ask when assessing the constitutionality of public support for faith-based social services—questions not about the goodness of religion in general or about its optimal role in public life, but rather about the distributional fairness of particular social service programs.

In cases involving religious displays and exercises—such as school prayer, crèche displays, the "under God" language of the Pledge of Allegiance—Equal Liberty's underlying concern remains the same; it insists on equal status for people with diverse spiritual views. But while that concern in social service cases translates into the requirement that government distribute its resources fairly, it assumes a different form when government sponsorship of religious symbols is at issue. People who object to public rituals or displays that have religious content typically express another kind of equality-based concern: they worry that by sponsoring religious displays or ceremonies, the government affiliates itself with or endorses a particular theological perspective and implicitly disparages other ones. Where that feeling is well justified, the government has failed to respect the requirements of Equal Liberty. How should we determine whether the feeling is well justified? We will argue that the answer to this question depends on what we will call the "social meaning" of the contested ritual or display, and further, that the cultural characteristics of religious belief and allegiance in America make the risk of disparagement high when government sponsors displays or rituals with religious content.

Equal Liberty thus provides ways for both proponents and opponents of faith-based social services and publicly sponsored religious displays to reframe their arguments as claims about what constitute fair public arrangements in a community of religiously diverse persons. It invites them to reconfigure their claims, so that they focus not on the historical pedigree of the separation concept, or on grand ideological questions about the value of religion, but upon the distributional characteristics of a subsidy plan (in the case of tuition vouchers) and the cultural significance of religious symbols (in the case of crèches). There is no natural coupling between these questions: one's answer to the question about cultural significance in no way determines or prejudices one's answer to the question about distributive characteristics. One might accordingly uphold the constitutionality of religious displays but not the constitutionality of faith-based social services, or vice versa. Equal Liberty thus calls for rethinking linkages that appear inevitable under the regime of separation, which suggests that one ought either to favor or to oppose government involvement with religion in general, be it through symbols or through dollars.

Our hope is that Equal Liberty, by focusing attention on equality and removing it from imponderable questions about the goodness of religion, can reduce the partisanship and confusion that now plague America's public argument about religious freedom. We do not mean to suggest that Equal Liberty will be uncontroversial among Americans. There are undoubtedly people in the United States who believe that you cannot be fully American unless you believe in God, or go to church regularly, or are a Christian, and so on. They will undoubtedly reject some of what we say in this book—and the more qualified their commitment to equality, the more of the book they will reject. But it is a sign of America's progress in the domain of religious freedom that most Americans prefer to defend their views on grounds that assume or are at least consistent with the equal status of all believers and non-believers, rather than on the ground that some subset of believers should enjoy a preferred constitutional status. For that reason, we hope and believe that the basic principles of Equal Liberty will provide an attractive starting point for resolving the issues about religion that divide Americans.

Separation and Its Cousins

A FEW YEARS AGO a television producer asked us to participate in a debate about whether it was desirable to "lower the wall of separation" between church and state. She needed somebody to argue in favor of "lowering the wall." Was that our position? We did not know what to say. In our view, the Supreme Court had been too restrictive of government voucher plans but too willing to permit publicly sponsored holiday displays. "Oh, that's perfect," the producer replied. "You think that the wall should be *lowered* but not *destroyed*." But that was not at all what we believed. If forced to speak in terms of a "wall," we believed that it should be *raised* in some places and *lowered* in others. Or that it should have holes in it. Or, since most people attribute the metaphor to Thomas Jefferson, that the wall should be *serpentine,* snaking around to separate some things (such as crèche displays and prayer rituals) but not others (such as tuition payments at private religious schools) from government influence and sponsorship.

Rather than push these strained metaphors, we declined the producer's invitation. What we really believed, and what we continue to believe, is that metaphors and slogans about "walls" and "separation" can never provide a sensible conceptual apparatus for the analysis of religious liberty. Churches—to say nothing of religion in general—can never be wholly separated from the state. Churches own property, employ workers, run childcare centers, broadcast television programs, and interact with the secular world in a myriad of other ways. They espouse doctrines and exhort actions that thrust clerics and believers into the political arena—sometimes for better and sometimes for worse. The question that matters is *how* church and state should mix, not *whether* they will do so.

Still, we were not surprised that the television producer wanted speakers to argue about "lowering" or "raising" the "wall of separation." The wall metaphor dominates American thinking about religious liberty. Historian Philip Hamburger observes that "Jefferson's phrase . . . provides the label with which vast numbers of Americans refer to their religious freedom. In the minds of many, his words have even displaced those of the U.S. Constitution, which, by contrast, seem neither so apt nor so clear."[1] The appeal of the metaphor is easy to understand. It captures a basic institutional difference between the United States and countries such as Great Britain and Iran that recognize an official national church or faith. It also crisply expresses two different ideals associated with religious freedom—first, that individuals and churches should be free to pursue their theological convictions and practices without undue interference from the state; and, second, that citizens and public officials should be able to conduct politics without inappropriate interventions by religious institutions and groups. In this double sense, the sphere of church-related activities should be "separate" from the state and its legitimate concerns.

That said, the crucial questions are about which state actions amount to "undue interference," what kinds of religious behavior might constitute an "inappropriate intervention," and what kinds of objectives are "legitimate concerns" of the state. The separation metaphor does nothing to answer these questions.

In an effort to make sense of the idea of separation and its wall, judges and scholars have typically begun their analysis with the idea that religion should be treated as beyond the reach of the state. From this idea of leaving religion alone, it follows that government should neither benefit religion nor interfere with it. If government either aids or hinders religious organizations, persons, or practices, then it has breached the "wall of separation" and violated the Constitution. At first, this sounds fine. Above all, the "neither aid nor hinder" formulation appears evenhanded: by definition, it seems neither to favor religion nor to disfavor it. Perhaps for that reason, the doctrine has attracted many adherents, including, as we shall see, some who share our doubts about the separation metaphor.

Yet, the "neither aid nor hinder" formula is deeply problematic, demanding treatment of religion that is anything but equal. On the one hand, government routinely aids many important projects and commitments of its citizens—why else would we want government? But if we take the "no aid" principle seriously, religious projects and commitments must be deprived of the aid that these other endeavors receive. On the other hand, government routinely burdens its citizens with regulations and exactions deemed important for the improvement of the overall good. But if we take the "no hindrance" half of the separation-inspired formula seriously, religious projects and commitments must be exempt from the burdens of democratic membership that the rest of us routinely bear. As a result, what the separation metaphor has led to is a strange view of religious liberty pursuant to which religion is on some occasions treated much more favorably than other important human projects and commitments, and on other occasions is treated much less favorably. This strange pattern of anything-but-equal treatment shows just how wrong reasoning by metaphor can go.

Why should religion elicit this strange, two-faced constitutional response? We might think that religion is distinctly valuable, in which case we would want to favor it; or that it is distinctly dangerous, in which case we would want to disfavor it. Perhaps we could think that it is both—in which case we might favor its good aspects and disfavor its bad ones. The "neither aid nor hinder" doctrine takes none of these positions. It assumes instead that there is some natural but precarious equilibrium state for religion, and that the government does great harm if it disturbs that state in any direction. But we do not take that attitude toward other fundamental human activities that the state nurtures, regulates, and curtails in any variety of ways. And we do not really believe that religion is best left alone in this way: we do not believe, for example, that churches should be denied police and fire protection, or that religiously inspired men should have a special prerogative to abuse their wives or children. Why should we take guidance from the view that religion and religion alone is best isolated from contact with the state?

Not only is it hard to justify the "no aid" and "no hindrance" rules; it is also often difficult to know which one should apply in a given case. The no-aid/no-hindrance approach assumes that there is a sharp and recognizable difference between policies that remove a burden and those that provide a benefit; that difference, after all, marks the dividing line between actions that are constitutionally *obligatory* and those that are constitutionally *impermissible*. But the distinction between removing a burden and conferring a benefit is vanishingly thin, if not purely semantic. Nowhere else in constitutional law does so much turn on so little.

For example, in the early 1980s St. Bartholomew's, an Episcopal church in Manhattan, wanted to tear down its terraced, seven-story Community House, located adjacent to the main church building, and build a forty-plus-story office tower. Church officials planned to rent most of the space in the tower to generate money for church projects. But the Community House had been officially designated a historic landmark, so New York's preservation statute barred the project. The church claimed that the statute unconstitutionally burdened its religious practices. The church accordingly maintained that the "no hindrance" rule entitled it to an exemption.[2]

Yet preservationists have invoked the "no aid" rule to argue for exactly the opposite conclusion. Lawmakers in some states, including California and Illinois, have allowed churches to exempt themselves from landmark restrictions.[3] Critics of those exemptions have challenged them on the ground that they amount to inappropriate state "aid" for religion. In their eyes, the exemptions give churches a valuable benefit—freedom from burdensome land use restrictions—that every property holder would like to have. From this vantage, what St. Bartholomew's was asking for was an extraordinary and special benefit, measured by the economic value of being exempt from the land use restrictions that would otherwise apply to it.

The same exemption can thus appear to be either the removal of a constitutionally impermissible "hindrance" or the creation of a constitutionally impermissible "aid." It all depends upon how one looks at it—or, perhaps, upon *who* looks at it.

At least one of these views has to be wrong. An exemption cannot be simultaneously *constitutionally obligatory* and *constitutionally impermissible* (both views might be wrong—the state might have discretion about whether to include special accommodations for churches in its land use laws—but at least one *must* be wrong). How should we decide? It depends upon what counts as "aiding" or "hindering" religion. Or, more precisely, it depends upon what sorts of aids and hindrances are *undue* or *inappropriate*. Neither the separation metaphor nor the doctrines derived from it provide us with any clue about how to think about that issue.

The cases we have been considering thus far are severe but not unique. Indeed, the "neither aid nor hinder" doctrine generates problems in even the simplest cases. For example, American fire departments protect churches along with other propertyholders. That is a valuable kind of government aid—but as we have already noted, nobody thinks that the Constitution prohibits the government from extinguishing fires at churches. So, to be precise, proponents of the separation model would have to say that government should never "unduly" or "inappropriately" aid religion. But then we are back where we started, since the separation idea provides no principle for determining what kinds of aid are "undue" or "inappropriate."

In the last decade or so, several prominent scholars have criticized the separation idea. They have emphasized, as we have done, that government and religion cannot be separate—they will inevitably interact in many ways. Unfortunately, most of these scholars have tried to replace separation with other concepts that preserve its core thesis—that government should in some sense leave religion untouched, whether for better or for worse. As a result, their theories are at bottom close cousins of separation, and as a result they exhibit the same defects.

One popular theory insists that the goal of the religion clauses is what Douglas Laycock calls "substantive neutrality." According to Laycock, substantive neutrality demands that religion "should proceed as unaffected by government as possible."[4] Judge Michael McConnell contends, to like effect, that government action should aim to replicate "the hypothetical world in which individuals make decisions about religion on the basis of their own religious conscience, without the influence of government."[5] Proponents of substantive neutrality suppose that it provides a way to make sense of the "no aid" and "no hindrance" doctrines. In their view, government unduly benefits religion if it makes religion better off than it would be "without the influence of government," and, conversely, it inappropriately burdens religion if it makes religion worse off than it would otherwise be.

As it happens, Laycock and McConnell think that leaving religion as unaffected as possible by the state means that religiously motivated persons get a presumptive right to disobey otherwise valid laws, but they do not think that this means that religious enterprises must be starved of public funds. But this distinction in outcome between their views and other versions of the separation model is just a function of what they stipulate that it means for religion to be "unaffected." In fact, as Laycock himself has observed, the conceptual structure of their views is remarkably similar to that of separation,[6] and, in our view, that structure suffers from precisely the same difficulties.

The idea that government should leave religious choice "unaffected" makes no more sense than the idea that government and religion should be "separate." After all, what could it mean for religion to "proceed as unaffected by government as possible"? Absent government, churches could not count upon police forces and civil courts to protect their property. Nor could minority believers count upon government to protect them from persecution by members of other faiths. What would churches do in such circumstances? It seems unlikely that they would build expensive office towers, as St. Bart's wanted to do; military watchtowers to protect their members and property are more likely. Perhaps they would run collective farms, since labor would be cheap and food would be in short supply. Or perhaps they would simply collapse; we suspect, with Hobbes, that in the absence of government, life for churches and believers, along with everyone else, would be "nasty, brutish, and short."[7]

The fact is that government inevitably, and quite desirably, influences choices about religion. It provides security, resources, and stability without which many forms of religious faith would be resoundingly difficult, if not impossible, to pursue. It inculcates and enforces principles of morality—such as the principle that persons enjoy equal status regardless of their race, faith, or sex, or the principle that speech should be free—that are more congenial to some religions than to others. It is sensible, we think, to demand that government not affect religious choices out of hostility or insensitivity to the value of religious practice. But it is neither attractive nor coherent to demand that either religion or choices about religion be "unaffected" by government.

One suspects that Laycock, McConnell, and other proponents of "substantive neutrality" do not really mean what they say, which is that religious choices should be unaffected by government. They must mean instead that it is acceptable for religious choices to be affected by some policies—such as the laws protecting private property, enforcing civil order, preventing religious discrimination, and, perhaps, many more—but not by others. The real question is not whether government should affect religious choices but *how* it should do so, just as the real question is not whether government should be wholly separate from religion, but *how* the two should interact. And the idea of substantive neutrality does not answer that question any better than the separation metaphor does. On the contrary, substantive neutrality would seem to lead to the same two odd and competing obligations—to treat religion both better *and* worse than other interests—and no discernible standard by which to harmonize them. That Laycock and McConnell substantially soften the starve-religion-of-public-funds side of neutrality is a function of their stipulated view of how things should come out, not a natural consequence of substantive neutrality.

The effort to treat religion better *and* worse than other interests has generated indefensibly inequitable results and created intractable problems for courts. And how could it be otherwise? The "no aid" and "no hindrance" doctrines are a surefire recipe for inconsistency. These norms cut in opposite directions, and in some cases spectacularly collide. Moreover, the premise that religiously motivated persons enjoy a presumptive right to disobey the law, and the diametrically opposed premise that religious enterprises must be starved of public funds, are *each* so unattractive on their face that judges have strained to find grounds—however arbitrary—to avoid the implications of both. The result has been a crazy quilt of special privileges and restrictions that seem ad hoc at best and incoherent at worst. In addition to being internally inconsistent, the jurisprudence of religious liberty is at odds with other major constitutional doctrines. Its insistence upon treating religious viewpoints both better and worse than other viewpoints has collided repeatedly with other doctrines—especially those of free speech and equal protection, both of which join our natural intuitions in demanding a norm of equal treatment.

"No Aid"

The "no aid" principle was in trouble from the very beginning. The Supreme Court's first major Establishment Clause decision was *Everson v. Board of Education* (1947).[8] *Everson* dealt with a New Jersey statute that authorized local school districts to compensate parents for the cost of sending their children to school by public transportation; private schools, including religious schools, were included in the program.[9] Ewing Township's board of education created such a program; in practice, the only private school students who actually benefited from Ewing's subsidy were enrolled in Catholic schools.[10] A local citizen sued, contending that the New Jersey statute and Ewing's program amounted to an unconstitutional establishment of religion.[11] The case was intensely controversial. At the time, many Protestants viewed Catholic schools as a threat to American values; Catholics, on the other hand, regarded their schools as essential to their way of life. As a result, the case generated great emotion and captured national attention.[12]

Justice Hugo Black, writing on behalf of the Court, quoted Jefferson and waxed eloquent on the theme of an impenetrable wall separating church and state. The fact that the transportation program undeniably aided religious schools, Black observed, brought the program to the "verge" of unconstitutionality.[13] With that beginning, one would imagine that Justice Black and the Court for which he wrote were plainly headed to the conclusion that it was unconstitutional for government to subsidize the transportation of parochial school students.

But Justice Black was troubled. In a sense, he noted, what was being complained of was the evenhandedness of the New Jersey program: the benign benefit of school transportation was being made available to all students, including those attending a religious school. Moreover, Jefferson's wall of separation notwithstanding, it was perfectly clear that not all government benefits to religious projects were unconstitutional; after all, no one thought that making police and fire department services available to churches was unconstitutional. And Justice Black was concerned by one other thing: the Court had held that the Constitution gave parents the right to send their children to private schools, including religious schools; it would be strange if the Constitution *insisted* that government penalize any parent who exercised that right by denying benefits like public transportation.[14]

All this made good sense, and in the end it persuaded Justice Black and the Court for which he wrote to reject the claim that a program that made public transportation available to all students violated the Constitution. Justice Black and the Court should have realized what the *Everson* case so vividly demonstrated: the separation metaphor was a very bad source of constitutional judgment. Instead Black struggled to find a way of making the school transportation program fit the separation metaphor. The question, he announced, was whether the government was pursuing secular goals that provided religion with incidental benefits, or whether it was aiding religion directly. He concluded that the New Jersey program was in the former category rather than the latter: its true objective was to provide students with safe transportation, not to provide them with a religious education.[15] Hence it was akin to providing churches with fire protection rather than to providing a direct subsidy.

Of course, it made little sense to ask whether New Jersey's subsidy paid for transportation or aided religion. It obviously did both. The real question in *Everson*—and in every Establishment Clause case that followed it—was not whether religion had been aided, but whether it had been aided in impermissible fashion. The clumsy metaphor of "separation" obscured rather than clarified that question.

What began badly in *Everson* grew worse. For several decades the Supreme Court continued to pursue the hopeless quest of the *Everson* Court: it tried to figure out which government programs "really" subsidized secular goods (such as transportation) and which ones "really" aided religion. Since the honest answer in every Establishment Clause case was that the program did both, the inquiry was jurisprudential quicksand. The justices' struggles only sank them deeper into the muck. They held, for example, that government could permissibly provide secular textbooks, but not maps, to religious schools; textbooks, apparently, were like transportation, but maps were too much like direct aid (Senator Daniel Patrick Moynihan wondered what the Court would say about atlases, which are books of maps).[16]

An especially dizzying pair of cases dealt with tax benefits for educational expenses. In one case, the Court held that it was unconstitutional for states to provide tax *credits* to parents of children attending religious schools, even if those credits were also available to parents of children attending secular private schools.[17] About a decade later, the Court held that it was permissible for states to provide such parents with tax *deductions* for their children's educational expenses, so long as the state also made those deductions formally available to parents who sent their children to public schools.[18]

The Court also drew a sharp distinction between subsidies and tax exemptions. In *Walz v. Tax Commission* (1970), the Court upheld a New York law that provided religious organizations a property tax exemption for land used solely for religious purposes. In the eyes of the Court, tax exemptions did not provide a benefit; they removed a burden.[19] Hence they were permissible.

The resulting hodgepodge of decisions prohibited New York City from using federal funds to send public school teachers onto religious schools' premises to provide remedial reading lessons,[20] but permitted the state to award valuable tax benefits to churches owning millions of dollars of property. In other words, poor churches could not share in nondiscriminatory public benefit plans (such benefits would amount to government "aid" for religion), but wealthy churches could get a tax break (that was simply the removal of a burden). Arguably, under the "no hindrance" and "no aid" combination, the rich got richer—by constitutional mandate.

By the mid-1980s the Court's jurisprudence had become so incoherent that when new lawyers studied for the bar exam, they were taught that state benefits to religious secondary schools were constitutionally permissible only if they took the form of something beginning with a "T"—transportation, textbooks, tax exemptions, tax deductions, and tuna fish. "Tuna fish" was a proxy for school lunches. The mnemonic was thus both artificial and untidy (woe to the student who confused tax credits with tax deductions, or who included "tuition" in the "T" list!), but it was the best that teachers could do with jumbled cases so bereft of any principled foundation.

This rickety jurisprudential edifice might eventually have collapsed of its own weight, but it was helped along by collisions with other, more stable doctrines. Beginning in 1981, the Supreme Court considered a series of free speech cases in which religious groups demanded equal access to venues and resources available to other groups. The free speech doctrine about such matters is clear: if the government makes a forum available to private groups, it cannot discriminate among them on the basis of viewpoint.[21] So, for example, if a university allows the student chapter of the Democratic Party to use its meeting rooms free of charge, then it must extend the same benefit to the Campus Republicans—or, for that matter, the Society of Young Communists.

The point of this free speech doctrine is to prevent government from using its resources to censor unpopular viewpoints. The rule occasionally generates hard questions—about, for example, whether the government can exclude speakers who advocate violence or who disparage particular students or groups of students. In general, though, the rule works well, and most people find it attractive. Yet the equality norm at the doctrine's core fits uncomfortably with *Everson*'s "no aid" idea, which suggests that government *must* treat religious viewpoints *worse* than others if equal treatment would benefit religion.

Public universities and schools often responded to *Everson*'s shadow by denying access and funding to religious groups and speakers, even while favoring secular groups with precisely those benefits. They did so in the name of avoiding the strictures of the Establishment Clause. Religious groups chafed under the inequity of these arrangements and began to turn to the courts, contending that their free speech rights had been violated.

The first such case to reach the Supreme Court was *Widmar v. Vincent,* decided in 1981. The University of Missouri had refused to permit a student religious group to meet anywhere on its grounds, even though it permitted nonreligious student groups to use its classrooms and other facilities. By an eight-to-one vote, the Supreme Court sided with the student group against the university. The justices concluded that free speech principles controlled: Missouri had an obligation to treat religious speech and nonreligious speech *equally,* and the Establishment Clause would not be violated by such evenhanded treatment.[22]

Widmar could not fully dispel the confusion generated by the intersection of free speech norms, which required *equal treatment* for religious viewpoints, and the *Everson* doctrine, which compelled *worse treatment* when government benefits were at stake. More than a decade after *Widmar,* the Supreme Court decided a similar case, *Lamb's Chapel v. Center Moriches Union Free School District* (1993). *Lamb's Chapel* addressed a Long Island school district's policy that made classrooms available in the evenings to community groups wanting to use them for social, civic, and recreational purposes—but not religious ones. As in *Widmar,* the school thought that its policy was required by the "separation of church and state": because public schools and churches should be separate from one another, religious groups could not meet on school property. A federal appellate court upheld the school's policy. The Supreme Court reversed. This time the opinion was unanimous; Justice White, the lone dissenter in *Widmar,* wrote for the Court, holding that free speech norms required equal treatment. It was impermissible to treat religious viewpoints better *or* worse than nonreligious ones; if all nonreligious groups had access to the classrooms, then so too should religious groups.[23]

Widmar and its progeny, decided under the Free Speech Clause, said that government had to treat religion equally when awarding groups access to meeting sites. By contrast, the Court's Establishment Clause cases about aid for parochial education required the government to radically disadvantage religion when distributing money. These outcomes created an odd division of prescriptive labor: access to facilities was governed by free speech principles, and hence was subject to the requirement that religious groups receive access on equal terms; funding, however, was controlled by the Establishment Clause, and hence was subject to the clashing requirement that religious groups be denied funds that were available to nonreligious groups.

This strange state of affairs was arbitrary and unstable. One of these two opposing lines of cases had to give way. The collision came in *Rosenberger v. Rector and Visitors of the University of Virginia* (1995).[24] Before *Rosenberger,* the policy of the University of Virginia was to provide financial support for a wide range of student groups but not to fund groups engaged in "religious activity." "Religious activity" was defined as any activity that "primarily promotes or manifests a particular belie[f] in or about a deity or an ultimate reality."[25] A religious student group, publishers of a newspaper titled *Wide Awake,* sued, demanding funding on equal terms. The university defended its policy as an effort to implement the "no aid" policy of the Establishment Clause.[26] In effect, *Rosenberger* was *Widmar* all over again, except that now the issue was about access to money rather than access to rooms. Ultimately it was the Establishment Clause/funding line of cases that yielded.

Rosenberger split the Court. Five justices thought that *Rosenberger* was a free speech case governed by the doctrine of *Widmar.* In an opinion written by Justice Kennedy, they held that the university's policy was unconstitutional because it violated the equality principles inherent in the Free Speech Clause: the University of Virginia had a constitutional obligation to treat religion equally with other viewpoints.[27] Four dissenters, in an opinion authored by Justice Souter, disagreed sharply with the majority. They argued that money was different from speech, so that *Everson's* "no aid" principle controlled *Rosenberger*. In Souter's view, providing university dollars to *Wide Awake* would involve using "public funds for the direct subsidization of preaching the word."[28] The disagreement between the majority and the dissenters could hardly have been more extreme: the majority thought that Virginia was not only permitted but indeed constitutionally obliged to subsidize religious viewpoints along with other viewpoints, whereas the dissenters believed that Virginia was constitutionally prohibited from doing so.

Meanwhile the "no aid" doctrine was coming under fire in another domain dominated by equality norms. State and federal agencies offered a variety of programs to ensure equality of opportunity for Americans with disabilities. Special scholarships were provided, and some recipients wanted to use those scholarships in religious programs. For example, the State of Washington subsidized vocational rehabilitation for blind people. Larry Witters wanted to use his benefits to prepare for a career in the ministry. Likewise James Zobrest, a student in Tucson, Arizona, invoked the federal Individuals with Disabilities Education Act in order to request funds to pay for a sign-language interpreter at his Catholic high school. In both cases, public officials refused to provide the benefits. The officials thought that they were only doing what the Supreme Court had instructed them to do—ensuring that "no aid" flowed to religious interests or institutions. In both cases, the Supreme Court disagreed.[29] If the state's policy promoted the secular goal of equal opportunity for persons with disabilities, the state could facilitate religious opportunities along with other ones. So long as benefits flowed to religions only through private choices by individual beneficiaries, there was no Establishment Clause problem.

The free speech and equal opportunity lines of decision put tremendous pressure on some of the Court's "no aid" precedents. Most vulnerable was the Court's 1985 decision in *Aguilar v. Felton*, which prohibited New York City from sending remedial reading teachers into religious schools to help disadvantaged students. In an especially literal application of the separation model, the Court said that if New York wanted to provide remedial instruction to parochial school students, it had to do so outside the school building on a "neutral site"—such as a trailer parked by the school playground.[30] The Court's later decisions in *Zobrest* and *Rosenberger* made this conclusion seem very odd. If it was possible for the state to send sign-language interpreters into religious schools, and if it was possible (indeed, obligatory) to allow religious groups access to a student activities fund, then why not allow disadvantaged students at religious schools equal access to remedial education?

This logic proved irresistible to the New York City Board of Education, which, at the time *Rosenberger* was decided in 1995, was still laboring under a consent decree issued a decade earlier in *Aguilar*. By invoking an unusual procedural device, the city managed to return *Aguilar* to the Supreme Court in 1997, this time under the name *Agostini v. Felton*. Five justices voted to overrule *Aguilar*. Justice O'Connor, writing for the Court, contended that the 1986 decision in *Aguilar* had forced New York City to "spend millions of dollars on mobile instructional units and leased sites when it could instead be spending that money to give economically disadvantaged children a better chance of success in life by means of a program that is perfectly consistent with the Establishment Clause." Her opinion applied an equality paradigm rather than *Aguilar*'s "no aid" rule: so long as aid was made available to all children needing assistance, it did not matter that some children, by consequence of their parents' private choices, received that aid at religious schools. The four justices who dissented in *Rosenberger* did so again in *Agostini* and renewed their insistence upon the "no aid" rule.[31]

Rosenberger, Agostini, and their predecessors were important cases; but a more explosive issue loomed on the horizon. There was growing political support for voucher plans that would allow parents to use public dollars to purchase private school education, including religious education, for their children. Under *Everson*'s "no aid" rule, vouchers were the classic example of an unconstitutional state program: they used state dollars to subsidize religious education. The majority opinions in *Rosenberger* and *Agostini* suggested, however, that the Court—or at least a five-justice majority—might be ready to abandon the "no aid" rule and hold that vouchers were permissible so long as they were allocated to parents on the basis of criteria that did not favor religion over nonreligion. The issue remained in doubt for five years, until June 2002, when the Court finally upheld a tuition voucher plan in *Zelman v. Simmons-Harris*.[32] The Court split five to four, as it had done in *Agostini* and *Rosenberger*. The majority upheld the constitutionality of the voucher plan, reasoning that public dollars reached religious institutions only as the result of private, uncoerced choices by parents. The crooked wall erected in *Everson* thus seemed to have crumbled at last. Since *Zelman,* state dollars may flow even to core aspects of religious education, so long as they do so through a state program that serves valid secular purposes and does not discriminate on the basis of religion.

Later, in Chapter 6, we will examine *Zelman* and the voucher issue in more detail. We regard the *Zelman* rule as imperfect but nonetheless a considerable improvement upon *Everson*. For the moment, though, our purpose is only to emphasize the incoherence of the separation paradigm. The "separation" and "no aid" concepts provide no basis upon which to defend *or* to criticize *Zelman* and its predecessors. Separation simply makes no sense: because many Americans are religious, church and state inevitably intersect.

For example, the modern state seeks to accommodate the needs of handicapped persons; many handicapped persons are religious, and hence they may want to use state aid for religious purposes. If the state allows handicapped persons to do so, the state will, in effect, benefit religion—yet not one justice was willing to regard such aid as an unconstitutional establishment of religion. Or, to take another example, the modern state provides meeting rooms to private groups;

some groups are religious, and hence they will want to use the rooms for religious purposes. If the state allows them to do so, the state will, in effect, aid religion—yet in the Long Island public school case, all nine justices agreed that such aid was not only permissible but, indeed, constitutionally mandatory when the state opened its rooms to a wide range of nonreligious groups.[33]

Of course, if the Establishment Clause means anything at all, it means that some subsidies to religion will indeed be unconstitutional. But the idea of a "wall of separation between church and state" tells us absolutely nothing about how to identify those subsidies. By insisting that "no aid" is permissible, it gives us no way to tell *which* aid is permissible—it gives us no way, in other words, to tell the difference between uncontroversial forms of aid, such as those in *Witters* and *Lamb's Chapel,* and other, unconstitutional benefits to religion.

Indeed, although the Supreme Court decisions in *Witters* and *Lamb's Chapel* were unanimous, both decisions reversed judgments by other appellate courts. The Washington State Supreme Court and the U.S. Court of Appeals for the Second Circuit had held that the Establishment Clause prohibited states from allowing religious groups equal access to public benefits. Those courts thought that they were following the instructions of the Supreme Court—only to find themselves reversed unanimously on appeal. The Washington State and Second Circuit judges were not stupid. On the contrary, their confusion was the inevitable by-product of a "no aid" rule that was incoherent, inconsistent with the basic equality norms that dominated other domains of constitutional law, and hence impossible to apply.

"No Hindrance"

The "no hindrance" rule has generated a legacy of conflict and confusion in free exercise cases that matches or surpasses the wreckage wrought by "no aid" in Establishment Clause jurisprudence. For several decades, the Court sought to implement the "no hindrance" principle by holding that any government policy burdening religious practice was unconstitutional unless justified by a "compelling state interest," thus giving religiously motivated persons a presumptive right to violate otherwise valid laws. The Court announced this doctrine in 1963, when it decided *Sherbert v. Verner,* the unemployment benefits case that we encountered in the Introduction.[34] South Carolina denied unemployment benefits to Adell Sherbert, a Seventh-Day Adventist who quit her job rather than work on Saturday, her Sabbath. To be eligible for benefits, one must have "good cause" for turning down available work. In the state's view, Sherbert lacked "good cause" because she could have kept her job if she had been willing to work on Saturday.

Justice Brennan wrote the opinion of the Court in *Sherbert v. Verner,* and he pointed out that South Carolina law flagrantly discriminated against those who observed their Sabbath on Saturday. South Carolina prohibited employers from firing workers who refused to "work on Sunday on account of conscientious . . . objections," but it provided no comparable protections to those whose Sabbath fell on other days. Had Sherbert been a member of the majority faith, she would never have been forced to choose between her job and her religious commitments. This discrimination surely sufficed to render South Carolina's treatment of Sherbert unconstitutional, but Brennan eventually analyzed the constitutional question by asking whether any "compelling state interest . . . justifies the substantial infringement of [Sherbert's] First Amendment right."[35]

The compelling state interest test has long had talismanic significance in American constitutional law. Traditionally, its invocation signaled that the Court intended to subject the government's policy to the highest possible level of constitutional scrutiny. Very few interests qualified as "compelling"—"national security" was the rare example of one that did. In a famous law review article, Gerald Gunther described the compelling state interest test as "strict in theory but fatal in fact."[36] Some justices—most notably Justice O'Connor in two opinions about affirmative action—have recently developed a softer, more flexible version of the test.[37] But for many years the call for a compelling state interest created a strong presumption of unconstitutionality. In most of the domains where the test applied, that presumption made perfect sense. For example, policies that discriminated against racial minorities were subject to the compelling state interest test. There was virtually no good justification for such policies, and so it seemed sensible to presume them unconstitutional.

Given that South Carolina discriminated against those who worshiped on Saturday, it would have been possible to see Justice Brennan's use of the compelling state interest test in *Sherbert* as analogous to its role in race-discrimination cases: if states discriminate against religious minorities, their policies ought to be treated with the same suspicion accorded to racial discrimination—that is, they ought to be presumed unconstitutional and stricken unless they meet the nearly unattainable standards of the compelling state interest test. Brennan's opinion was, however, ambiguous. Subsequent courts and commentators interpreted it as a robust statement of the "no hindrance" principle: anytime government substantially burdened religious exercise or practice—whether or not it discriminated against religion or against religious minorities—its policy was subject to the compelling state interest test.

So understood, the compelling state interest test was wildly impractical. Laws burdening religious practice are both commonplace and inevitable. For example, zoning laws affect the freedom of churches to erect new buildings, expand their parking lots, and conduct business operations that might fund their charitable projects. It makes little sense to presume that every such law is unconstitutional (if we did, almost none would survive the rigors of the compelling state interest test: zoning laws are indispensable to good government, but the interests behind them are almost never sufficiently pressing or extraordinary to qualify as "compelling"). Moreover, religious practices in the United States are so diverse, and so pervasive, that nearly any law may burden somebody's religious exercise. Thus religious persons have demanded exemptions from laws that require photos on their drivers' licenses, laws that require employers to pay a minimum wage, and laws that require separated parents to pay child support for their children.[38]

Not surprisingly, courts, while paying lip service to the *Sherbert* case and its compelling state interest test in free exercise cases, in practice shied away from this radical prescription. Confronted with the prospect of presuming ordinary laws unconstitutional, courts either diluted or evaded the test. Sometimes they inflated government interests to make them seem compelling. For example, in *United States v. Lee* (1982), an Amish carpenter and his employees sought to opt out of the social security system on the ground that they believed it was "sinful not to provide for their own elderly and needy and therefore [we]re religiously opposed to the national social security system." The Court denied the claim on the basis that the government had a compelling interest in sustaining a viable scheme of social insurance.[39] Undoubtedly it does, but, as Justice Stevens pointed out in a concurring opinion, the system was unlikely to be threatened by the exemption sought by the Amish—indeed, since they were low-wage workers and wanted to opt out of benefits as well as taxes, allowing them to do so might actually have saved the government money.[40] The Court's rationale thus had to rest on administrative problems that might arise if other groups demanded exemptions—a good enough reason, perhaps, to deny the benefits, but not one that would have satisfied the compelling state interest test in any other domain of law.

On other occasions the Court somewhat disingenuously declared that a challenged policy had not burdened religious exercise at all, despite the mistaken impressions of the believers themselves. The Court took that route, for example, in a case involving a nonprofit religious organization, the Tony and Susan Alamo Foundation, whose members worked for the organization in exchange for food, shelter, clothing, transportation, and medical benefits. The government sued the foundation for failure to comply with minimum wage laws; the foundation defended on the ground that its workers had religious objections to receiving cash wages for their work. The Court rejected this argument, saying that it would not really violate the workers' beliefs to receive higher wages, since they would be free to donate them to the foundation.[41] A defensible result, we think—but not for the reasons the Court gave. From the perspective of a secular accountant, it might make little difference whether workers never receive wages or instead receive and return them; but from a religious believer's viewpoint, controlling the cash might be wholly impermissible.

In other cases the Court simply created ad hoc exceptions to the compelling state interest test. When the army fired a Jewish psychologist for wearing a yarmulke with his uniform, the Court said the compelling state interest test did not apply to the military. When the Interior Department elected to run a Forest Service road through a Native American burial ground on federal land, the Court said the compelling state interest test did not apply to government decisions about how to use its own property. When Muslim prison inmates complained that the warden no longer allowed them to attend certain worship services, the Court said the test did not apply to the treatment of prisoners.[42]

And so it went. As the cases piled up, it became clear that winning a free exercise exemptions case was extremely difficult. Elsewhere, the compelling state interest test was "strict in theory but fatal in fact"; in religious liberty cases, it was strict in theory but feeble in fact.

In the Supreme Court, free exercise claimants won only four times after *Sherbert*. Three of the cases were near-clones of *Sherbert* itself— cases in which claimants were denied unemployment benefits because they refused work on religious grounds.[43] The fourth involved Amish parents who successfully sought exemption from a state law requiring that all children attend school until age sixteen; the Amish won their right to pull their children from school at age fourteen.[44] Everybody else lost. Matters were equally bleak in the federal courts of appeal, where free exercise claims were consistent losers.[45]

The "no hindrance" doctrine, like its "no aid" counterpart, was both internally inconsistent and at odds with other, fundamental constitutional doctrines—most notably, again, with free speech jurisprudence. The "no hindrance" rule insisted that religious perspectives should sometimes be treated *better* than other perspectives: religious interests must be exempt from burdens the state could legitimately impose upon other interests. By contrast, free speech doctrine insists upon *equal* treatment for diverse perspectives. Suppose, then, that a state applies a general sales tax to books and magazines along with clothing, appliances, and most other goods. Are religious publications eligible for, or perhaps even entitled to, an exemption? The "no hindrance" rule suggests that the answer is yes—religion has a unique constitutional claim to be freed from burdens and hindrances. But free speech doctrine points in the opposite direction: the state must not prefer religious viewpoints over nonreligious ones. So which is it?

The Supreme Court confronted exactly that question in *Texas Monthly v. Bullock* (1989). Texas had exempted religious magazines and books from its sales tax. The publishers of the *Texas Monthly*, a secular publication, challenged the law, contending that its preference for religious speech violated the Free Speech Clause. The case fractured the Supreme Court, which produced four separate opinions. Nevertheless, a majority of the justices held that it was unconstitutional to prefer religious publications.[46] Thus when the "no hindrance" doctrine collided with free speech norms, it met the same fate as did the "no aid" rule: the muddled, impractical idea of treating religion both better and worse collapsed upon contact with the clear, consistent equality principles of free speech jurisprudence.

In 1990 five justices surveyed this string of precedents and stated the obvious—that although the Court had long given lip service to *Sherbert's* compelling state interest test, it had never applied it faithfully and, what is more, could not possibly do so. It made no sense to presume that every law burdening religious exercises was thereby unconstitutional, and it was no surprise that courts had not done so. The case was called *Employment Division, Department of Employment Services v. Smith.*[47] Justice Scalia, who wrote the opinion of the Court, characterized *Smith* as a clarification of the law and denied that he was overruling any past decisions. Whatever else was true, the majority left no doubt that henceforth the compelling state interest test would not be applied, and that laws burdening religion would be upheld if they were "neutral and generally applicable."[48]

The *Smith* decision sparked a firestorm of controversy. Critics insisted that the Court had unseated rather than clarified the twenty-seven-year experience of the Court under the guidance of *Sherbert's* compelling state interest test. (This claim of course was at once true and false: *Sherbert* had been the Court's nominal guide, but it was honored only in the breach.) Civil liberties groups and churches lobbied Congress to pass legislation to reverse the effects of *Smith*. The tone of critique grew quite shrill, with some critics going so far as to say that *Smith* had rendered the Free Exercise Clause meaningless and that religious freedom would cease to enjoy constitutional protection.

These claims were absurd. After *Smith*, courts continued to enforce the Free Exercise Clause. Rather than trying to apply the compelling state interest test, courts instead asked whether laws were "neutral and generally applicable." Just three years after its decision in *Smith*, the Supreme Court used the new standard to hold unanimously that Hialeah, Florida, acted unconstitutionally when it prohibited Santerians from sacrificing chickens but allowed other, nonreligious forms of slaughter within the city.[49] Rarely, if ever, had such an unpopular religious group scored a Supreme Court victory in a free exercise case.

Nevertheless, *Smith* set in motion an extraordinary series of events and created a sustained conflict between Congress and the Supreme Court. By the time the Supreme Court ruled in the animal sacrifice case, *Smith*'s critics had found a receptive audience in Congress. Ironically, though *Smith* prompted hysterical accusations that the Court was eliminating free exercise rights, minority religious groups probably had more political clout in the early 1990s than ever before.[50] Denominational divisions had been declining for decades, but America remained very religious.[51] Politicians who might once have praised the importance of being Protestant now spoke of the importance of faith in general. Told that the Supreme Court was threatening religious freedom, Congress seized the opportunity to rebuke the Court and demonstrate its own respect for religiosity. It passed the Religious Freedom Restoration Act of 1993 with only three dissenting votes in the Senate and none in the House.[52] The act, which came to be known as RFRA (pronounced "riff-ra"), contained a robust statement of the "no hindrance" rule. It stipulated that no government policy—local, state, or federal—could "substantially burden" religious exercise unless the imposition of the burden was "the least restrictive means" to further a compelling state interest.

Not surprisingly, RFRA precipitated more confusion in the courts. As we have seen, it restored a test that talked tough but packed no punch in practice. Congress said nothing to clarify the meaning of this schizophrenic standard. Instead, it bluntly asserted that the test had proven "workable" in the past. Saying this did not make it so, of course. Indeed, after RFRA became law, even some professors who testified on behalf of the bill admitted that Congress had never recognized, much less addressed, the inconsistencies that beset the Court's pre-*Smith* cases. It simply left courts to sort out the mess.

It took the Supreme Court less than five years to hold that much of RFRA was unconstitutional. Parts of the statute survived the Court decision, however. The Supreme Court ruled on federalism grounds; that is, it held that Congress had no power to impose RFRA's restrictions on state and local governments.[53] The decision did not examine whether RFRA was unconstitutional as applied to national laws and regulations. Courts have therefore continued to apply RFRA to national policies.[54] Moreover, the Supreme Court's decision about RFRA prompted another round of hysterical accusations and legislative proposals. One leader of a religious lobby, Oliver Thomas, actually compared the Court's decision to *Dred Scott*, the infamous nineteenth-century case that struck down the Missouri Compromise and held that African-Americans were not persons within the meaning of the Constitution.[55] Several states passed "little RFRAs" that recreated the Religious Freedom Restoration Act as a matter of state law.[56] Congress itself passed the Religious Land Use and Institutionalized Persons Act of 2000, or RLUIPA (pronounced "R-loopah"), which resurrected RFRA's compelling state interest test for state and local regulations dealing with land use and prison inmates.[57]

The journey from *Sherbert* to *Smith* to RFRA and beyond resembles Alice's adventures in Wonderland. First, the Supreme Court invented a test that sounded exceptionally rigorous but protected almost nothing. Then, when the Court abandoned the empty test, people cried that religious freedom was in mortal danger. Next, Congress responded by declaring that the broken test was workable and always had been. The Supreme Court struck down the test again, and people claimed that we were reliving *Dred Scott*. Accompanying this extreme talk was a haphazard series of decisions: the Court had protected religious practice aggressively on a few occasions and not at all on others.

These bizarre results are no accident. They are the inevitable legacy of the separation metaphor and the "no hindrance" rule. Those concepts leave us without any coherent way to discuss or analyze the scope of free exercise rights. Because religious practice intersects with the legitimate concerns of the state in countless ways, the two cannot be separate. State regulations will inevitably constrain—which is to say, "hinder"—religious practices along with all the other conscientious practices that we as a people value. The relevant questions are *which* hindrances are permissible and *why*. Separation and its cousins give us no traction on that issue.

Religion in Politics

When we present the arguments of this chapter in workshops and lectures, some members of our audience offer a qualified defense of the separation metaphor. They concede that the metaphor has inspired some wrongheaded thinking about religious freedom; nevertheless, they insist, separation captures something distinctive and important about the relationship between politics and religion in the United States. Their arguments go this way: "Surely there is more to the idea of separation than you allow. For example, in some Islamic countries, courts routinely enforce the *sharia,* or religious law. It would be un-thinkable—and distinctly unconstitutional—for an American court to give the Bible the same sort of authority, wouldn't it? And doesn't the idea of 'separation of church and state' capture this difference?"

Yes and yes. In the United States, no religious text has the status of law. "Separation" describes this fundamental feature of our Constitution and various others—such as the absence of any official national church. Americans usually take these blunt features of their constitutional practice for granted, but from the perspective of world history they were remarkable innovations, and—as recent confrontations with fundamentalist terrorism make clear—they remain controversial in today's world. If the point of the separation metaphor were to call attention to ways in which the U.S. Constitution contemplates a role for religion far different from that which prevailed in eighteenth-century England or still prevails in modern-day Iran, then we would have no quarrel with it.

But no respected participant in American legal debate disputes these basic features of our constitutional arrangements. When judges and other American public officials disagree about the constitutional status of religion, they are concerned instead with the sorts of questions that we have discussed in this chapter, questions about whether and when government can aid or hinder religion. And with regard to those questions, as we have seen, the separation metaphor leads us on a wild-goose chase, searching for an ideal that is neither coherent nor attractive.

Those who continue to feel attracted to the separation metaphor sometimes suggest that, even if it rarely makes a beneficial contribution to Supreme Court cases, it might nevertheless illuminate one specific, nonjudicial topic. They propose, in particular, that the separation metaphor can tell us something about the propriety of public officials' drawing on their religious convictions as a guide to choices they make in their official capacities. After all, many people feel that public officials have some responsibility to distance their public acts and speeches from their personal religious convictions, and the idea of separation might help to explain that intuition about "distance."

The problem is this: once we agree that it would be wrong for an official to treat the Bible as binding law enforceable by American courts, we confront a series of more nuanced questions, questions that don't usefully respond to the blunt demand for separation. In the past, some judges have interpreted ambiguous secular laws to reconcile them with the Bible, and their opinions have cited biblical text in support of their conclusions. Is that practice constitutionally permissible? The practice is rare today, and we suspect that many people would regard it as inconsistent with the Constitution (we certainly would). But then what of a Christian judge who invokes his religious beliefs to defend his jurisprudence not in a judicial opinion, but in a public speech, as Justice Scalia did a few years ago?[58] Some might believe that Scalia behaved unconstitutionally. If so, would they have the same view about an elected official who justified his conduct on overtly religious grounds? For example, Alabama governor Bob Riley, a conservative, invoked the Bible and Christian teaching to justify reforms shifting tax burdens from the poor to the rich.[59] Was he behaving unconstitutionally? If so, would his behavior be more acceptable if he acted upon his Christian convictions but refrained from expressing them in speech? If Governor Riley's conduct raises constitutional problems, then what about Abraham Lincoln's Second Inaugural Address, which is rich with theological language?[60] And what of the Reverend Martin Luther King? He drew upon his religious authority to lead the civil rights movement. Was it wrong for him to mix religion and politics? Some officials heeded his call for justice (we wish that more had done so). If those officials were moved by religious components of King's appeal, did they thereby act improperly?

If separation is taken literally, and read to insist that all penetrations of religious thought into public life are improper, then it proves too much. Among the many difficulties of a ruthless separationist view would be the radical inequalities it would generate: political argument and justification flowing from a wide variety of nonreligious sources would be heard, but the public official or citizen whose moral compass was religiously inspired would be silenced.

We suspect that most of those who hold out for separation would be reluctant to take the idea so far as to condemn all these invocations of, or responses to, religion. Rather, they—like us—would work to draw lines between what is appropriate and what is not. Here as elsewhere, the metaphor of separation offers no help. In a country as religious as the United States, it is impossible even to imagine a politics wholly separate from religion.

The issue for judges, legislators, and citizens in the United states is not whether church and state can permissibly interact, but rather how they should interact—for interact they surely will. The metaphor of separation is a bad guide to thinking about that issue: it and its conceptual cousins have offered the implausible counsel that religion must be treated either far better or far worse than other commitments and projects. Judges have understandably been unwilling to take that counsel in many cases, with the result that separation and its cousins have left a legacy of confusion.

· II ·

Equal Liberty

ALMOST EVERYBODY BELIEVES that religion requires special treatment in some circumstances. Sometimes it seems that religion should be subject to special *prohibitions*. For example, the government funds artistic enterprise through the National Endowment for the Arts, but it would obviously be problematic—if not plainly unconstitutional—for the government to set up a National Endowment for Religion. Conversely, in other contexts it seems appropriate to grant religious believers special *permissions*. For example, churches may refuse to hire women as ministers even though antidiscrimination statutes forbid employers from making sex-based distinctions.

These common views about the place of religion in our politics and in our Constitution beg for an explanation. Indeed, the otherwise implausible notion that we should sharply separate church and state derives much of its appeal from the vain hope that it might reconcile these two seemingly disparate intuitions: some forms of government funding of religious enterprises are plainly inappropriate and so too are some forms of employment regulation as applied to religious enterprises. Separation folds these two intuitions into its metaphor of mutual disconnectedness, the "wall" between church and state, and then derives from it two implausible and clashing commands: no funding of churches, and virtually no regulation of them, either. We have argued that this strategy is doomed to fail. Separation and its cousins have sown confusion throughout religious liberty jurisprudence. But if separation and its contradictory commands are not the right way to account for our intuitions that *some* special prohibitions and permissions apply to religious enterprises, then what is?

Fortunately, if Americans can shake themselves loose from the grip of the separation model, they will find more helpful ideas readily at hand. We saw evidence of that fact in Chapter 1, when we examined what happened when the separation model collided with free speech and antidiscrimination law. The baroque, paradoxical doctrine of treating religion both better and worse quickly yielded to the sturdy equality principles underlying these other areas of law. The Court abandoned the separation metaphor, but it did not thereby abandon religious liberty. On the contrary, the Court protected religious liberty effectively by insisting that government treat religious and nonreligious expression equally.

In this chapter we elaborate an alternative understanding of religious freedom that is above all shaped by concerns of equality. The model, which we call "Equal Liberty," has three distinct components. First, it insists in the name of equality that no members of our political community ought to be devalued on account of the spiritual foundations of their important commitments and projects. Religious faith receives special constitutional solicitude in this respect, but only because of its vulnerability to hostility and neglect. Second, and again in the name of equality, Equal Liberty insists that aside from this deep and important concern with discrimination, we have no constitutional reason to treat religion as deserving special benefits or as subject to special disabilities. Finally, Equal Liberty insists on a broad understanding of constitutional liberty generally. It demands that *all* persons— whether engaged in religiously inspired enterprises or not—enjoy rights of free speech, personal autonomy, associative freedom, and private property that, while neither uniquely relevant to religion nor defined in terms of religion, will allow religious practice to flourish.[1] We will refer to Equal Liberty's first two components as its antidiscrimination and neutrality principles, respectively, and its third component as its general liberty principle.

Equal Liberty begins with a fundamentally different question than does the separation-inspired approach to religious freedom. Separation and its cousins ask how government should behave toward *religion;* Equal Liberty asks how government should treat *persons* who have diverse commitments regarding religion (including, in some cases, a commitment to reject religion) and for whom those commitments are important components of identity and well-being. Equal Liberty seeks terms of fair cooperation for a religiously diverse people.

As it happens, Equal Liberty has a venerable constitutional pedigree. Philip Hamburger, in his exhaustive history of the Establishment Clause, reports that founding-era disestablishmentarians used "equal liberty," rather than "separation," to summarize their view of religious freedom.[2] We are pleased by this discovery but do not attach much weight to it. We began using the phrase "equal liberty" before we learned that it had been invoked at the founding. We were drawn to "equal liberty" because we thought it fit well what we regard as the best understanding of religious freedom, not because the name had a good pedigree. Indeed, it is debatable whether and to what extent our theory tracks the eighteenth-century concept. People may disagree about how to understand "equality," "liberty," and "equal liberty." There is thus no magic in the phrase.

On the other hand, we do not think it purely coincidental that the words "equal liberty" appealed to Americans more than two centuries ago. In virtually every domain of constitutional law aside from religious liberty, where the separation ideal holds sway, liberty and equality are the basic building blocks of constitutional justice. "Equal

Liberty" signals that religious freedom must be understood in light of America's foundational commitments to these ideals, and that we should be concerned about both the *scope* of religious liberty and its *distribution*. In a country that is at once very religious and very religiously diverse, we must not only ensure that people have a fair opportunity to practice their religion, but also prevent the government from favoring or disadvantaging people on account of their religious affiliation (or lack thereof).

The appeal of the Equal Liberty approach to religious freedom is underscored by the self-contradictory nature of the separation model and its conceptual cousins. At the heart of the separation model is a very attractive idea: it is no business of the state what god or gods people choose to worship, what they believe about the nature of that god or those gods, and what they choose to believe is the appropriate way to worship or otherwise honor that god or those gods. But if we try to implement that idea through the separation model, we run into immediate and deeply troubling problems.

Recall the two hypothetical Ms. Campbells, neighbors whom we first met in the Introduction. Both Ms. Campbells want to run soup kitchens for the hungry out of their homes, and both are debarred from doing so by zoning ordinances that narrowly define what activities can be undertaken in a residential zone. One of the women is impelled by her religious commitments, which include a powerful commandment to "treat those less fortunate as you would treat your own," coupled with her personal belief that she has been called by her god to live out this commandment by feeding the poor from her home. The other woman is impelled to act by what she describes as "a deep and abiding concern for those who suffer the misfortunes of poverty and hunger, and my sense that this is one small way that I can help." Now, the separation model commends our attention to the religious requirements of the first Ms. Campbell, but is uninterested in the second, who is not motivated by what in any ordinary sense could be called religion. For the separationist, the first woman has a substantial claim to be left alone by the state to pursue her religious projects, and hence, a strong claim to be exempt from the zoning laws that stand in her way; the second Ms. Campbell, presumably, is left to the mercy of the local board of zoning appeals.

Note the unfortunate circle we have traveled: we began with the idea that religious belief is no business of the state, but now we find ourselves examining the reasons the two Ms. Campbells have for wanting to feed the poor, and deciding whether one or both women are "religious" in the right way, so as to qualify for the substantial immunity from regulation that separation means to confer upon cases like these. Suddenly, the state has to decide who is religious and who is not, to the disadvantage of the second woman—not on account of her sincerity or depth of commitment, but rather on account of the moral or religious content of her commitment. In the name of keeping the government out of matters of belief, the separation model requires the government to categorize and selectively advantage some citizens over others precisely on the basis of the substance and structure of their beliefs. The separation model thus finds itself in painful self-contradiction.

The point is not to take one last swipe at separation as a way of thinking about religious freedom; rather, the point is to note how close to the surface of our widely shared ideas of religious liberty the ideal of equal treatment is. The antithesis of religious liberty is religious persecution; and the essence of religious persecution is the systematic disadvantaging of persons because they are not loyal to the "right" religious beliefs. In the antipersecution core of religious freedom, liberty and equality are alternative ways of stating the same important principle of justice.

Equal Liberty has the great virtue of putting the constitutional ideal of religious freedom in harmony with other prominent and prized features of our constitutional tradition, most notably free speech and equal protection. More to the immediate point, it has the virtue of putting the constitutional ideal of religious freedom in harmony with itself.

Of course Equal Liberty, like any nontrivial theory of religious freedom, will be controversial. Some people will flatly reject the ideal of equal treatment that is at its core. For example, some Americans may regard the United States as a Christian nation and believe that Christianity is in some way constitutive of full citizenship. Other Americans may wish that the United States were an Islamic nation. Not all members of our political community and not all religious groups are committed to the twinned ideals of liberty and equality that pervade our constitutional tradition.

We believe, however, that the most important challenges to Equal Liberty are likely to come not from radical critics of its basic principles, but from people who share the model's concern with equality. After all, we have already seen, in Chapter 1, that equality principles appeal across ideological lines.[3] Indeed, in at least three cases that excited public controversy, equality principles enabled the Supreme Court justices to reach unanimous rulings. The Court's opinion in *Church of the Lukumi Babalu Aye,* the Florida animal-sacrifice case, exemplified Equal Liberty's antidiscrimination principle: the Court prohibited the city of Hialeah from discriminating against religious forms of animal slaughter.[4] In *Witters,* the case about the blind seminarian, the Court applied a version of Equal Liberty's neutrality principle: the justices agreed that the Establishment Clause did not require Washington's scholarship program to distinguish between religious and secular programs of study.[5]

Finally, in *Lamb's Chapel,* the case involving the religious organization that wanted to use public school classrooms for its evening meetings, the Court combined Equal Liberty's neutrality principle with its antidiscrimination principle.[6] The Court first rejected the school district's contention that it was constitutionally obliged to treat religious groups differently from other groups seeking access to its facilities. The Court went on to rule that drawing such a distinction amounted to unconstitutional discrimination. The Court invoked the Free Speech Clause rather than the Free Exercise Clause to justify this result, so we might regard *Lamb's Chapel* as illustrating Equal Liberty's third principle—the importance of broad general liberties—as well as its antidiscrimination and neutrality principles.

In the *Lukumi–Witters–Lamb's Chapel* trio, the Supreme Court reached consensus by emphasizing the need to treat religion and nonreligion alike. Such cases present formidable problems for separation and its cousins, which insist upon treating religion and nonreligion differently; but Equal Liberty, with its emphasis on equality and fair cooperation, has no problem explaining them.

A critic of Equal Liberty, however, may worry that this approach to religious freedom has precisely the vices of its virtues. Such a critic might suggest that Equal Liberty easily explains cases, such as *Lukumi–Witters–Lamb's Chapel,* in which it seems entirely appropriate to treat religion and nonreligion identically, but runs into trouble in those circumstances in which our instincts insist that religion and nonreligion should be treated differently. And, as we noted at the outset of this chapter, almost everybody believes that in some cases religion requires special treatment. Almost everyone believes, for example, that, unlike other private employers, a church should be able to insist that its priests be men. Can Equal Liberty account for these cases?

This is a serious challenge to Equal Liberty. To be sure, Equal Liberty is meant to do more than just collect our existing intuitions about how various questions concerning religious freedom should be resolved; if we are convinced that Equal Liberty is the best approach to religious freedom, then our views about some questions will change in response to the directions that Equal Liberty provides. But our feelings about some cases of special religious permissions or prohibitions are very durable, and unless we can account for these cases, many people who are otherwise drawn to our basic concern with equality neverthe-less will conclude that our model is wrongheaded or, at best, incom-plete. The temptation will be to renounce or modify Equal Liberty's neutrality principle in order to accord religion some distinct constitu-tional status not fully captured by a concern with discrimination.

The stakes here are high: if we can make sense of our durable intu-itions about religious freedom only by adding some distinct constitu-tional status for religion into our conceptual mix, then we are back to the contradiction that so badly undermines separation. In the name of keeping the state's hand out of the spiritual lives of its citizens, we will be obliged to fashion constitutional tests that require the state to say who or what is in the right way religious, and then attach distinct ad-vantages or disadvantages to the resulting judgment. Equal Liberty's spareness does not flow from a fetishistic preoccupation with equality; it grows out of our desire to fashion an attractive and coherent ap-proach to religious freedom.

In the next section we explain how Equal Liberty, even while insist-ing on the foundational importance of equality, can explain the distinct treatment of religion in some circumstances. Ultimately we will need to consider a wide range of controversies about religious freedom in America in order to demonstrate that Equal Liberty offers sound guid-ance for resolving them. That enterprise will occupy us throughout this book. But it is not too early to see how, in general, Equal Liberty can account for durable intuitions about the need to treat religion spe-cially.

Special Prohibitions and Permissions

Equal Liberty accounts in two ways for religion's apparently special status within our constitutional tradition. First, in some circumstances, its antidiscrimination principle will justify special constitutional solici-tude for religion. There is nothing contradictory or paradoxical about this. Antidiscrimination principles in both law and common morality routinely focus on what we could think of as cultural fault lines. They focus, that is, on chronic social circumstances that leave some groups peculiarly vulnerable to deep and undeserved disadvantage. Modern constitutional doctrine reflects this by making laws that distinguish among persons on the basis of race or gender formally "suspect" and subject to a strong presumption of unconstitutionality.[7] Fair housing and equal employment laws reflect this as well, by flatly barring adverse treatment based on race, gender, and a small list of other prohibited criteria.[8] In these legal contexts, it makes perfectly good sense to single out vulnerable groups for special concern precisely because of their vulnerability to discrimination. The aim of such laws is parity, not advantage. In just this way, religion is sometimes singled out for distinct treatment in our constitutional tradition, precisely with the goal of protecting persons from discrimination.

Consider one of the examples with which we began this chapter, the creation of a National Endowment for Religion (the "NER"). On first blush, the idea seems highly problematic. But why? Separationists have an easy answer: Directing public money towards religion is a singularly disfavored breach of the "wall of separation." This proves much too much, of course, since it also calls into question providing police and fire protection to churches, and immediately disqualifies religious groups from receiving public funds for any projects, including projects with laudable secular aims like feeding the poor or combating substance abuse; it would also imply that the state of Washington could never give scholarship dollars to a blind seminarian—which is the conclusion that the Supreme Court unanimously (and quite rightly) rejected in *Witters*. But, for all its patent difficulties, separation can at least offer reasons for doubting the constitutionality of the NER. What can Equal Liberty offer?

Well, a great deal, actually. Even in the absence of any details about its mandate and operation, the prospect of an NER immediately conjures up the vision of a solemn group of commissioners deciding which projects or groups are appropriately religious to qualify for consideration, and then, in turn, deciding which religious groups or projects are most worthy of public support, *qua* the aim of helping religion to flourish. The problem, it bears emphasis, is not simply that religious enterprises get funded and others do not; the NER, after all would exist in an institutional environment already populated by the National Science Foundation, the National Endowment for the Arts, and the National Endowment for the Humanities. Nor, emphatically, is it the problem that religious enterprises are among those which now will receive public monies. The problem is that the mandate of the NER will presumably be something on the order of funding projects that are worthy as religious projects, which are valuable for the state of religion in the United States, or in some other closely-related sense have "religious merit."[9] And that will put government in the position of saying what religion is, what is good for religion, and, ultimately, something very much akin to what is a good religion.

Now the NER is just a figment of our conversation, and perhaps there could be some version of the NER that would not threaten to make the government the arbiter of good religion or good religious projects. Perhaps in operation the NER could embrace a wide swath of enterprises including yoga, new-age spiritualism, and perhaps even secular humanism; and perhaps the formal and functional criteria of funding choices could turn away from religious worth and towards general secular goals like health, morals, and general welfare of the American people. It would seem a great deal more natural to call this revised entity the National Institute of Health and Morals rather than the NER, and the choice of name should give us cause to be a bit skeptical, but that is not our present problem. Our concern is with understanding how Equal Liberty can account for our immediate sense that a National Endowment for Religion is constitutionally problematic, and our immediate sense is based on what we all imagine the purpose and real-world function of an NER would be.

One could try to conceive of an entity that could sensibly be called the NER but whose commissioners could somehow avoid deciding what religious projects are worthy of support, but that heroic effort would be simply beside the point.

The skeptical reader might not be satisfied. She might respond to our Equal Liberty case against the NER in this fashion: "Absolutely. You're quite right to locate our unease with the NER in the prospect that its commissioners would be forced to make judgments of religious worth. But all that you've done so far is make the problem of special treatment more precise. The National Endowment for the Arts has to decide which artists and what projects merit funding, and we don't get in an uproar about that. So you must explain our special sensitivity with regard to governmental judgments about religion. Can Equal Liberty do *that* job?"

We might respond first by noting that although public funding of the arts is widely accepted, some commentators have worried about the inevitable consequences of the government making the sort of choices required by such funding. But more to the present point, there are reasons to think that government funding choices with regard to the worth of religious projects would be far more threatening to constitutional concerns about discrimination than are government choices implicating artistic worth. We discuss these reasons at greater length in Chapter 4, but we can preview them here. In our society, religious belief and affiliation are important components of individual and group identity. Religious affiliation typically implicates an expansive web of belief and conduct, and individuals often feel and are seen as either "in" or "out" of such webs. In a variety of ways the perceived and actual stakes of being within or without these webs of belief and membership can be very high: being fulfilled and redeemed or eternally damned; being welcomed as a member of the community or shunned. Moreover, it is in the nature of religion that persons outside a given faith will on occasion fail to understand or appreciate matters internal to that faith, and so will be inappropriately indifferent, suspicious, or even repelled and hostile to beliefs and practices central to that faith. These are matters of sociological fact, and they justify distinct constitutional concern that governmental conduct will valorize some beliefs at the cost of disparaging others, and further, that in the course of such conduct, government will valorize some citizens at the cost of disparaging others.

The object of this concern is to avoid governmental acts that constitute or encourage discrimination among members of our political community on the basis of their systems of belief. On the Equal Liberty account, the Constitution neither specially celebrates nor denigrates religion. Religion is one important source of commitment and fulfillment among many, and the Constitution's goal is to protect members of our political community from discrimination on account of their spiritual commitments. The vulnerability of non-mainstream religious views—including views that repudiate religion in any of its recognizable forms—to discrimination is what justifies the special constitutional treatment of religion on some occasions, of which our fictive National Endowment for Religion is one instance. In this way, Equal Liberty's equality principle both accounts for and requires the special treatment of religion under some circumstances.

There is a second way in which Equal Liberty can support what appears to be the special treatment of religion. At the beginning of this chapter, we offered a second example that seemed to insist on the distinct constitutional treatment of religion: Some churches, including the Catholic church, refuse to hire women as ministers. This practice appears to violate statutes prohibiting employment discrimination on the basis of sex (Title VII, the federal law prohibiting sex discrimination, makes no exception for the clergy).[10] Yet, most people—including many who lament these discriminatory practices—believe that church policies about clergy should be constitutionally exempt from antidiscrimination statutes.

The separation model explains this widely-shared belief by treating religion as constitutionally unique, as the beneficiary of a remarkable regulatory immunity. Separation advances the "no-hindrance" principle—the idea that, in principle, government ought never to burden religious practice. This is what gives rise to the disturbing possibility we talked about earlier in this chapter, the possibility that two women who wanted to feed the poor from their suburban homes in contravention of local zoning restraints could be treated in radically different ways, depending on whether they satisfied a test of having the right kind of reasons for wanting to engage in their humane exercise. Separation, in other words, justifies permitting the Catholic church to refuse to hire women as priests by giving religion a fundamentally distinct—and in this context a distinctly advantaged—constitutional status.

Equal Liberty, in contrast, seeks to understand the widely-held view that churches should be free from state interference in their choice of clergy by drawing on constitutional values of autonomy and freedom of association that run to the benefit of all members of our constitutional community. The idea, in rough, is this: If the state told its citizens whom to turn to as mentors, as best friends, as role models, as moral advisors, as sources of consolation in times of need—for example, by requiring that we make such choices without regard to gender or race—we would easily conclude that the state had overstepped the boundaries of its authority and entered a domain the Constitution preserves for private choice. Ordinarily, we do not confront problems of autonomy of this sort because the state has neither the inclination nor the capacity to intrude into the lives of its citizens in this way.

But organized religions like the Catholic church are structural anomalies in this regard. Priests and their counterparts play an amalgam of these relational and guidance roles: They act as moral advisors, as sources of consolation, as role models, best friends, and mentors. But they do so in formal, visible, compensated, group environments. Under these circumstances, the possibility of state regulation is real; and under these circumstances, the latent constitutional values of associational autonomy suddenly become important, and inform both our instincts about what is just and the behavior of judges and legislators charged by the Constitution with the duty to respect the fundamentals of political justice.

This account is reinforced by two closely-related strands of constitutional doctrine. First, for nearly a century, the Supreme Court has traced a thin but durable line of cases recognizing the existence of a right of personal autonomy against an overreaching state. In the 1920s, the Court found that while the state could insist that children attend elementary and secondary school, it could not require them to attend public schools. In the same era, and in the same vein, the Court found that the state could not bar private schools from teaching the German language.[11]

Since the 1960s, and for some, more controversially, the Court has found that state cannot prevent either married or unmarried persons from buying or using contraceptives;[12] that in many circumstances it must permit women to secure abortions,[13] grandparents to live with and indeed, take custody of their grandchildren,[14] and same-sex couples to engage in benign and consensual sexual relations.[15] The Court has referred to this constitutional principle of personal autonomy as "the right of privacy."[16]

The second strand of constitutional doctrine may well be distinct from the first only in the passing judgment of the Supreme Court. Recently, the Court held that the Boy Scouts of America were constitutionally exempt from a New Jersey law that prohibited discrimination against homosexuals.[17] The Boy Scouts, reasoned the Court, were free to choose their members in a way consistent with the principles that defined the organization. Because the Scouts defined their organization to require a commitment to heterosexuality, they were free to exclude homosexuals. In reaching this conclusion, the Court appeared to rely heavily on earlier cases where it had derived a "right to association" from the First Amendment right to free expression—the right to band together for political—or, more generally, expressive—purposes.

The Boy Scouts case was controversial, both off the Court and on it. Four of the nine Justices dissented from the ruling, albeit on a narrowly factual ground: They maintained that being a Boy Scout, as judged by the Boy Scout organization's own past practices and statements, had very little to do with one's sexual orientation. All nine justices appeared to agree on the broader question of principle raised by the case: expressive organizations—including religious organizations—have a constitutional right to choose their members in a way consistent with their mission and principles.[18]

These two lines of cases are best viewed as responses to the same important constitutional principle, namely, that there are a variety of personal relationships in which members of our political community are free to choose their partners, associates, or colleagues without interference from the state. On this view, the Boy Scout case would better be understood without reference to the purported "expressive" function of the scouting enterprise; if the outcome in that case is correct, it is correct because the Constitution bars the state from some forms of interference in voluntary private associations which provide variations on our now familiar list of private relational benefits: role-modeling, mentoring, guidance, and friendship. The case should thus turn on questions about the structure of activities and leadership in the Boy Scouts, and upon the nature of the expectations of parents who choose the Boy Scouts for their sons.

But for our present purposes, we need not resolve this controversy about the conceptual basis of associational freedom. The important point is that contemporary constitutional law endorses associational freedom, and further, that the constitutional immunity of the Catholic church from equal employment opportunity mandates in the choice of priests can readily be explained as an instance of that freedom.[19]

Not everyone will agree that the Catholic church should enjoy this immunity. For example, Professor Ira C. Lupu argued some years ago that churches should have the freedom to decide for themselves whom to admit as members, but that, once having made that decision, they were obliged to respect antidiscrimination laws with regard to the treatment of their members. He thus concluded that the Catholic church, having permitted women to join, has no constitutional right to discriminate against its women members when choosing priests.[20] On its face this seems a strange view: Why concede to the Catholic church the freedom to exclude persons on the basis of gender, but not permit the Church to assign differentiated roles of leadership on the basis of gender? What matters most at the moment, though, is what a debate between Lupu and us would be about: it would focus upon the shape of associational liberty and its application to religious organizations.[21] That is the lesson of Equal Liberty.

So with the help of the two examples with which we began this chapter, the fictive National Endowment for Religion and the not-at-all fictive license of the Catholic church to insist that only men serve as priests, we have seen how Equal Liberty supports our strong sense that religion sometimes requires special treatment. In the case of the fictive Endowment, we drew on the equality principle of Equal Liberty; when considering the license of the Catholic church, we drew on the general liberty principle. We should note that some cases may involve the combined force of these principles. We do not, for example, require that priests, rabbis, ministers, or other clerics be licensed by the state. Our sense that clerical licensure would be inappropriate may well draw on both associational liberty and the concern that the state could not say who is qualified to be a good religious leader without saying what religious beliefs are good.

By now, you are probably thinking of other examples that Equal Liberty might have trouble explaining. "O.k.," you might think, "Equal Liberty can make sense of our intuitions about the NER, or about the freedom of churches to discriminate when they hire ministers, but can it make sense of the way we treat religion in the schools? Or the need to exempt religious believers from some laws that apply to everyone else? Or the debate about charitable choice and tuition vouchers?" If you are asking questions like these—terrific. They are, we think, exactly the right kind to ask. To test Equal Liberty, we must dive into practical political and constitutional arguments about religion in American life, uncover the intuitions that motivate them, and ask whether Equal Liberty enables us to understand and analyze them. What we are seeking is a kind of balance, or equilibrium, between our durable instincts about these various cases and attractive principles that can both explain these instincts and help to shape them at their margins. We are satisfied that Equal Liberty offers the best account of religious liberty. Our project in the chapters which follow will be to persuade you that this is so, and in so doing, argue for the best outcomes in the most pressing and interesting religious liberty controversies that our community now faces. We will proceed from the inside out, beginning with concrete problems and intuitions and using them to assess the abstract principles laid out in this chapter.[22]

Two Preliminary Objections

But before we embark on this enterprise, we need to consider two threshold objections that, according to some critics, disqualify Equal Liberty as an interpretation of the Constitution from the very outset, however attractive it might otherwise prove to be. One of these threshold objections is a legal argument; it maintains that Equal Liberty is inconsistent with the text and history of the Constitution. The other threshold objection is a moral argument; it asserts that Equal Liberty cannot count as a conception of religious freedom because it is not sufficiently neutral among religious perspectives.

The Objection from Text and History

Some critics contend that the constitutional text rules out "Equal Liberty." Their argument runs something like this:

The framers knew how to use words, and, if they had wanted to say "equality" or "equal liberty," they could have done so. But the Constitution does not say "equal liberty"—it says "free exercise" and "no law respecting an establishment of religion." "Free exercise of religion" sounds like a guarantee of liberty, not (just) equality. Besides, the Constitution does speak of "equal protection" later on, in the Fourteenth Amendment; the Equal Liberty interpretation would thus render the religion clauses of the First Amendment redundant and superfluous.

To be sure, the Constitution does not actually say "equal liberty." So we find ourselves explaining the religion clauses in a vocabulary not contained within them. That, however, does not distinguish us from other theorists who are trying to interpret the religion clauses. The First Amendment does not say "separation of church and state," for example. Nor does it say "neutrality" or "compelling state interest." In order to explain the meaning of the First Amendment (or any other constitutional provision, or, for that matter, any text), one must translate it into other terms. One might imagine, in the spirit of Hugo Black or Humpty-Dumpty, a "free exercise theory" of the Free Exercise Clause, which posits that when the Constitution guarantees the free exercise of religion, it means precisely the free exercise of religion—nothing more and nothing less.[23] This theory would never depart from the language of the Constitution, but it would never offer any comprehensible explanation of it, either.

Although Equal Liberty (like any other theory of religious freedom) goes beyond the plain language of the First Amendment, the interpretation it propounds is fully consistent with that text. The Free Exercise Clause, for example, refers to laws that prohibit the "free exercise" of religion. Free from what? From all burdens whatsoever? Nobody takes that position—nobody supposes, for example, that government is obliged to subsidize religion so as to render it costless. From all legally imposed burdens? Nobody takes that position, either—government can criminalize murder even if it thereby interferes with religions that endorse human sacrifice. So does the Free Exercise Clause guarantee that religion will be free from all but those legally imposed burdens that are necessary to advance a compelling state interest? From unequal treatment? From intentional discrimination? The Free Exercise Clause thus poses a question, and Equal Liberty—like its competitors—proposes an answer to that question. It proposes that the exercise of religion is "free" when it is free from burdens imposed through hostility toward or neglect of particular theological perspectives. That is an interpretation of the text, not a departure from it.

This line of argument also answers the claim, made by Douglas Laycock and Stephen Pepper (among others), that free exercise is a "liberty" right, not an "equality" right.[24] As we suggested earlier, religious persecution, at its very core, consists in the adverse treatment of persons on account of their religious beliefs and affiliations. Freedom from burdens not shared equally by others is a substantial and valuable form of freedom. It makes sense of the phrase "free exercise of religion," and, as we shall show in the chapters ahead, it provides religious believers with considerable space in which to practice their faith. If Equal Liberty fails as an account of religious liberty, it cannot not be because of the semantic demands of the words "free exercise."[25]

Just as the Free Exercise Clause demands a judgment about what religious exercise must be free from, so too the Establishment Clause requires a judgment about what it means to make a law "respecting an establishment of religion." Does it mean designating some church (or group of churches) as the nation's official church (or churches)? If so, even preferential funding programs might be consistent with the Constitution's disestablishment norm. Or does it mean providing benefits to a church (or group of churches, or to religion in general) on a preferential basis? Or does it mean providing tax dollars to a church (or group of churches) on any basis whatsoever, whether preferential or not? Equal Liberty selects a particular answer—namely, that "establishment" means advantaging or disadvantaging persons or groups because of the spiritual foundations of their deeply held beliefs and commitments. Once again, this is an interpretation of the First Amendment, not a departure from it.

This leaves to be considered the threshold objection of redundancy. Should we be disturbed by the fact that, on our interpretation, the religion clauses express equality norms that, though limited to the specific domain of religion, are much like the more general norms in the Equal Protection Clause? It is entirely possible, of course, that while both the Equal Protection Clause and the religion clauses are concerned with equal status, one might be more or less demanding than the other in some respect; indeed, as we shall note in our extended discussion of Equal Liberty in action, we think that Equal Liberty's antidiscrimination principle calls for more robust doctrine than the Supreme Court currently applies in equal protection cases. But suppose this were not the case: Would it be a problem if the religion clauses turned out to be nothing more than specific versions of more general norms included within the Equal Protection Clause?

Not at all. When the Bill of Rights—including the religion clauses of the First Amendment—was ratified in 1789, the Equal Protection Clause did not exist. It is entirely sensible to think of the religion clauses as one of the Constitution's first encounters with concerns over the equal status of members of our political community. A century later, in the wake of the Civil War, the Fourteenth Amendment extended equality concerns to African-Americans. Ultimately, the Equal Protection Clause has been broadened to include gender equality and concerns of equal status and equal rights more generally. That the Equal Protection Clause, as interpreted by the modern Court, might do much or all of the work of the religion clauses seems neither surprising nor disturbing. It is, if anything, an advantage of Equal Liberty that it harmonizes the religion clauses with other important constitutional precepts. This is especially so since the religion clauses, by their own terms, apply only to the federal government; lawyers and judges understand them to apply to states and local governments only because the general guarantees of the Fourteenth Amendment "incorporate" most of the provisions in the Bill of Rights and apply them to the states.[26]

More generally, even absent the evolution of a constitution over time, it makes perfectly good sense for constitutional provisions to overlap and in effect redundantly secure important protections.[27] Suppose, for example, that a new country drafts a Bill of Rights that includes a provision guaranteeing "equality" and another guaranteeing "religious freedom." At the constitutional convention, a delegate rises to express his concern that the provisions are redundant because "religious freedom" is in fact a subset of "equality." Two delegates then rise in defense of the proposed Bill of Rights. One defender agrees that she understands religious freedom as a species of equality, but wants to retain both guarantees. Why? So that the constitution will protect the best version of "religious freedom," regardless of whether it turns out to be coterminous with "equality" rightly understood. The second defender rises and says he is absolutely sure that full protection of equality would assure religious freedom. But, he continues, the matter is too important to leave to the interpretive judgment of the courts. Better to be redundant and insure the protection of religion against discrimination. Surely both defenders have offered perfectly good reasons for keeping both provisions in place.

Another legalistic objection to Equal Liberty focuses not on text but on history. "Equal Liberty," say some critics, "is not an acceptable conception of the Constitution's religion clauses because it is not consistent with the intentions and expectations of the people who drafted and ratified the Constitution." In fact, we think that, if it matters, Equal Liberty's historical pedigree is pretty good. We have already mentioned that, according to Philip Hamburger, the generation that framed the Constitution used "equal liberty" more frequently than "separation of church and state" to describe its views (though we also cautioned that the framers' understanding of the phrase might differ considerably from our own). More generally, and more importantly, there are strong historical grounds for affirming that one purpose of the religion clauses was to protect religions from discrimination. The framers knew well the bitter divisions engendered by religious conflict, and they sought to protect American believers from persecution.

That said, we do not wish to lean heavily on the historical case in favor of Equal Liberty. We believe that the most honest assessment of the historical record requires a conclusion more or less like the one offered by Donald Drakeman in his study of the Establishment Clause—namely, that the record provides no answers to the normative questions raised by the plain text of the religion clauses.[28] History cuts neither for nor against "equal liberty" as the operative conception of religious freedom.

Ambitious efforts to prove otherwise lead pretty much to the same conclusion, despite the earnest protests of their authors. So, for example, Michael McConnell has written an exhaustive and widely cited history of the Free Exercise Clause.[29] In it he argues that Thomas Jefferson and James Madison were the two guiding geniuses behind the clause;[30] that Jefferson expressed "disdain . . . for the more intense manifestations of religious spirit" whereas Madison took a "more affirmative stance toward religion";[31] and, finally, that Madison, "with his more generous vision of religious liberty, more faithfully reflected the popular understanding of the free exercise clause that was to emerge both in state constitutions and the Bill of Rights."[32] One might suppose that this stark divergence between Madison and Jefferson would by itself suffice to vindicate an assessment rather like Drakeman's conclusion about the Establishment Clause—namely, that history leaves all the big questions unanswered. Suppose, though, that we accept McConnell's conclusion, which is that we should follow Madison rather than endorsing Jefferson's "disdain for religion." Where does that get us? Nowhere. Constitutional interpreters must choose between conceptions of religious freedom such as Equal Liberty and "separation of church and state," and both of these are conceptions of how we should respect (rather than disdain) religion. Ruling out Jefferson's view of religion (or, more precisely, Jefferson's-view-per-McConnell) amounts to ruling out a red herring. Even McConnell, who would clearly have wanted to invoke the authority of history on behalf of his views, could in the end only argue that history did not rule out his position on the question of religious liberty.

We have thus far met the textual and historical arguments on their own terms—we have met them, in other words, with competing textual and historical arguments, arguments showing that text and history raise important questions of political justice rather than resolving them. We confess, though, to finding this exercise a bit exasperating. Despite pious proclamations to the effect that we must follow text and history wherever they lead, commentators seem invariably to find that text and history lead to exactly those conclusions that they elsewhere defend on normative grounds. We suspect that their normative convictions are doing the real work here—that their interpretation of ambiguous text and multivocal history depends on, rather than constrains, their convictions about what counts as a satisfactory conception of religious freedom. Those normative questions are the ones we ought to be arguing about—not because we are free to ignore the Constitution's text and history, but because it is obvious that Equal Liberty and a whole slew of competitors are equally consistent with that text and history insofar as they are constitutionally relevant.

The Neutrality Trap

There is another, very different threshold critique of Equal Liberty that rests on philosophical rather than legal grounds. It adopts the bracing position that there is no such thing as a satisfactory theory of religious freedom because no theory can be equally acceptable to all religions. Equal Liberty must fail as a theory of religious freedom because every such theory must fail. Steven D. Smith, one academic proponent of this view, says that efforts to find and justify a constitutional principle of religious freedom are "foreordained failure[s]";[33] Professor Stanley Fish says, to like effect, that they are "mission impossible."[34]

It is, of course, true that no theory of religious freedom could be acceptable to all religions. Some versions of Islam insist that other religions must be proscribed or restricted.[35] So do some versions of Christianity. For adherents of these faiths, the freedom of religion is the freedom to be Islamic, or the freedom to be Christian, or the freedom to be some other more-or-less specific faith. These conceptions of religious freedom are inconsistent with one another and, obviously, with pluralist views such as Equal Liberty.

Equal Liberty presupposes a commitment to respect theological (and nontheological) perspectives different from one's own. Those who reject that commitment confront a very different range of interpretive problems from the ones we consider here. For example, thoroughgoing theocrats would find themselves uncomfortably constrained by the text of both the Establishment and Free Exercise Clauses, since, whatever the ambiguities of those clauses, they seem to proscribe Congress from designating a particular religion as the nation's official church and from outlawing the practice of competing faiths.[36] Theocrats might accordingly believe that interpreting the First Amendment is a very different matter from theorizing about religious freedom, since the plain text of the amendment is inconsistent with their view of religious freedom. If so, perhaps they would accept Equal Liberty as an interpretation of the religion clauses, even though they would not accept it as a theory of religious freedom. At any rate, our arguments in this book are not directed to theocrats or others who believe, as a matter of justice, that one or another faith deserves a privileged status;

our argument is directed to readers who take for granted that people of diverse faiths are entitled to equal citizenship.

Significantly, the skeptical philosophical critique launched by Smith and Fish aims at this same audience. It observes that no theory of religious liberty will satisfy everyone, which is true, but it does not stop there. It contends that because of this fact, there can be no satisfactory theory of religious liberty at all. Why? Because all theories of religious liberty aim to treat religions equally, or neutrally, and no theory can do that—because, as we have just seen, any theory of religious liberty will treat some religions sufficiently badly so as to be unacceptable from the standpoint of those religions.[37]

We think this argument depends upon something like a pun on words such as "equality" and "neutrality." It is true that all persuasive accounts of religious freedom will pay some homage to equality, and Equal Liberty in particular is deeply committed to that value. Equal Liberty insists that government must respond to the needs and interests of all its citizens with equal regard; it demands, for example, that if government regulations make special accommodation for the dietary needs of pluralist faiths, then they must also accommodate the dietary needs of theocrats to the same degree. It likewise demands that people be equally free to preach pluralist religious doctrines and theocratic ones. Government must extend these rights to all religions without passing judgment on their theological content.

That said, no regime of equality can or should aspire to be equally congenial to all persons: there will always be some who are most prosperous or best satisfied only when basic norms of equality are transgressed. So too, religious freedom cannot assure that all faiths will flourish equally in America. Nor can it assure that the rights protected in its name will be equally attractive to all religions. As we have already seen, efforts to achieve that kind of equality would indeed be "foreordained failures" or "mission impossible." But it is for just that reason implausible to ascribe such quixotic ambitions to the ideal of religious freedom by stipulating at the outset a paradoxical, self-denying form of equality.

Of course, one might discover, after detailed examination of American intuitions and opinions about religious freedom, that they contradict one another in some fundamental way, so that no coherent conceptual framework can accommodate them all. If so, then skeptics such as Smith and Fish could reformulate their objections to Equal Liberty and other theories of religious freedom. They could base their skepticism not on an implausible stipulation of what "equality" demands of religious freedom but on an analysis of concrete intuitions and judgments about religious freedom that seek their warrant in concerns of equality. But this form of skepticism would obviously provide no ground for making a threshold objection to the investigation of specific problems in the domain of religious freedom; on the contrary, the skeptics would have to offer their objection as the upshot of such an investigation.[38]

That investigation is the heart of the matter, and in the chapters that follow we turn to it. We hope to show that the Equal Liberty account of religious liberty in our constitutional tradition brings with it three substantial advantages. First, Equal Liberty helps us to identify and understand areas of common ground, such as those involved in the equal access cases (*Widmar* and *Lamb's Chapel*) and the chicken-sacrifice case (*Lukumi*), as well as our shared sense of how to resolve cases like the Endowment for Religion or the Catholic church's only-males-need-apply rule for the selection of priests. Second, Equal Liberty builds on that improved understanding to offer normatively attractive guidance in areas where uncertainty and tentative disagreement now reign, areas like public school voucher programs and the inclusion of "under God" in the Pledge of Allegiance. Finally, Equal Liberty helps us to understand what Americans disagree about when they disagree about religious freedom. Despite their rhetoric, Americans do not really disagree about whether church and state should be "separate," or about whether to "lower" or "raise" some imaginary wall. Instead, we will argue, Americans disagree about how to apply the three components of Equal Liberty. They disagree, for example, about what the antidiscrimination principle means, about how to implement it, and about whether or not discrimination is occurring in particular cases. These disagreements are real and durable, and the conceptual machinery of Equal Liberty cannot make them go away. It might, however, permit the contestants to enhance their understanding and respect for one another and, in some cases, to enlarge the common ground they already share.

· III ·

The Exemptions Puzzle

AL SMITH'S LOSS of his job as a substance abuse counselor spawned one of the most important Free Exercise Clause cases of the twentieth century. Smith, who was employed by the Oregon government, had participated in a Native American Church religious ritual that involved the ingestion of peyote, a banned substance in Oregon.[1] Smith's boss found out about the ceremony and fired him. Smith sought unemployment benefits, which Oregon denied to him on the ground that he had lost his job through criminal misconduct. Smith responded by claiming that Oregon had penalized him for participating in a religious ceremony and thereby violated his right to the free exercise of religion.

Smith's claim eventually reached the Supreme Court. The formal name of the case at that stage was *Employment Division v. Smith* (1990), but we will refer to it as the *Peyote Case*. The Supreme Court did not favor Mr. Smith. It held that religiously motivated persons have no special right to violate otherwise valid laws, provided that the laws are general in application and do not single out religiously motivated behavior for adverse treatment.[2] With regard to the specific issue of Native American religious rituals, the *Peyote Case* quickly became a dead letter: both Congress and the Oregon legislature responded to it by passing legislation to protect the sacramental use of peyote.[3] With regard to free exercise jurisprudence more generally, however, the impact of the *Peyote Case* was dramatic indeed. The Supreme Court's decision sparked a firestorm of protest and set in motion a serious confrontation between Congress and the Court, about which we will have more to say later, both in this chapter and in Chapter 7.

The collision between straightforward legal regulation and religious practice that gave rise to the Court's decision in the *Peyote Case* is by no means unique. The modern state has many legitimate regulatory concerns, including, for example, providing public education, preventing discrimination in the workplace and the housing market, protecting the environment, coordinating land use, assuring that foods and drugs are safe, and protecting people from violence or exploitation. Religion, for its part, assumes many forms and comprises many beliefs. Not surprisingly, in America, which is home to a diverse range of religious beliefs and practices, it is not uncommon for persons in the grip of their religious commitments to discover that those commitments are at odds with public regulations. As Marci Hamilton has recently documented, these conflicts are manifold and sometimes severe.[4] Here are some real-world examples that fall within this vexed category of religious liberty issues:

1. *Dress code cases.* A recurring pattern involves religious claimants who seek exceptions from uniform and grooming regulations. A Jewish Air Force officer wants to wear a yarmulke with his uniform, but a military regulation prohibits the wearing of headgear while indoors.[5] A student at a public high school believes on religious grounds that wearing shorts is immodest and immoral, and she accordingly refuses to comply with a rule requiring her to wear shorts in gym class.[6] Two Muslim police officers believe that their religion obliges them to wear a beard, but the

police department's grooming code prohibits them from doing so.[7]

2. *Zoning cases.* Churches often seek exemptions from burdensome land use regulations. Sometimes they simply want permission to build a church in a district zoned exclusively for other purposes. In other cases they want to build large parking lots or high-rise office buildings, ignore historical preservation statutes or environmental regulations, or even erect broadcasting antennas. These churches invoke their underlying religious missions as constitutional grounds for their right to ignore historical preservation statutes, environmental regulations, or routine zoning ordinances.[8]

3. *Medical care cases.* Some Christian Scientists believe that one must trust in God to cure disease and that it is immoral to accept medical treatment. They have sought exemption from laws requiring them to provide medical care to their children, sometimes under circumstances in which, in the judgment of medical experts, the lives of their children are at grave and imminent risk.[9]

4. *Prison diet cases.* Prisoners have religious and other moral restrictions upon what they can eat. For example, some are vegetarians, and some must keep kosher. They have insisted that prisons supply them with meals that are consistent with their religious and moral views.[10]

For the most part, these collisions between public regulation and religion have not captured public attention in the way that, for example, school prayers, tuition vouchers, and the Pledge of Allegiance have done. But for the individuals and groups involved in these cases the stakes are sometimes very high, and for many religious and civil rights groups these issues are at the very heart of what the Constitution should offer religion. These cases thus loom very large in a sustained and heated debate about the nature and scope of religious liberty. Judges, legislators, and scholars have been caught up in the question of whether religiously motivated persons are entitled to be exempt from the reach of otherwise valid laws, most prominently in the context of the historic confrontation between Congress and the Supreme Court sparked by the Court's decision in the *Peyote Case.* That confrontation, which has been characterized by more fire than light, has been raging for more than a decade and is not likely to enjoy resolution soon. If Equal Liberty can help untangle the conundrum of legal exemptions for religiously motivated persons, it will have gone a great distance toward proving its worth.

The Balancing Approach

We can begin to address the question of legal exemptions for religiously motivated persons by thinking about why we are even tempted to grant such exemptions. Two closely related reasons come to mind. First, as a people, we strongly resist state-imposed orthodoxy, and we know from experience that religious belief is especially vulnerable to such impositions. And second, we sympathize with the plight of persons who must choose between their deepest personal commitments and obedience to the law; accordingly, we think that the government behaves unjustly if it needlessly puts persons to such choices.

Unfortunately, these observations, without a good deal more, cannot take us very far. To be sure, some common cases have obvious appeal as candidates for exemptions, perhaps even constitutionally required exemptions. Many of the dress code cases are like that: on the face of the matter it seems highly unlikely that public schools have anything like a good enough reason to require a girl bound by religious strictures of modesty to wear shorts in her gym class. The apparent indifference of the state to such a girl's claims of religious conscience seems lamentable and, further, looks like the sort of overbearing state behavior for which the Constitution is meant to provide a remedy.[11]

But we have good reason to pause before following the impulse toward exemptions for religiously motivated persons from otherwise valid laws. Our laws do not descend arbitrarily from an alien entity called "government." They are the product of legislative and administrative concerns, enacted by our representatives in service of what those representatives deem good and sufficient reasons. And very often those reasons are indeed both good and sufficient. We generally recognize and act upon the obligation to honor those laws even when our private projects and convictions, however important or sincere, are thereby thwarted. Our sense that people must respect the law is particularly strong where life-and-death issues are at stake and where private convictions conflict with broadly endorsed public judgments. Few of us, for example, would be tempted by the idea that parents should have the right to deny life-saving treatment to their children, whatever the nature of the parents' convictions might be.

The reader might think that extreme examples like this are misleading. We could, after all, hold that religious believers are normally entitled to disregard laws that get in the way of their religious convictions but still recognize limits on this get-out-of-jail-free privilege. There could be in effect a presumption that persons are free to act as their religions dictate, but that presumption could be overborne in cases in which the public interest behind a legal regulation was very strong. The interest in protecting children from parents who are bent on denying them critical medical treatment would surely qualify as one that overrides a presumption of religious license.

This is not at all a new idea. Give or take, it is the approach announced by the Court in 1963 in *Sherbert v. Verner,*[12] renounced by the Court twenty-seven years later in the *Peyote Case,* and made the object of Congress's attempt in the Religious Freedom Restoration Act to force the Court to return to the rule to which it gave lip service in *Sherbert.* The idea is that religiously motivated persons are constitutionally entitled to disregard otherwise valid laws unless the government can demonstrate that a state interest of the highest order is at stake. There is a legal term of art for such overriding state interests: they are called "compelling state interests," and the constitutional test that requires the government to demonstrate the existence of such interests is often called the compelling state interest test.

If we were to take seriously the idea that religiously motivated persons have a constitutional right to disregard any legal rule that falls short of satisfying the compelling state interest test, there would be radical consequences. Churches would be free to disregard most if not all land use restrictions, despite community concerns about traffic, parking, reasonable height standards, and historic preservation. These are weighty public interests but are unlikely to rise to the level of importance demanded by the compelling state interest test. Individual religiously motivated conduct would also be constitutionally exempt from a wide variety of other laws—such as laws requiring photos on drivers' licenses, laws mandating contempt sanctions for persons who violate judicial decrees, some laws imposing taxes, laws banning products or practices on environmental grounds, and even laws prohibiting some forms of discrimination, to name just a few.

Darkening this picture would be the patent inequity of granting religious exemptions from the laws that most people have to obey. A church could build a lucrative skyscraper where a secular organization committed to the welfare of orphaned children could not; a religiously motivated individual could run a food kitchen in defiance of contrary zoning ordinances where an individual whose humane impulses were not in any recognizable way grounded in religion could not; a monk could insist on illustrating books with materials banned on environmental grounds, but a passionately committed artist who had no religious basis for her insistence on using those same materials could not. We could multiply such examples as far as our imaginations and our readers' collective patience run.

Most people would consider this pattern of results decidedly unattractive, and, as we suggested in Chapter 2, it seems to contradict some of the most important reasons that we are attracted to religious liberty in the first instance. All this helps to explain why the Supreme Court never gave more than lip service to *Sherbert's* compelling state interest standard.

The point goes deep: we are regularly called upon to act in ways that we dislike. We pay taxes, even when they go to support projects that do us no benefit or which we actively oppose. We obey land use laws, even when it would be very much to our advantage to disregard setback requirements or height restrictions or use limitations. We may even find ourselves compelled to participate in military ventures that we regard as imprudent or wrongful. We accept the imposition of a myriad of rules, even though those rules often deflect us from the course we would otherwise pursue; and even, in some cases, when we regard the collective projects that underwrite the rules as misguided. We accept the imposition of these rules because our society—indeed any modern society—could not function without reciprocal sacrifices of this sort.

Against this backdrop of the modern regulatory state, it is remarkable to grant some persons broad exemptions from the rules that everyone else is required to follow—and more remarkable still if eligibility for this privileged status is made to depend upon the spiritual infrastructure of a person's reasons for resisting a rule. That, presumably is what Justice Scalia had in mind in the *Peyote Case,* when he characterized "a private right to ignore generally applicable laws" as a "constitutional anomaly."[13]

Local zoning cases illustrate Scalia's point nicely. Homeowners occasionally find themselves subject to land use restrictions they consider oppressive or unfair, but they must obey them anyway. Few people believe that churches should be in a radically different position. It seems desirable for land use authorities to accommodate the religious needs of churches and individuals to some extent, but it is not attractive to suppose that churches should enjoy a blanket exemption from zoning regulations—and that is so even though zoning often serves aesthetic purposes rather than life-saving ones.

Sensible defenders of the balancing approach retreat in the face of these difficulties. Judge McConnell, for example, observed after the *Peyote Case* that the justices had always applied not the compelling interest but "a far more relaxed standard" in exemptions cases.[14] In his view, they were "correct to do so."[15] McConnell recommended that the Court "recast the 'compelling interest' test in a more realistic form" that avoided "rhetorical overkill."[16] His own preferred version was that the government should have to grant an exemption unless it would be "repugnan[t] to the 'peace and safety of the state.'" This suggestion is a step in the right direction, but it is almost certainly still too robust to be satisfactory. For example, unless we take a very expansive view of "safety," most zoning laws and many tax laws will again fail to meet the threshold.

We suspect that no balancing formula will be remotely plausible unless it applies a proportionality standard rather than a threshold test: the formula would, in other words, have to be sensitive to the nature and weight of the burden imposed on religious exercise as well as to the gravity of the state's interest. Whether or not that is so, it should be clear that as we move away from the relatively absolute standard of the strict compelling state interest test, a good deal of indeterminacy and ad hockery enters the picture. We are supposed to show some degree of solicitude for the needs of religious believers, but how much is unclear. In the absence of a clear standard, judges and other public officials may give preferential treatment to mainstream, familiar claims of conscience at the expense of more exotic ones, raising serious concerns about a failure of equal treatment.

These problems are symptoms of a deeper pathology: the balancing approach lacks a coherent normative foundation. Most defenders of the balancing approach have tried to justify it by reference to some version of the separation model. McConnell, for example, contends that we should test exemption claims by reference to "the hypothetical world in which individuals make decisions about religion on the basis of their own religious conscience, without the influence of government." But as we saw in Chapter 1, that goal makes no sense. It is impossible to know what religious convictions people would have in the harsh world that would exist if government were absent. Government inevitably and quite desirably influences religion in myriad ways—such as by providing the property rights and security without which religious organizations would be difficult or impossible to sustain.

Might one defend the balancing approach on the simple ground that accommodation increases the capacity of people to practice their religion, and that we should accordingly presume accommodations desirable unless the government can demonstrate that they are not? Viewed as prudent counsel to policymakers, this suggestion has much to recommend it. Policymakers should accommodate religious practices where possible. Of course, religious needs are by no means unique in this regard; policymakers should also accommodate the special needs of parents, the handicapped, and cultural minorities (to name only a few examples) where possible. But the "balancing approach" to exemptions goes well beyond this sort of banal, generally applicable advice. It does not merely tell policymakers to try to accommodate the special needs of the persons they serve, but insists that—*in the special case of religious believers*—they bear the burden of proving that their refusals to make accommodations are well justified. The approach thereby puts a thumb on the scale in favor of religious accommodation at the expense of other public interests. The Constitution does not impose any such preference in favor of, for example, the special needs of parents, even though Americans generally regard parental commitments as dignified and valuable.

There is no good reason to award such an across-the-board privilege to religious commitments. Bear in mind that claims for religious exemptions arise in the first instance only when a set of religious practices conflicts with some aspect of the common good. More specifically, constitutional claims for free exercise exemption arise only if two conditions hold: first, the public has judged the conduct in question to be so harmful to the common good that it must be proscribed; and second, the public has judged the harms sufficiently serious that no exception can be made for the benefit of individual believers with special needs. If either of these conditions fails, no free exercise claim would be necessary: if the first condition failed, the practice would not be proscribed; and if the second condition failed, the claimed exemption would already exist. Yet if both conditions apply, then we are dealing with conduct (whether it be refusing medical care to children or something less extreme, such as erecting broadcast antennas in residential neighborhoods or refusing to pay a certain kind of tax) that has been judged harmful enough to warrant regulation or even proscription. There is no reason to suppose that it is generally desirable to facilitate this special subset of religious behavior, even if we think that religious behavior in general is likely to be valuable and benign.

Equal Liberty and the Exemptions Problem

Equal Liberty recommends a fundamentally different approach to the exemptions problem. As always, Equal Liberty begins with the idea that religious liberty, above all, requires that persons not be treated unequally on account of the spiritual foundations of their deep commitments. Equal Liberty thus calls on government to exempt religious observers from burdens that are not shared fairly with others. Equal Liberty also insists that religious persons, organizations, and practices must share fairly in the burdens and limitations that go along with membership in organized society. Equal Liberty forsakes the benighted quest to find a constitutionally specified balance-point between "enough accommodation" and "enough sacrifice for the common good."

This conceptual framework clarifies important features of the exemptions problem. In particular, Equal Liberty's antidiscrimination principle responds differently to laws that deliberately and inevitably share burdens among all variety of life plans, and those that negligently or maliciously impose unique burdens on religious life plans. Tax laws and zoning laws typically fall in the first category. It should come as no surprise that such laws will sometimes burden the religious projects of churches and individuals. Taxes and land use laws deliberately impose restrictions upon life projects of all kinds—philosophic, political, educational, familial, vocational, artistic, and religious projects among them. The whole point of these laws is to impose burdens and to share them fairly. They do so in order to provide services and options without which many (if not all) such projects would be impossible. We all feel the bite from such laws, sometimes quite keenly. If churches and religious practices received a blanket presumptive exemption from burdens of this sort, the result would be an indefensible special privilege, not equal treatment.

But there are other occasions on which official actions may unjustly impose burdens on religious projects. Consider again the dress code cases. Laws prohibiting basketball players from wearing headgear or requiring police officers to be clean-shaven impose modest and entirely reasonable restrictions on the personal choices of many would-be basketball players and police officers, but they can have drastic consequences for some. An Orthodox Jew would be unable to play basketball without transgressing his religious obligation to wear a yarmulke, and a Muslim whose beliefs demanded that he grow a beard would be barred from service as a police officer.

Laws are not unjust simply because they impose a minor burden on some and a much greater burden on others. Laws do that all the time. A law that makes it illegal to ride horses on the main streets of a town, for example, may well be supported by quite sensible traffic-flow and sanitation policies. Such a law will impose only a minor burden on some, and no burden at all on many. Yet there could be some persons who will be substantially inconvenienced by such a law. Their circumstance is surely unfortunate, but, without more, there is no reason to suppose that an injustice—much less an injustice of constitutional significance—has been done.

From the vantage of Equal Liberty, the potential for injustice in the basketball-headgear and policeman-beard cases lies elsewhere. It is very likely that the officials who authored the regulations in those cases would have reshaped them to accommodate the deep concerns of Orthodox Jews and devout Muslims (and others caught out in the same way) if (1) the officials had anticipated the impact of the regulations on the life plans of these claimants and (2) they were disposed to treat the religious commandments of unfamiliar faiths as giving rise to deep and worthy personal commitments. In such cases, the failure to provide such an accommodation for the Orthodox Jews and devout Muslims involves what we will call a failure of *equal regard*—a failure by the state to show the same concern for the fundamental needs of all its citizens. In a regime of Equal Liberty, failures of equal regard are unconstitutional when they devalue some citizens' interests or commitments on the basis of their spiritual foundations.

Equal Liberty thus explains why dress code cases are such appealing candidates for claims of accommodation. These cases typically involve situations in which burdens on religion have been overlooked or callously ignored and in which, as a result, the possibility of a failure of equal regard is high. The accommodation of religious needs in cases of this sort will often be necessary to avoid such a failure. Equal Liberty also counsels against too quick a move from settings like dress code cases to other settings like zoning cases, where there is good reason to suppose that accommodating the needs of religious groups will sometimes unjustly privilege such groups.

The balancing approach, in contrast, ignores and obscures the difference between these two sorts of cases, for it asks only about the weight of the burden on religious practice and the importance of the government's interest, without attending to the distribution of burdens within society. In political argument, proponents of special exemptions for churches have sometimes capitalized on the resulting obscurity. They have pointed to appealing cases like those involving dress codes, and then argued for special exemptions from land use restraints for churches, on the grounds that land restrictions cast burdens on religion that are roughly similar and the state purposes involved seem comparably weighty. That argument is a non sequitur, and Equal Liberty enables us to see why.

Equal Liberty demands principled consistency across cases rather than conformity to some idealized, theoretically specified regulatory equilibrium. Equal Liberty recognizes that it is an important function of democratic government to determine what the appropriate balance between collective regulatory concerns and individual interests should be, and to shape public regulations accordingly. But, crucially, Equal Liberty insists that government treat all hardships and commitments fairly once that balance has been struck.

Equal Regard and the Role of Benchmarks

Failures of equal regard are especially easy to recognize when the state has accommodated serious mainstream religious or secular interests but refuses to provide an equivalent accommodation for the comparably serious interests of minority religious groups or individuals. That was true in the real-world version of the police case we have been discussing. Two Sunni Muslims, Faruq Abdul-Aziz and Shakoor Mustafa, were officers in the Newark, New Jersey, police force. Their religious beliefs required them to wear beards, and they accordingly sought exemption from a departmental grooming regulation that required officers to be clean-shaven. The department refused their request, and they sued, asserting that Newark's actions had violated their constitutional rights. The U.S. Court of Appeals for the Third Circuit agreed; the opinion was written by Judge Samuel Alito, whom President George W. Bush would later nominate to the Supreme Court.[17] Alito pointed out that Newark's regulations contained an exemption for officers who suffered from folliculitis, a skin condition that made it painful for them to shave. If Newark was willing to make an exception to accommodate the special health needs of its officers, then it had to show equal regard for the special religious needs of its officers.

It is also easy to find comparable benchmarks in real-world versions of the basketball case. For example, an association of virtually all of Illinois's public and private high schools had a rule that prohibited high school basketball players from wearing "hats or other headwear, with the sole exception of a headband no wider than two inches, while playing." In litigation, the association justified the rule on safety grounds: if hats fell off, players might slip on them.[18] Yet Illinois—and every other state—accommodated the need of players who must wear corrective lenses, even though glasses are a kind of "headwear" that might slip off, break, or jab an opposing player.[19] States permit glasses but require that they be held in place with retaining straps. There is no reason to treat yarmulkes any differently: players should be able to wear them but should be obliged to minimize the safety risks in any way possible. And that is more or less the solution that has been worked out: Jewish students are permitted to wear yarmulkes while playing, but they have been required to devise safer and more secure ways of fastening the yarmulkes to their hair.[20]

When, as in the Newark police case and the Illinois basketball case, the government has already accommodated secular needs that are plainly analogous to a religious one, it is easy to recognize a failure of equal regard. But the requirements of Equal Liberty apply even in the absence of ready-made comparisons. If, for example, the Forest Service chooses to locate a new road on federal lands in a way that needlessly desecrates a Native American religion's most sacred site, it is pretty clear that the officials did not treat the religion's interests seriously. There is an implicit counterfactual question lurking in the background, of the form "If the location of the road threatened a well-recognized conservationist interest (by killing off some of the last great redwood trees, say) or was a site sacred to a small but well-acknowledged group of Catholics or Orthodox Jews, would the Forest Service have pushed ahead with its plans?" The answer to that question is almost certainly no. In the real-world version of the Forest Service road case, the Supreme Court—about two years before it decided the *Peyote Case*—failed to think of the problem as one of unjust inequality and refused to intervene in the Forest Service's decision.[21] Congress, however, was considerably more sympathetic with the Native Americans' religious claim, and it promptly defunded the proposed road.[22]

The *Peyote Case* itself is another example of a situation in which Equal Liberty may insist on accommodation in the name of equality, despite the absence of an obvious benchmark. Oregon's law banning peyote was completely general; it contained no exceptions comparable to Illinois's allowing basketball players to wear glasses or Newark's permitting policemen with a certain skin condition to wear beards. Oregon's laws regulating alcohol, however, contained an interesting wrinkle. In several places, the laws made exceptions for the sacramental use of wine. For example, Oregon had what are called "local option dry laws": state statutes gave counties the option to decide whether to ban the purchase and consumption of alcohol. State law expressly exempted sales "of wines to church officials for sacramental purposes" from local dry laws. Oregon also exempted the sacramental consumption of wine from its prohibition of underage drinking.[23] Thus, while Oregon did nothing to accommodate the use of peyote during Native American religious rituals, it expressly accommodated the use of another drug, alcohol, during Christian religious ceremonies. This disparity in treatment could signal a failure of equal regard. Of course, it might be possible for Oregon to justify its disparate treatment of peyote and alcohol by reference to the different characteristics of the two drugs. Perhaps peyote is more dangerous than alcohol, so that an exemption for peyote rituals would be substantially more damaging to state interests than an exemption for Christian communion ceremonies. People might reasonably disagree about that question. But in the end the Equal Liberty approach might lead to the conclusion that Oregon acted unconstitutionally when it refused to make exceptions to its ban on peyote, despite the absence of an immediately applicable benchmark.

In both the comparatively easy cases like the Illinois basketball controversy and the Newark police case, and the hard cases like the Forest Service road case and the *Peyote Case,* the approach commended by Equal Liberty is the same. The Constitution requires accommodation when and only when a failure to accommodate bespeaks a failure of equal regard.

Enough Liberty?

In the cases we have described thus far, Equal Liberty provides an attractive and practical approach to protecting religious liberty. It avoids the conceptual quandaries that plague the separation model and the balancing approach, and it provides courts with a sound rationale for upholding free exercise rights in cases—such as the case about the Forest Service road and the Native American cemetery—in which judges have been too timid in the past. Readers might nevertheless wonder whether Equal Liberty can do justice in the full range of cases that seem to call for accommodation. We tend to believe, for example, that people should be free to practice their religion if doing so does no substantial harm to others. Equal Liberty does not seem to guarantee that result. It offers a "mere" antidiscrimination principle—a powerful one, to be sure, but an antidiscrimination principle nonetheless. If Equal Liberty exhausts the requirements of religious liberty, isn't it possible that the Constitution might sometimes permit the government to suppress religious practices that are profoundly valuable to participants and not much trouble to anyone else, provided that the state does so evenhandedly? And if so, shouldn't that possibility count against Equal Liberty?

This line of argument is very important in understanding the scope, justification, and practical reach of the Equal Liberty approach to religious liberty, and we will respond to it at some length. Our answer, in brief, is that Equal Liberty is not merely an antidiscrimination theory. As its name suggests, it is also a liberty-based theory. Indeed, it incorporates and depends upon two different kinds of liberties. The first are constitutional in character. The second are a matter of ordinary lawmaking and regulation: the various specific measures and exemptions that legislatures, judges, and agencies have crafted to meet the needs of diverse groups in society. Liberties of this second form are not constitutionally entrenched, but neither are they accidental. They are—as we shall soon explain in more detail—the inevitable product of lawmaking in a free, democratic, and pluralistic society, and a sound constitutional theory of religious freedom must build upon the foundation they provide.

We have already described how Equal Liberty incorporates general constitutional liberties. Its third principle, what we in Chapter 2 called its general liberty principle, insists on a robust set of constitutional rights available to all persons and groups, without any reference to their religious, nonreligious, or antireligious commitments. Prime among these liberties are the right to freedom of expression and the right to privacy (which is the label in our constitutional tradition for a general right of autonomy over a number of matters of deeply personal concern). We all benefit from these general liberties, but minority religious groups are especially advantaged by them. Many of the most important constitutional entitlements enjoyed by minority religious groups—for example, the right to make many important decisions about educating children, the right to speak openly and controversially and to solicit support and membership, the right not to participate in civic exercises like the Pledge of Allegiance—owe their existence to these general liberties. Equal Liberty would be incomplete without them.

The question then is what special or additional protection should be afforded to religious groups and individuals. Equal Liberty's reply is that groups and individuals are entitled to be free from discrimination on the basis of the spiritual foundations of their deep commitments and important projects. That protection is at the very heart of religious liberty, and it brings us to the second kind of liberty that matters to Equal Liberty. The basic idea is this: if American law in general respects liberty and accommodates individual needs, then a sufficiently powerful equality principle will ensure that it also respects religious needs in particular.

Interestingly, the wave of criticism generated by the Court's 1990 decision in the *Peyote Case* tacitly accepted the validity of an equality-based approach to the issue of accommodation. Many of the Court's critics seized on this provocative passage in Justice Scalia's opinion: "It may fairly be said that leaving accommodation to the political process will place at a relative disadvantage those religious practices that are not widely engaged in; but that [is an] unavoidable consequence of democratic government."[24] Critics correctly pointed out that this passage seems to renounce the Court's "traditional role as protector of minority rights against majority oppression. The 'disadvantaging' of minority religions is not 'unavoidable' if the courts are doing their job."[25] Complaints along these lines were offered as a reason for returning to the *Sherbert* case, with its compelling state interest test and presumptive right to disobey the law. But this was a non sequitur: if the fair treatment of social minorities was the nub of the problem in the *Peyote Case*, then what it called for was a robust equality principle like that sponsored by Equal Liberty, not a special and extreme privilege running only to those who are religious.

The problem with the *Peyote Case* is that it did not set forth a sufficiently robust equality principle, and did not recognize that the disparate treatment of sacramental wine and sacramental peyote in Oregon law gave rise to the suspicion that there was in fact a failure of equality. From the vantage of Equal Liberty, the *Peyote Case* was half right and half wrong in its approach to the question of religious accommodation. The Court was entirely correct in rejecting the idea that religiously motivated persons are presumptively entitled to disregard the laws that the rest of us are obliged to obey. But the Court was wrong in treating that as the end of the matter; as we have observed, Oregon's treatment of sacramental wine gave rise to the possibility that the state's failure to make comparable space for the sacramental use of peyote represented a failure of equal regard. Even before the *Peyote Case,* many other states, as well as the federal government, specifically exempted the ritual use of peyote from their controlled-substance laws, and, in the wake of the case, Oregon also did so;[26] the alacrity with which this initiative was adopted bespeaks a legislative judgment that the interests of the church members had previously been unfairly neglected.

The appropriate repair of the *Peyote Case* is the construction of a more articulate and robust principle of equality. Some of those unhappy with the *Peyote Case* worry, however, that no equality principle will have sufficient traction in cases like those involving dress codes. The problem they see is that in cases of this sort, important religious commitments will have no secular analogues: it is hard to imagine, for example, how a wholly secular person could feel gripped by a compelling moral duty to wear a beard or a special kind of hat (such as a yarmulke).

Yet, while it is improbable in the extreme that secular moral commitments will give people reason to wear beards or hats, health-related needs can and will supply reasons to engage in this or equivalent conduct. The state is likely to be appropriately responsive to health concerns, and the resulting accommodations can easily form the basis of

Equal Liberty claims on behalf of religious accommodation. We saw precisely this in the basketball-yarmulke case and the police-beard case. Worries about dress code cases are thus misplaced. Not only will Equal Liberty call for exemptions in most dress code cases, but it—unlike the balancing approach—helps to explain why they provide such attractive opportunities for accommodation: the burdens imposed in such cases are especially likely to result from neglect, rather than from an effort to share societal burdens equally.

Health-exemption analogies are an especially fruitful source of comparisons for Equal Liberty's antidiscrimination principle, but they are not unique. The state may sometimes provide special accommodations for the needs of working parents or the poor, for example. Moreover, the state may sometimes accommodate some religious interests while ignoring others. That was true, for example, in the case of Adell Sherbert, the mill worker who quit her job rather than work on Saturdays. South Carolina law expressly accommodated the interests of persons who worshiped on Sunday but not those of persons who worshiped on Saturday.

In our society, special needs are ubiquitous, and accommodations for them are common. Truly generally applicable laws are thus relatively rare: many laws contain some exceptions to accommodate special hardships. Exceptions, one might say, are pretty much the rule. For example, a Nebraska state college had a rule requiring freshmen to live on campus, but it made exceptions for all sorts of needs and interests—for freshmen who wanted to live with their parents, freshmen who had jobs, even freshmen who had connections to trustees of the college. But when a freshman sought an exception so that he could live off-campus at a Christian fellowship house, the college refused his request. He sued, contending that he was constitutionally entitled to an exception like the ones the college made for nonreligious interests—and a federal judge agreed.[27]

Other laws authorize public officials to make individualized determinations about whether exemptions are appropriate when ordinary rules impose hardships. Land use laws are often like that: for example, land owners who feel specially burdened by a zoning regulation typically have the right to apply for a variance (though it is usually difficult to get one). Exceptions of this kind must be available for religious and nonreligious needs on equal terms. Thus a Maryland federal judge held that if a historic preservation statute exempted owners in cases of financial hardship, it must likewise exempt churches when it imposed a hardship upon their religious mission.[28]

Unemployment benefits statutes also involve a kind of individualized hardship determination. Unemployment benefits are available only to people who meet three conditions: they were employed, they lost their jobs, and they continue to seek (and be available for) suitable employment. Claimants who quit their jobs or who turn down other jobs must show they had "good cause" for doing so. States typically assess claims of "good cause" through individualized hearings. This individualized process helps to explain why the unemployment benefits cases were virtually the only free exercise claims to prevail in the Supreme Court.[29] The claimants in each of those cases complained because states had refused to recognize religious reasons as "good cause" for leaving a job. For example, Eddie Thomas was a Jehovah's Witness and a pacifist who worked at a foundry. When he was transferred to a new job that required him to make tank turrets, Thomas quit on the ground that his religion prohibited him from participating so directly in war-making. The state denied him benefits on the ground that he had quit his job without good cause, and Thomas raised a free exercise claim.[30]

Thomas can be understood to have made a kind of antidiscrimination argument. If Thomas had a medical reason for rejecting the new assignment (if, for example, he had a severe allergy to a chemical used to make the turrets), the state would presumably have recognized it as "good cause." By treating his religious "allergy" to tank-building less favorably than it would have done a physical allergy, the state arguably discriminated against Thomas. Some Supreme Court justices have interpreted *Thomas* and the other unemployment benefits cases in much this way. Thus, Chief Justice Burger said that the cases stood for the principle that where a state has "created a mechanism for individualized exemptions . . . its refusal to extend an exemption to an instance of religious hardship suggests a discriminatory intent."[31] Likewise, Justice Stevens observed that treating "a religious objection . . . as though it were tantamount to a physical impairment that made it impossible for the employee to continue work . . . could be viewed as a protection against unequal treatment rather than a grant of favored treatment for the members of the religious sect."[32]

Because exceptions and accommodations are so common in American law, critics of the Supreme Court's decision in the *Peyote Case* have had to retract their early, dire predictions about its consequences. Soon after the case, a parade of witnesses—including liberals such as Nadine Strossen, president of the ACLU, and conservatives such as Michael Farris, president of the Home School Legal Defense Association—testified before Congress, claiming that the decision had "all but repealed the Free Exercise Clause."[33] These critics of the *Peyote Case* apparently assumed that most American laws were "neutral and generally applicable," so that virtually all exemptions claimants were doomed to fail after the *Peyote Case*. Yet, as we have seen, that is very far from being the case, and as a result claimants have found it possible to fashion compelling cases under the equality principle in the *Peyote Case*, a principle that is less protective than the one recommended by Equal Liberty.

Of course, judges applying Equal Liberty might sometimes fail, for good reasons or bad, to vindicate free exercise claims that seem, on their face, to be appealing. But that is no less true of any other approach, including the balancing approach that the Court abandoned in the *Peyote Case*. It bears remembering that free exercise claims had a truly wretched success rate under the old compelling state interest test in the Supreme Court and the federal appellate courts: almost everybody lost.[34] As a result, it is far from clear that free exercise claimants are worse off after the *Peyote Case* than they were before it.[35] Equal Liberty recommends an equality principle more robust than the one in the *Peyote Case,* and it would accordingly enhance the scope of constitutional protection. The result would be an approach to religious freedom that is not only normatively coherent (in a way that separation and the balancing approach are not) but powerfully protective of individual liberty.

Are Religious Obligations Unique?

Critics have offered more specific reasons why, in their view, Equal Liberty's antidiscrimination principle is not a trustworthy foundation for exemptions jurisprudence. Some have contended that religious interests and commitments are unique, so that the comparative project that Equal Liberty recommends is impossible to undertake. Others object that Equal Liberty makes the accommodation of religion a matter of accident rather than a matter of justice, because it makes the availability of exemptions for religious conduct dependent upon the state's entirely discretionary choice to create exemptions for other, nonreligious hardships. A third group argues that Equal Liberty improperly demotes free exercise rights to a secondary constitutional status in relation to other rights, especially free speech rights. In the next several sections, we consider these three objections in turn.

Professor Douglas Laycock is among those who have attacked antidiscrimination approaches to the exemptions problem on the ground that "religion is unlike other human activities." To buttress this claim, he points out that there is no comparison between the desire to wear a yarmulke and the desire to wear a Budweiser promotional cap.[36] True enough. But neither is a teenager's desire to look cool in a promotional cap comparable to a disabled American's need to wear special clothing or protective equipment. As we have already seen, health-related concerns and other serious secular commitments generate useful analogues for religious needs and obligations. Our theory depends upon the idea that the state must not discriminate between religious convictions and comparably serious secular convictions; it does not depend on the idea, which is manifestly false, that religious convictions are comparable to any secular conviction or impulse, however frivolous (like the impulse to don a Budweiser cap).

Several critics of Equal Liberty have complained that we do not offer a framework within which religious and nonreligious interests can be compared. One such critic, Michael McConnell, suggests that such comparisons are simply impossible, and that it follows that the equal-regard/accommodation leg of Equal Liberty is incoherent.[37] A related objection has been advanced by Andrew Koppelman, who argues that our exposition of Equal Liberty is crucially incomplete because we do not specify any theory that explains which secular interests are comparable to religious ones and which are not.[38] McConnell and Koppelman are thoughtful and forceful analysts, but here they both go astray in roughly the same way, by assuming that Equal Liberty requires courts or legislatures to make precise comparisons of the interests that its citizens have.

What Equal Liberty demands of the state is that it attend to the deep minority religious commitments of its citizens with the same regard that it brings to bear on other, more mainstream concerns. But to insist on equal regard is not to imply that diverse human commitments and projects—religious and nonreligious, minority and mainstream—come equipped with "price tags" that specify their subjective weight for those who have them. Interpersonal comparisons of this sort are notoriously difficult, whether or not the interests being compared straddle the religious/nonreligious divide. Equal regard does not depend on the capacity of rulemakers to weigh the interests of their citizens with mathematical precision. Nor does equal regard stipulate that religiously inspired interests automatically go to the head of the class, to be treated as though they were inevitably as weighty as the most weighty of human interests. Equal regard is a public stance or posture, an attitude. Disparities in treatment between what seem roughly comparable secularly grounded interests and religiously grounded interests, or between interests grounded in mainstream beliefs and those that derive from minority beliefs, suggest a failure of equal regard. Hence the force of the claims in the basketball eyeglass/yarmulke comparison and the police-beard example. The question is whether a government that was alert and sympathetic in principle to the religiously inspired interests of a particular minority faith could have fashioned the contested disparity in accommodation.

Accordingly, Equal Liberty does not depend on the possibility of close comparisons of religious and secular interests or of a theory by which such close comparisons could be guided. We do not need to elaborately explain or calibrate the weight of a folliculitis-sufferer's interest in avoiding pain versus a devout Muslim's interest in honoring his religious obligation to wear a beard. Both are put to an unfortunate choice when the opportunity to serve as policemen in Newark is at stake; and both will almost certainly be denied that opportunity by dint of the force of their reasons for not being clean-shaven.

Equal Liberty *does* depend on our ability to see these interests as sufficiently comparable to indict a government that accommodates one and flatly rebuffs the other. So, if someone were tempted to deny that a breach of a religious mandate could be as important to some persons as the avoidance of a nasty rash, Equal Liberty could not gain traction in the police-beard case. Indeed, this deflationary view of religious conviction would pretty much silence Equal Liberty. But this is a view that almost no one holds, and one that we feel comfortable in dismissing.

More common—though to us no more credible—is the view that

no secular need or commitment, no matter how serious, can ever be comparable to a religious obligation. Advocates of this view observe that, from the perspective of a religious believer, divine commands take precedence over all other needs and obligations. Believers who flout such commands risk eternal damnation or other awesome punishments that dwarf any harms one might suffer in the earthly world. Moreover, laws that conflict with divine commands put believers in an exquisitely difficult position by forcing them to disobey either divine or secular law. Secular citizens, these commentators contend, never face any comparable dilemma.[39]

This claim has a rather metaphysical character to it, and, if we wanted to pass on the truth of it, we would have to make some uncomfortable choices among theological perspectives. From an external, secular perspective, there is no reason to assume that any specific religious practice (particularly one prohibited by law) is *really* commanded by God. Nor is there any reason to assume that as a matter of real-world phenomenology, religious convictions exercise a more powerful grip upon the individual psyche than do deeply felt secular convictions. From a secular perspective, the comparative force of religious and secular convictions is a matter for empirical scientific inquiry. Likewise, if examined from the perspective of *other* religions, a believer's commitments may appear to be the product of foolish mistakes rather than divine command. Many religious Americans, for example, regard the Santerian practice of animal sacrifice as a superstition with gruesome entailments. And even within the perspective of a sympathetic religious believer, not all burdens on religious practice will involve direct conflicts between religious and secular obligations. Some religious activities are elective rather than compulsory; participation in a sacrament, for example, may be regarded as a privilege rather than a duty. Other practices are in some relevant sense substitutable, like the many ways available to a Christian believer who takes herself to be deeply obligated to do good works.

Fortunately, we can avoid all of this. We need not engage in the dubious enterprise of finding some ground from which to make sweeping metaphysical or phenomenological comparisons between religious and secular commitments. It suffices to observe that secular commitments can be sufficiently compelling that people will die rather than compromise them (think of parents' love for their children), and that secular needs may be so unyielding as to render ordinary courses of action unthinkable. So, for example, skin irritation may be a trivial burden by comparison to the wrath of Allah, but if a police department prohibited all officers from wearing beards, the regulation would have much the same impact on folliculitis sufferers and Muslims: neither group could serve in the police force.

More generally, any persons who hold that divine law trumps civil law will be strongly inclined to obey God rather than the state. Such persons will suffer the penalty imposed by civil law rather than betray their religious commitments. As a result, the price they pay will not be eternal damnation or whatever other terrifying punishment their deity (or deities) might mete out for noncompliance with divine commands, but the mundane sanctions of the state: loss of a job, ineligibility for benefits, or, in some cases, imprisonment. That price is identical with the one paid by individuals who are unable to comply with the law for nonreligious reasons, such as disability, health, or secular conscience. Equal Liberty's antidiscrimination principle requires that the state show equal regard for the religious and nonreligious needs of citizens when it distributes these burdens—by which we mean the burdens of civil law, the only burdens that the state has any power to impose.

Accidental Justice?

Some people contend that our approach makes the availability of exemptions depend upon arbitrary coincidences. For example, Equal

Liberty's antidiscrimination principle helped Officers Abdul-Aziz and Mustafa to get an exemption from the Newark police department's grooming regulations, but only because Newark already made an exemption for the benefit of officers who suffered from folliculitis. Isn't it just good luck that such an exemption existed? Suppose Newark made no exception for officers with folliculitis. Or, for that matter, suppose that there were no such skin condition. It might then seem that, according to the doctrine of Equal Liberty, the officers would be entitled to no relief. Yet most observers (ourselves included) would feel unhappy with that result: they (and we) would feel a strong tug from the accommodation intuition when confronted with Newark's treatment of its Muslim officers. So somebody might conclude that Equal Liberty offers only a kind of "accidental justice." Or, worse yet, someone might decide that our approach recommends a kind of parlor game, in which a believer's fate depends on hiring a lawyer clever enough to identify real or hypothetical nonreligious analogues to the believer's distinctive religious needs.[40]

It is true, of course, that the existence of folliculitis is a morally arbitrary accident. If there were no such condition, or if Newark made no exemptions for the benefit of those afflicted with it, then we would have to look for analogies that were further afield. That is what we did when we discussed the case of the yarmulke-wearing basketball players. We knew of no basketball players who had to wear hats for medical reasons, so we analogized wearing a hat to wearing eyeglasses. And when we analyzed the ritual ingestion of peyote, we invoked an even rougher comparison: we noted that Oregon exempted the ritual consumption of alcohol from its local-option dry laws, but we conceded that alcohol and peyote had different properties.

As these analogies become less exact, they allow more room for argument and disagreement. Thus Oregon's exemptions for the sacramental uses of wine provide evidence that Native American religious practitioners are entitled to an exemption for their peyote ceremony, but the differences between alcohol and peyote provide Oregon with a counterargument. At the furthest extreme of such difficulties are cases like that of the Forest Service road, in which there may be no discrete instance of accommodation to point to as a point of comparison. All that is available in such cases is the counterfactual question of whether more mainstream concerns would have been treated more favorably. Arguably, what gives us confidence about such counterfactual judgments in suitably extreme cases is our experience in the world; but by hypothesis that experience is too diffuse and attenuated from the case in question to permit serving up concrete points of comparison.

In this sense, the Newark police officers were indeed lucky: they wanted exactly the same exemption that Newark had already granted to folliculitis sufferers, and they accordingly could offer powerful proof that Newark had flouted Equal Liberty's antidiscrimination principle. But it does not follow that the officers' entitlement to an exemption depended *in principle* upon the existence of a skin condition like folliculitis. It means only that the existence of such a condition, and the exemption created in response to it, made it especially easy for the officers to show that their interests had been unconstitutionally neglected. Or, to put the point more generally: some people who suffer from discrimination will be lucky enough to have knockdown proof of discrimination, and others will not. That banal observation holds true for *every* antidiscrimination principle. It is not a reason to reject antidiscrimination principles in general or Equal Liberty in particular.

Suppose, however, that a critic of our position tries to push the "accidental justice" objection further. Imagine, says this critic, that the Newark police department never made any exemptions to accommodate any individual hardships of any kind. (We note that this supposition is very strongly counterfactual, since the Americans with Disabilities Act would probably require the department to accommodate disabilities.)[41] Or, since we are now playing at thought experiments, imagine that nobody had physical disabilities, so that there was no need to allow basketball players to wear glasses or sensitive-skinned police officers to wear beards. In such a world, would we not still feel that the yarmulke-wearing Jewish basketball players and the beard-growing Muslim police officers deserved exemptions? And, if so, doesn't this thought experiment show that, ultimately, the antidiscrimination principle cannot fully account for common intuitions about accommodation?

It may be enough to say that the imaginary world of this thought experiment is nothing like our own. In our world, as we have noticed before, special needs are ubiquitous and accommodations for them are common. As a result, it is nearly impossible to devise an example of a minority religious practice for which there is no secular or mainstream religious analogue. Our claim is that in this world, the world we actually inhabit, religious needs and obligations are not at all unique, and the right principle for analyzing exemptions claims is therefore a kind of equality principle. By contrast, in the imaginary world in which the only special needs are religious needs, religious commitments would (by hypothesis) be different from all other commitments (because they, and they alone, would require accommodation through exemptions). What one might say about such a radically different world is not our concern: we are writing constitutional theory for this world, not for some fanciful alternative to it.

There is a deeper point to be made here, one that answers both the "accidental justice" and "parlor game" objections to the model of Equal Liberty. The critic's thought experiment calls upon us to assume away some crucial conditions that make constitutions necessary. Constitutional theory is about (among other things) how to structure governments for a people with heterogeneous needs, commitments, obligations, talents, and desires. Constitutional governments must produce laws to coordinate the pursuit of divergent life projects by diverse citizens. There is thus nothing "accidental" about the dazzling array of special needs and responsive accommodations that provide traction for Equal Liberty's antidiscrimination principle. On the contrary, they flow directly from the basic goals of constitutional governance in a complex, modern society.

The constitutional enterprise inevitably promises both benefits and burdens for citizens who participate in it. The laws provide the "ordered liberty" without which citizens could not hope to pursue any life project successfully (save, perhaps, for a kind of survivalist fantasy), but the laws also restrict their liberty to carry out any such project. The right of religious freedom is *not* the right to an exemption from this general state of affairs. It is not, for example, the right to benefit from zoning laws insofar as they create flourishing residential neighborhoods, but then to escape those laws insofar as they restrict one's religious projects. Instead, the right of religious freedom is the right to participate in the constitutional project on fair terms, so that one is neither privileged nor disfavored on the basis of the religious (or nonreligious) character of one's commitments. Participating on fair terms entails, among other things, having one's religious needs accommodated on the same terms as comparably serious religious and nonreligious needs. Thus, when the state accommodates small burdens on secular and mainstream religious commitments, it should likewise accommodate small burdens on more unusual religious practices. And, conversely, when state interests are deemed so important that no exemption is made even for large burdens upon secular or mainstream religious commitments, then the state should also be free to impose large burdens on less common religious practices. That is why Equal Liberty's comparative inquiry is not in any sense a "parlor game." The relevant question is whether the government, in coordinating diverse life projects, is sharing burdens fairly among them. To ask about fair shares is to ask a question that is inherently comparative.

Free Exercise and Free Speech

People sometimes object to Equal Liberty's treatment of the exemptions problem in another way: they say that by relying on antidiscrimination principles, Equal Liberty demotes religious freedom to a lesser status than that of free speech, the other major right protected in the First Amendment. Justice Sandra Day O'Connor, for example, made such an argument in her concurring opinion in the *Peyote Case*. She noted that the Court used the compelling state interest test to evaluate free speech claims, and she contended that the Court ought therefore to apply the same test to free exercise exemption claims, since the free speech and free exercise rights enjoyed equal constitutional status.[42]

There is good reason to think that comparing rights in this way is a futile exercise. At the heart of free speech jurisprudence is the notion that belief and simple expression should not be the occasion for state reprisal, even if other persons are persuaded by that expression to perform damaging criminal acts. No one can be punished for believing that stealing from the rich and giving to the poor is entirely justified; and no one can be punished for distributing a leaflet that makes the case that this is so, even if the leaflet successfully persuades some persons who consider its arguments to emulate Robin Hood. On the other hand, anyone who undertakes to steal from the rich and give to the poor, even if the motive is exquisitely communicative ("No one will get my point unless I go out and do it!"), can be punished by the state. Free exercise claims get interesting and difficult at exactly the point where the heartland of free speech is left behind. Religious believers clearly can be committed to the view that God demands that they steal from the rich and give to the poor, and they can publish and circulate the interpretations of sacred scripture upon which their belief is founded, even if their beliefs and scriptural support successfully persuade some persons to emulate Robin Hood as a matter of divine obligation. Free exercise claims arise only at the point where someone acts on her belief and undertakes to force redistributions of wealth at gunpoint.

That contrast makes Justice O'Connor's argument about the equal status of speech and religion a stark non sequitur. There are many reasons why a jurisprudence of justice might distinguish between doing an act and inspiring others to do that act, without any regard to the status of free expression or religious liberty.

All that said, a comparison of free speech doctrine with free exercise doctrine as shaped by Equal Liberty makes Equal Liberty look very robust indeed. Free speech doctrine is at its strongest when the government treats speech adversely because of its content. So, for example, if the government penalizes the criticism of public officials, or if it prohibits racist speech, or if it suppresses speech about sex, the Court will usually invoke the compelling state interest test—and it will usually find the regulations unconstitutional. Equal Liberty and the Supreme Court's free exercise doctrine recommend precisely the same level of exacting scrutiny when government policy singles out a particular religion or religion in general for adverse treatment. So, for example, when the City of Hialeah prohibited the *ritual* slaughter of animals but allowed other forms of slaughter, the Supreme Court quite rightly applied the compelling state interest test and unanimously found the prohibition unconstitutional.[43]

The cases in which free expression comes closest to free exercise are those in which government is regulating speech not because of its content but because of its external impact—such as its noise or its impact on traffic. In those cases, the Court is highly deferential to government and its regulatory interests; "time, place, and manner" regulations almost always survive judicial scrutiny. This is so even with regard to regulations that single out expressive activity for special burdens. In an arguably analogous context, the Court has taken a very deferential attitude toward copyright laws, even though copyright regulates expressive activity and no other kind of activity. By contrast, any law that explicitly imposed special burdens or penalties on religious activity, and religious activity alone, would (and should) receive demanding scrutiny from the Court. To be sure, the Court defers to the government with regard to laws that disadvantage religion by excluding it from subsidy programs, but here again free exercise doctrine parallels, rather than deviates from, free speech doctrine: the Court also affords government wide latitude to decide what kinds of speech it will fund.

More to the point, free exercise doctrine (as recommended by Equal Liberty and as understood by the current Court) is considerably more generous to exemption claims than is free speech doctrine. Neither movie theaters nor libraries nor schools can invoke the Free Speech Clause to demand an exemption from local zoning laws, even though all of them are loci of expressive activity and even though land use regulations may make it difficult (or impossible) for them to operate. Newspaper publishers have no entitlement to exemption from taxes, labor laws, and safety regulations that burden their expressive activity and that may, in some circumstances, force them to stop publishing. Yet these are exactly the sorts of rights that are at stake in free exercise exemption cases, and Equal Liberty as well as current Supreme Court doctrine will sometimes recognize such rights. For that reason, Equal Liberty protects liberty in a way that is *more demanding* than current free speech doctrine.

There is a basic conceptual feature beneath the doctrinal details we have been discussing. A concern for equality suffuses free speech law, just as it does Equal Liberty's recommended version of free exercise law. Free speech concerns are greatest when the government discriminates against particular viewpoints, and they are almost as intense when the government burdens speech because of its content (by, for example, imposing special restrictions on pornography or advertising). Laws that discriminate against speech in general to the point of choking off speech activity may also trigger constitutional concern—as was the case when Los Angeles airport authorities enacted an absurd regulation prohibiting "all First Amendment activities" at the airport.[44] But other laws that restrict speech without regard to viewpoint or content will attract only limited judicial review; copyright laws are an example. And free speech concerns are at low ebb when laws applicable to conduct in general impose incidental burdens on expressive activity—as, for example, when land use regulations limit the freedom of movie theaters and newspapers along with the freedom of everyone else.

We do not mean that equality concerns can explain all of free speech law. Some cases—such as those insisting that government allow expressive activity to take place in public parks and on public streets—are not in any obvious way about equality. And there remains the basal question about why speech, like religion but unlike (say) recreation, is entitled to special constitutional solicitude. Nevertheless, our reflections in this section not only highlight important parallels between free speech and free exercise claims; they also provide concrete reinforcement for a point that we made more abstractly in the last chapter: there is no sharp distinction to be had between "liberty rights" and "equality rights." Being free from burdens that are imposed through discrimination, hostility, and neglect is an important form of liberty. Not surprisingly, the freedom of speech, often considered the preeminent and most securely protected "liberty right" in the American constitutional system, reflects that fact.

Daniel Seeger, Secular Thomas, and Related Characters

Thus far in this chapter, we have been concerned with the accommodation of religious practices. We close by considering the converse problem. Equal Liberty's antidiscrimination principle demands that people not be treated with hostility or neglect because of the religious or nonreligious character of their convictions. Suppose, then, that the government accommodates certain religious needs but refuses to provide comparable accommodation for secular interests. Should persons with secular needs be entitled to constitutional relief?

The answer depends upon the kind of secular need or commitment that is at stake. Secular moral commitments are much like religious commitments. Moral commitments may be subject to hostility or neglect precisely because of their nonreligious or irreligious character; for that reason, Equal Liberty's antidiscrimination principle demands that they receive special constitutional solicitude. By contrast, other secular needs, such as health needs, induce an asymmetric response. As we have already seen (in, for example, the case involving bearded police officers), the government's differential treatment of health needs and religious needs may give rise to a successful constitutional claim when the religious needs are treated less favorably: courts may conclude that the state is discriminating against religious needs because of their religious character. But the fact that the government accommodates religious needs does not automatically generate a constitutional claim that it must accommodate health needs. Because health needs are shared by religious and nonreligious people, there is no reason to suppose that government will discriminate against them by virtue of their nonreligious character.

Here again, examples help to clarify the idea. We begin with a well-known case from the Vietnam War era. At the time, federal law permitted young men to assert conscientious-objector status, and so to avoid military service, only if they could demonstrate themselves committed to pacifism by virtue of their "religious training and belief." The statute specifically defined "religious training and belief" to mean "an individual's belief in relation to a Supreme Being involving duties superior to those arising from any human relation, but [not including] essentially political, sociological, or philosophical views or a merely personal moral code." Daniel Seeger, who found and articulated the grounds for his pacifism in secular forms of moral reflection rather than in anything recognizably religious, sought exemption from the draft and challenged the constitutionality of the law. The Supreme Court ducked the constitutional issue, holding that Seeger's beliefs were religious within the meaning of the statute: the Court declared that the statutory exemption was available to anyone having a "sincere and meaningful belief which occupies in the life of its possessor a place parallel to that filled by the God of those admittedly qualifying for the exemption."[45] This was a rather strained reading of the statute, and it required the justices to ignore some powerful legislative history to the contrary. For our purposes, the crucial issue is the constitutional one that would arise if the statute discriminated against Seeger and other secular pacifists: Would such discrimination violate the principles of Equal Liberty?

We think that the answer is plainly yes. If the government granted conscientious-objector status only on the basis of religiously motivated opposition to war, it would be favoring some needs over others purely on the basis of their theological character or spiritual foundations. Seeger's pacifism might be no less sincere, no less intense, no less durable, and no less binding upon his conscience than the convictions of his religiously motivated counterparts, but the government would nevertheless favor their claims over his. In a country as religious as the United States, it is easy to understand how such favoritism might arise: radical moral dissent, and fervent moral commitment, will seem more familiar and more "American" to many citizens and legislators if predicated upon religious conviction rather than secular conviction. One of Equal Liberty's primary goals is to prevent the government from showing this kind of hostility and neglect to needs that seem, by virtue of their religious (or nonreligious) character, eccentric to most Americans.

Similar considerations apply to a hypothetical character whom we invented some years ago, Secular Thomas. Secular Thomas is the secular counterpart of Eddie Thomas, the petitioner in *Thomas v. Review Board,* who quit his job because his assignment to a tank-building operation conflicted with his understanding of his religious faith. Secular Thomas, like Eddie Thomas, is a pacifist, but on secular rather than religious grounds. Suppose that Secular Thomas quits his job (just as Eddie Thomas did), applies for unemployment benefits, and is denied. Is he entitled to constitutional relief?

We expect that some readers will find Secular Thomas an implausible character. Surely pacifist convictions might keep one from serving in the military, but would they bar one from helping to manufacture tank turrets? Skeptics might suspect that the moral convictions of Secular Thomas were at least partly the product of self-interest: having been transferred to (we might suspect) a less desirable job assignment, he "discovered" that his moral principles required him to quit. But it is a factual question whether Secular Thomas actually believes what he says he believes. A court will have to determine whether Secular Thomas is sincere, just as a court had to determine whether Eddie Thomas was sincere about the religious beliefs he claimed to have. Our hypothetical presupposes that we are convinced of the sincerity of Secular Thomas's belief: does the state then have a constitutional obligation to accommodate him?

Once he has overcome factual doubts about his sincerity, Secular Thomas seems to be exactly analogous to Daniel Seeger. His secular convictions prohibit him from participating in warfare, and there is a risk that the state will disrespect those convictions precisely because they are not religious in nature. If Eddie Thomas is entitled to constitutional relief, then so should be Secular Thomas.

Not all moral convictions will trigger the protections of Equal Liberty, however. For example, imagine a single mother whose employer, like Adell Sherbert's, asks her to begin working on Saturdays. The worker, whom we will call Mother Sherbert, has arranged childcare for Monday through Friday, but she is unable to find any affordable childcare on Saturday. She accordingly quits her job and looks for another that will not require her to work on weekends. Unable to find such a job, she files for unemployment compensation. The state refuses to grant benefits to Mother Sherbert. It finds that she lacked good cause for giving up her job. Mother Sherbert sues. She points out that had she refused to work on Saturday for religious reasons, as Adell Sherbert did, she would have been entitled to benefits, and she contends that the state is discriminating against her because her reasons for quitting are secular.

We think that Mother Sherbert should lose her case insofar as it is predicated upon constitutional claims of religious freedom. Unlike in the case of Daniel Seeger or that of Secular Thomas, we see no reason to suppose that the state is rejecting Mother Sherbert's claims because of their relation to religion. Indeed, we have thus far said nothing about the religious or nonreligious character of Mother Sherbert's commitment to her children. We can imagine at least three possibilities. First, Mother Sherbert might be a thoroughly irreligious person, and her commitment to her children might be entirely secular. Second, Mother Sherbert might be religious, but she might view her commitment to her children as growing out of secular reasons, such as her love for them and her secular moral convictions. Or, third, Mother Sherbert might be a religious person who self-consciously conceptualizes her duties to her children as part of her duties to God. If the state were to treat these three possibilities differently, we would of course have a religious liberty problem. But so long as the state treats the three cases identically, then it seems clear that Mother Sherbert has been denied benefits because of some judgment the state has made about childcare needs, not because of hostility or neglect toward either religion or irreligion.

This position may seem to saddle us with an embarrassing inconsistency. Suppose that Mother Sherbert viewed her commitment to her children as a matter of religious duty. Would her claim not be on a par with that of Adell Sherbert—different duty, same source? And since we defended the result in Adell Sherbert's case, are not we bound to hold for Mother Sherbert, too? No, for the two religiously motivated duties are importantly different. Adell Sherbert's convictions yielded an inflexible obligation not to work on Saturdays, whereas Mother Sherbert's do not. Mother Sherbert could take Saturday work if she could obtain childcare. In that regard, she (unlike Adell) is in exactly the same position as an entirely irreligious mother. The state's refusal to recognize childcare needs as "good cause" is presumably predicated on a judgment that, if the mothers tried a bit harder, they would be able to find a suitable caretaker on the weekends. That determination may be unrealistic and harsh, and it might reflect sex discrimination, since childcare burdens fall disproportionately on women. It does not, however, involve any imposition on religious freedom.

Finally, we consider what we deem an exceptionally difficult case. Suppose that the Newark Police Department had exactly the opposite policy from the one it actually enforced: suppose, in particular, that the department permitted officers to wear beards if they were religiously obliged to do so, but made no exception for those who suffered from folliculitis or other skin conditions. Imagine now a police officer—we'll call him Officer Beard—who alleges that the state has violated Equal Liberty by treating his secular, health-related reasons for wearing a beard less well than religious ones. (Officer Beard would have a claim for accommodation under the Americans with Disabilities Act, but let's assume that, for whatever reason, the ADA is out of the picture.) Should Officer Beard prevail?

It is hard to say. On the one hand, it is implausible to suppose that Officer Beard's religious status or beliefs have anything to do with the way he is being treated. Indeed, we have not specified Officer Beard's religious faith; he might, for all we know, be a member of a mainstream or majority sect. In this respect, Officer Beard's case is weaker than Daniel Seeger's, since it seems apparent that the state treated Seeger less favorably precisely because of the irreligious character of his beliefs. On the other hand, the state can violate Equal Liberty's antidiscrimination principle by preferring religious commitments over all others. That seems to be, in our hypothetical, exactly what Newark is doing. Why else would Newark deny Officer Beard the same accommodation that it allows to those who have religious reasons for wearing beards?

If we struggle mightily, we can imagine one nondiscriminatory justification for the policy. Officer Beard's objection to shaving, like Mother Sherbert's objection to working on Saturday, is conditional: if

Officer Beard could shave without pain, he would be willing to do so. As a result, his secular claim for accommodation is flexible compared to those of his religious counterparts, who recognize an absolute prohibition upon shaving. If Newark determined that proper treatment can cure folliculitis, or that those who have the condition can in fact shave with only minor pain, then it might have a reason to accommodate the Muslim officers but not Officer Beard.

As far as we can tell, these determinations would be flatly false. But Newark's hypothetical failings in this regard would not involve any violation of *religious liberty*. Newark would be treating Office Beard badly, but it would not be treating him badly by virtue of some judgment about his religious convictions (or about the comparative importance of other people's religious convictions). So the question in our hypothetical case would come down to how closely courts should look to see whether Newark's policy was based on mistakes of this kind rather than on a constitutionally invalid preference for religion.

To avoid the conclusion that the hypothetical policy discriminates in favor of religion, we would have to assume that the officials responsible for it were very foolish. We are reluctant to do that, and so we are inclined to regard the policy as preferring religious obligations because of their religious character. That is unconstitutional discrimination, and we would therefore uphold Officer Beard's constitutional claim.

We recognize, however, that different people—even among those who accept the model of Equal Liberty more or less wholeheartedly— might reach different results. Indeed, the entire problem of secular claimants is delicate and admits of multiple approaches producing a variety of results. But that circumstance is hardly disturbing. Officer Beard, Secular Thomas, and other secular claimants pose difficult cases. As we have said before, we should not expect theories of religious liberty to make hard cases seem easy; instead, their job is to explain why such cases are hard and what factors are relevant to their disposition.

Too Hard to Apply?

We hope that we have now shown that an equality-based approach can provide a robust basis for accommodating religious conduct. One of our academic critics once conceded in a private conversation that we had done so, but then he leveled another—and we think rather curious—objection against Equal Liberty. "Now that I understand your approach, I'm comfortable with it in theory," he said, "but I think that it is just too hard for judges to apply in practice." He meant that the process of identifying appropriate comparison cases—police officers with folliculitis, basketball players with eyeglasses, and so on—was just too demanding for the ordinary judge.

What a strange complaint! Concerns about the workability of a constitutional theory ought to count strongly in favor of Equal Liberty, and against its most apparent rival, the family of balancing tests. The compelling state interest test was so flagrantly and indefensibly partial to religion and destructive of important state interests that the Court never paid more than lip service to it. The result was a collection of cases that did no credit to the Court or to religious liberty, even according to the defenders of the test. And any effort to ratchet that test down to a more plausible demand for balance would lead into all the difficulties we canvassed at the beginning of this chapter, and put the Court in the role for which it has the least competence, namely, that of deciding in any given case whether the vector of sound social policy and compassion ought to result in a flat regulatory rule or in a more textured rule softened by various exemptions.

In contrast, Equal Liberty asks judges to compare different claimants and treat like cases alike, a task that judges have traditionally performed in common law systems, including the American one. We have good reason to expect judges to be good at this. The sad history of the compelling state interest test before the *Peyote Case,* and the success of litigants under equality-based tests after it, suggest that Equal Liberty is much the best hope of those whose religious convictions put them crosswise with regulatory demands.

It is true, of course, that as immediate and clear benchmarks for comparison in Equal Liberty cases (as in the Newark police beard case) give way to more remote and less clear benchmarks (as in the *Peyote Case*), and eventually give way still further to cases in which only our counterfactual judgment is available (as in the Forest Service road case), the job of judges will get progressively more difficult. Ultimately, there will surely be some cases which involve a genuine failure of equal regard but which evade judicial detection and invalidation. It is entirely reasonable to hope and expect that Congress and state legislatures will help at these margins of judicial enforceability of the Constitution, and in Chapter 7 we examine how legislatures might do just that. Before turning to that topic, however, we continue our exploration of the judicial enforcement of Equal Liberty by examining a series of Establishment Clause controversies that have roiled American politics for more than three decades.

· IV ·

Ten Commandments,
Three Plastic Reindeer,
and One Nation . . . Indivisible

EARLY ONE DECEMBER DAY some years ago, the principal of a public elementary school somewhere on Long Island called the executive director of the New York Civil Liberties Union. "Ira," he said, "Please don't tell anyone I'm calling you, but we're having an assembly next week, and I want to know whether it is okay for us to sing a few Christmas carols." Ira replied: "Joe, please don't tell anyone that I told you this, but just go ahead and do it!"

Some disputes about religious liberty can seem either deeply important to a pluralistic society or so trivial that the attention paid them is silly and exasperating. Constitutional questions about Christmas carols are like that, which is our point in recalling the brief telephone exchange between two men, who in different circumstances might have been courtroom adversaries. So too are the roiling controversies we take up in this chapter: Ten Commandments displays, crèches in public parks, and Pledge of Allegiance ceremonies. Perhaps this sense of vacillating between the profound and the irritating is inevitable: the stakes in these cases are purely symbolic, but religious conviction is a domain in which symbols are often very important to Americans.

Whatever else is true, public exhibitions of religious symbols excite intense and heated controversy. The resulting cases provide a starting point for exploring Equal Liberty's implications for Establishment Clause jurisprudence. At the outset of that exploration, we need an account of how religious symbols matter in American culture. It is to the task of developing such an approach that we first turn.

Public Displays

Cases about crèche displays, town-sponsored Christmas trees, and other public exhibitions of religious symbols came to the Court relatively late in its continuing effort to develop an attractive and workable approach to Establishment Clause cases. Cases about public aid to religious schools first reached the Court in the late 1940s, and the Court's first school prayer cases were decided in the 1960s; in contrast, the first Christmas display case arose in the 1980s. Now, however, the annual Holiday Wars—political and legal skirmishes over whether the government can sponsor displays celebrating Christmas, Hannukah, and so on—have joined eggnog, greeting cards, and fruitcake as staples of December culture in America.

When Supreme Court justices analyze cases about the public display of religious symbols, they tend to use reasons and concepts that fit nicely with the precepts of Equal Liberty. In particular, they usually invoke some version of the endorsement test that Justice O'Connor developed in the Court's very first holiday display case, *Lynch v. Donnelly* (1984). *Lynch* involved the display by the city of Pawtucket, Rhode Island, of a nativity scene or crèche in a park owned by a nonprofit organization and located in the city's shopping district.[1] Justice O'Connor said that the crucial question was whether the display amounted to an endorsement of religion (or of a particular religion):

> The Establishment Clause prohibits government from making adherence to a religion relevant in any way to a person's stand-

ing in the political community. Government can run afoul of that prohibition . . . [by its] endorsement or disapproval of religion. Endorsement sends a message to nonadherents that they are outsiders, not full members of the political community, and an accompanying message to adherents that they are insiders, favored members of the political community.[2]

Justice O'Connor's words are music to an Equal Liberty enthusiast's ears. Not everyone finds them convincing, though.[3] In *Lee v. Weisman* (1992), a case about a prayer at a public school graduation, Justice Scalia wrote a blistering dissent critiquing Justice O'Connor's endorsement test.[4] Scalia would recognize Establishment Clause violations only in cases in which somebody suffered "coercion . . . backed by threat of penalty."[5] Pawtucket had not forced anybody to say a prayer, or to participate in a ritual, or to visit its homage to the Christmas season. So where, Scalia asked, was the harm?

"Taxpayers were forced to pay for the display," someone might say, "even if they rejected its religious message." But this explanation is question-begging at best; Pawtucket had not spent much taxpayer money on its crèche display.[6] Suppose that the city had spent none at all, relying entirely on private contributions to pay the modest expenses associated with an officially sponsored display. Would that make a difference? Not under Justice O'Connor's endorsement rationale and not, we think, to most citizens. Complaints about the misuse of taxpayer dollars are a staple of American political rhetoric, but they do a poor job of capturing what is constitutionally troublesome about crèche displays.

If endorsement per se amounts to a constitutional violation, then the fact of disparagement must by itself—unsupplemented by any concerns about coercion or the expenditure of government money—be the relevant harm. To Scalia and other critics of the endorsement test, that injury seems too flimsy and subjective to deserve constitutional attention. After all, people can feel disparaged at the drop of a hat. Indeed, as we shall discuss later in this chapter, some religious believers feel themselves disparaged by the *absence* of religious symbols from public spaces. And governments might plausibly deny that they intend to disparage anybody with their displays; Pawtucket claimed that its purpose was simply to attract holiday shoppers to local stores, and that might have been so.[7] Why, then, should we single out the public display of religious symbols as a constitutionally impermissible form of disparagement?

We believe that this question has a sound answer, one consistent with Justice O'Connor's reasoning in *Lynch*. The answer pertains to what we will call the *social meaning* of religious symbols in American culture. To answer Justice O'Connor's critics fully, we need to develop the idea of social meaning in some detail. Our treatment of it will involve some subtle distinctions, but the basic idea has a venerable pedigree in American constitutional jurisprudence and ought, we believe, to resonate with our readers' understandings. We begin our discussion with a simple example, one to which we will return several times.

Religion, Social Meaning, and Disparagement

Imagine that the officials of a small town—let's say "Fineville"—have decided to erect a handsome highway-spanning arch as the portal to their municipality. Now imagine two different inscriptions they might choose to blaze across their arch. One imagined slogan would be "Fineville—A Nuclear-Free Community." The other would be "Fineville—A Christian Community." Now it is certainly possible that in the Fineville of our imagination questions of nuclear power and/or weapons are a matter of controversy—possibly even heated controversy—and that advocates of things nuclear might be irked at the highly visible side-taking implicated in the nuclear-free-community sign. But it would be odd in the extreme to regard the losing side in the nuclear debate as disparaged in a way that should invoke our constitutional sympathies. When we shift our attention to the Christian-community sign, it is not at all odd to think that non-Christians are so disparaged.

What accounts for this difference? We suggest that public endorsements of religious belief must be understood against the background of four structural features of religion in our society, features that, even if not common to everything that might be called "religion," are nevertheless common to most of American religion. These features affect the social meaning of religious displays—that is, they affect the meanings that competent participants in American culture may reasonably associate with the government display of religious symbols.

First, religions tend to be comprehensive; they are not discrete propositions or theories, but large, expansive webs of belief and conduct. Second, despite the real diversity within American churches, there are still important respects in which one is either "in" or "out" of a religion. In some of the most cohesive faiths, churches distinguish insiders and outsiders in a strictly enforced, institutional sense: the Mormon church, for example, excommunicates those whom it deems unfaithful. Most American churches are more loosely structured. Catholics can be relatively orthodox or quite secular, and it is possible to be a "secular Jew." Still, it makes little sense to "mix and match" religions, and groups that pretend to do so, such as the evangelical Christian group Jews for Jesus, only underscore the point. Third, open ritual is prevalent in religion, and participation in ritual—standing up or staying seated, bowing one's head or not, repeating designated words or remaining silent—plays an important role in signifying who is "in" or "out" of these comprehensive structures in the eyes of individual believers, church communities, and the more general public. Fourth, the perceived stakes of being within or without these structures of belief and membership are often momentous: being chosen or not, being saved and slotted for eternal joyous life or condemned to eternal damnation, leading a life of virtue or a life of sin, acknowledging or repudiating one's deepest possible debt, fulfilling or squandering one's highest destiny. Or the stakes may be less transcendental and more mundane, but no less categorical, such as being like us or very different from us, or being or not being perniciously under the sway of particular leaders or worldwide movements.

As we have observed throughout, Americans are keenly sensitive to distinctions in religious identity. Though most American faiths are reconciled to the fact of religious pluralism and to the consequent need for religious tolerance, they nonetheless continue to insist on the unique truth of their beliefs and the special significance of their religious identity. In the late 1950s the sociologist Will Herberg said that in the United States, the question "What are you?" usually calls for an answer drawn from the list "Protestant, Catholic or Jew."[8] The list may have grown—to include, for example, "Muslim"—but the basic point still holds: in the United States, religion plays a major role in defining civic identity.

All this means that public endorsements of religion carry a special charge or valence. Such endorsements signify who is "in" and "out" of competing large-scale social and ideological structures, and assign powerful and pervasive judgments of identity and stature to the status of being in or out. Religious endorsements valorize some religious beliefs and those who hold them, and thereby disparage those who do not share those beliefs.

There is thus a deep and crucial difference in the meaning of the two Fineville signs, and the disparagement of non-Christians implicated in the social meaning of the second sign is inconsistent with the requirement of evenhandedness—of what we have called "equal regard"—that lies at the heart of the Establishment Clause.

This understanding of public religious endorsements is not just a matter of a statistical generalization about personal sensibilities. Sensitivities vary across groups and over time. Moreover, by making constitutional law so dependent upon personal reaction, we would risk creating a "tyranny of the squeamish": an especially thin-skinned group would have a better chance of getting doctrines offensive to it excised from publicly sponsored speech. It might seem more reasonable to tell the group to toughen up a bit.

Nor does this understanding of a public religious endorsement depend on what the public officials had in mind when they chose to make the endorsement. A particular official or group of officials may not intend to contribute to the disparagement of persons in their community and yet do or say something that constitutes such a disparagement, just as an individual speaker might overlook or misunderstand the linguistic meaning of her words.

The pernicious element of disparagement that inheres in public religious endorsements like Fineville's sign is a product of the social meaning of such endorsements. The social meaning of an event or a public expression is the meaning that a competent participant in the society in question would see in that event or expression. Social meaning is in this respect like linguistic meaning, which depends upon the understanding and use of language by a competent practitioner in the relevant linguistic community. In our national community, the structure of religious belief and affiliation is such that endorsements carry with them the taint of disparagement. And in our national community, "Fineville—A Christian Community" disparages non-Christians, while "Fineville—A Nuclear-Free Community" merely irritates nuclear advocates.

The concept of social meaning—whether invoked by that name or explicitly invoked at all—is important in thought and discourse about justice in political communities, and in fact it has a venerable pedigree in constitutional jurisprudence. The first Justice Harlan called upon it in his justly famous dissent in *Plessy v. Ferguson* over a century ago. *Plessy* involved a constitutional challenge to a Louisiana law mandating that whites and blacks ride in separate railway cars. The majority of the Court rejected the challenge, insisting that no harm to constitutional equality was at stake. At one point, the majority came close to the heart of the case, only to demonstrate a peculiar inability to see the world as it clearly was:

> We consider the underlying fallacy of the plaintiff's argument to consist in the assumption that the enforced separation of the two races stamps the colored race with a badge of inferiority. If this be so, it is not by reason of anything found in the act, but solely because the colored race chooses to put that construction upon it.[9]

In response, Justice Harlan insisted that "the real meaning" of the Louisiana law was unduckable, namely, "that colored citizens are so inferior and degraded that they cannot be allowed to sit in public coaches occupied by white citizens."[10] Harlan thus saw "separate but equal" railway cars as carrying an insidious social meaning that contributed to the perpetuation of social caste, and for that reason, as plainly unconstitutional.

We think Harlan's invocation of social meaning was morally precocious, and that his concept of such meaning was very similar to the one we are using here. Like us, he believed that certain practices had a disparaging effect that was "real" and not reducible either to the personal intentions of their sponsors or to the personal perceptions of observers.[11] These practices pertain to important constituents of identity—most notably, race and religion—that, within American culture, function as especially significant markers of social division.

A Double-Edged Sword?

When we discussed Justice Scalia's dissent in *Lynch,* we adverted briefly to one frequently heard objection to the endorsement test. Some people contend that the test is incoherent because government cannot help but endorse some sort of controversial message about religion. Governmental embrace of religious symbols might disparage nonbelievers, but the absence of religious symbols might equally well disparage believers. If so, there is no getting away from the problem.

We think this argument wrong in a number of ways. Let's go back for a minute to Fineville, with its portal sign "Fineville—A Christian Community." Suppose several residents of Fineville take the town to court, and ultimately secure a judgment to the effect that the sign is unconstitutional because it has the social meaning that persons other than Christians of a certain sort are not full members of the community—because, in our conceptual vocabulary, it disparages nonmainstream believers. The town officials take down the sign and replace it with another: "Fineville—Home of the Riding Lawnmower." (It's a long story; don't ask.)

Now, some, possibly many, residents of Fineville may be irked by this turn of events; they may feel that the first sign was a valuable means of expressing their solidarity with regard to a matter of great importance to them. But it would be bizarre to say that the social meaning of taking the sign down is that mainstream Christians are not full and respected members of the community. And that is so whether we take the relevant community to be Fineville, the state, or the nation. In what possible sense could persons in Fineville who wanted the old sign plausibly claim to be disparaged?

Two possibilities suggest themselves, the first more palatable than the second. First, when the court in question ruled that the old sign violated the Constitution because it disparaged non-Christians, it determined that Fineville had behaved wrongly with regard to persons other than mainstream Christians in the community. Thus, there is an opprobrious dimension to the Court's judgment. But that is just a function of constitutional adjudication generally: there will often be a moral dimension to constitutional disputes, and persons on the losing side may understand themselves to have been criticized by an official organ of the state. The social meaning of the court's decision does not on this account include the message that anyone is less than a full member of any relevant community.

Second, we could imagine a claim of disparagement that ran as follows: "We, the fellowship of like-thinking religious believers who live in Fineville are entitled to recognize what we have in common and to take pride in what makes us special; nonbelievers can choose to live here as less than full members of our community, or they can choose to live elsewhere . . . it's a free country. When the court insisted that we suppress our public celebration of who we are, it denied our specialness. That is a form of disparagement." It is certainly possible that the social meaning of the court's decision and the resulting removal of the Christian-community sign in our hypothetical includes the proposition that mainstream Christians have no pride of place in Fineville or elsewhere in our country, that persons who are not mainstream Christians enjoy equal constitutional stature. Yet, if insistence on equal status offends a group of persons because it demotes them from a superior status, their taking offense, obviously, is not what we would or should regard as a constitutionally cognizable harm.

When Is a Display an Endorsement?

In *Lynch*, after propounding the endorsement test, Justice O'Connor went on to observe that not all public displays of religious material constitute endorsements—or, as we would put it, that not all displays of this sort have a social meaning that includes the disparagement of some members of the community on the basis of their religious beliefs.

We agree with Justice O'Connor about this point (though not with the conclusion she ultimately drew from it). To see why, we return again to the fictional hamlet of Fineville and imagine two more cases. First, it is the Christmas season, and the Fineville City Council directs the Parks Department to display a large crèche in a prominent location in the public park that surrounds the City Hall; and second, in a remarkable coup, the Fineville City Art Museum borrows and displays one of Fra Angelico's paintings of the Annunciation as part of its "Treasures of the Italian Renaissance" exhibition. These two events are likely to have very different social meanings. The social meaning of the crèche includes disparagement of those who do not embrace Christianity as their religious belief, while the social meaning of the art exhibition does not. Why is this so?

We can begin to understand the difference when we realize that the proper question is "What is the meaning of the display?" as opposed to "What is the meaning of the object that is being displayed?" Ordinarily these questions produce the same answer, because governments will properly be understood to express the meaning of the symbols they invoke. So when a government erects a crèche, that act will have the social meaning of celebrating the birth of Jesus Christ and thereby affirming those faiths that embrace Jesus Christ as a figure of reverence. When this is true, the social meaning of the display will be more or less the same as the meaning of the object displayed, and with a sectarian object like a crèche, that meaning will include the disparagement of nonbelievers.

Sometimes, however, governments will properly be understood in effect to be holding a religious object at arms length, to be putting quotation marks around a religious text or a contextual frame around a religious object. Our story about the Fineville City Art Museum's display of one of Fra Angelico's paintings of the Annunciation is like that. The content of the painting is exquisitely religious: the Annunciation—in which the Angel Gabriel tells Mary that she will conceive the child Jesus—is a an event depicted and celebrated most prominently within Catholic theology. And Fra Angelico's depictions are faithful to their subject—Gabriel is undeniably an angel, and his message spills forth in explicit Hebraic text. But Fra Angelico is a great painter, and his works are widely appreciated for their extraordinary artistic force and their importance in the evolution of Western art. The display of the painting in a museum, as a great and important work of the Italian Renaissance, would properly be understood as an instance of framing rather than embracing the religious content of the painting, and thus the display would not carry the bitter social meaning of disparagement.

This distinction—between invoking the sacred meaning of a religious object and framing that meaning—more or less tracks the distinction in the philosophy of language between "using" and "mentioning." In a later section we will present some excerpts from the Ten Commandments. Were our project in this book different than it is, we might be offering the Commandments to support a claim about theological truth. We would then be *using* the Commandments. In fact, though, we include these quotations simply as a reminder of what the Commandments say, so that we can go on to discuss the constitutional status of their public display. We are not using the Ten Commandments; we are *mentioning* them.

There are many examples of the public quoting or framing of religious material. The federal government maintains the San Antonio Missions National Historical Park, which preserves for public appreciation four missions, the greatest concentration of Catholic missions in North America. These were established by Franciscan friars bent on extending the influence of Spain and of the Catholic church. The historical and architectural significance of these buildings makes them worthy objects of public appreciation. Their public presentation by the Park Service—from the name of the park onward—makes them a clear instance of historical framing.

The name San Antonio itself is an instance of the framing of religious content. "Saint" or its equivalent is something of a commonplace in community names in the United States; other prominent examples include St. Paul, San Diego, and San Francisco. There can be no doubt that these names have religious origins, but we think it would be just plain silly to suppose that any constitutional violation results. "St. Paul" now has at least two meanings: it refers to a Christian saint and to a city in Minnesota, and the latter meaning is secular. Acceptance of the city's historical name does not imply that residents or officials admire or venerate the eponymous saint—any more than use of the name Germantown, Maryland, implies that current residents are from, or support, Germany.

Fig Leaves versus Frames

Having used the Italian Renaissance and Fra Angelico as our prime example of the public framing of objects with religious content, we are tempted to borrow from an adjacent tradition of Italian painting: in the late 1600s and thereafter for a century or so, church functionaries—more prudish than their predecessors had been—ordered the addition of fig leaves to quite prominent works of art, like Michelangelo's Sistine Chapel ceiling and Masaccio's depiction of Adam and Eve in the Brancacci Chapel in the church of Santa Maria del Carmine in Florence. Modern restorations have removed these fig leaves, leaving the human figures in their original undressed state; but the fig leaf has survived as a metaphor for a fairly flimsy disguise.

Fig leaves come to mind because sometimes public officials stick a kind of fig leaf on religious displays. These cover-ups do nothing to deflect the social meaning of the displays; in fact in some instances these thin disguises may have the perverse effect of emphasizing the religious social meaning that lies just underneath. This problem has been very much at the center of the Supreme Court's unwieldy jurisprudence about crèches, Christmas trees, and other holiday displays. The justices seem in those cases to be struggling to find a way to distinguish between frames and fig leafs—between, that is, thinly disguised cases of endorsement/disparagement, on the one hand, and cases in which the community in question is framing or mentioning religious materials, on the other. To date, the results have been a bit clumsy. Consider what some commentators have come to think of as the "three plastic animals rule," which is yet another product of *Lynch,* the case about Pawtucket's crèche display.

We have thus far emphasized the more abstract parts of Justice O'Connor's opinion, including its endorsement test. When it came time to decide upon the constitutionality of Pawtucket's display, Justice O'Connor produced a conclusion about which we are less enthusiastic. She emphasized that the crèche was part of a larger display, along with such items as colored lights offering "Season's Greetings," a Santa, flying reindeer, a clown, an elephant, and a teddy bear. Justice O'Connor—who cast the decisive vote in the case—suggested that by surrounding a crèche with a few Santas and flying reindeer, a town frames it in a way that separates the crèche's theological content from the government's authority.[12] That, we think, is a mistake. The reindeer do subtly change the meaning of the crèche display—they suggest a less theologically rigorous, more commercialized form of religious belief, one that will be offensive to some devout Christians as well as to some non-Christians. But the Santa and his reindeer neither secularize the crèche nor mark it as only one of several competing religious and philosophical symbols valued by citizens. They are at best a fig leaf, not a frame.

As we said earlier, a public display of religious material carries the meaning that a competent member of the community would attach to the display. Some lower federal courts seem to have exactly this in mind when they ask whether "a reasonable observer would believe that a particular action constitutes an endorsement of religion." Such an observer may in part be attributing a purpose to the officials who chose to mount the display, but the question of whether a competent observer would believe the officials to have intentionally lent their support to religion is not the same as the question of what the officials actually had in mind. So, if our much-referenced officials of Fineville choose to erect a crèche in a prominent place in the park adjacent to their city hall solely out of the belief that doing so will put people in a holiday mood and boost the sales of local merchants, this craven but secular impulse is to a large degree beside the point. That the Fineville officials happen to be singularly obtuse does not determine how members of their community will or should read their actions.

That some observers take offense on religious grounds to a public display, however, does not justify the conclusion that the display's social meaning is that of endorsement or disparagement. Some residents of Fineville may take offense—on religious grounds—at the display of the Fra Angelico. But Equal Liberty is about finding fair rules of cooperation among a religiously diverse people. From the vantage of Equal Liberty, we have to be concerned not only about disparagement but also about the tyranny of the thin-skinned.[13]

Similarly, social meaning is not deflected by poorly informed public reaction. Suppose Fineville has a public display area in the park adjacent to the City Hall, where private groups are permitted to erect displays; qualifying displays are chosen in some content-neutral way—say, on the principle of "first come, first served" or by drawing lots. A church group receives a permit to use the space and puts up a controversial, and explicitly religious, exhibit. Under these circumstances, Fineville hasn't endorsed anything other than the principle of free and robust expression. The religious content of the display comes from a private choice; indeed, it is entirely possible that the government's officials, as well as a large majority of voters, will disagree with the church group's message.

It is possible, of course, that a passerby, recognizing the site as public property, will mistakenly believe that the government has sponsored the display. But it would be impractical and unwise to base the government's constitutional obligations not on whether it has in fact endorsed a religious or theological position, but on whether some citizens might mistakenly think it to have done so. After all, citizens who see a religious display in a government-sponsored public forum might mistakenly believe that government has endorsed the display; other citizens who see a public school or public park without religious symbols might mistakenly believe that the government has discriminated against religion. The government would have a constitutional obligation to defer to the confusion of both groups. Such a rule would saddle us with a tyranny of the poorly informed, in which the government's most fundamental obligations would be controlled in significant part by the befuddlement of whatever groups least understood its actions.

Hence the importance of the idea of an "objective" social meaning, turning on the way that a reasonable (and reasonably well-informed) member of a community would understand the actions of public officials who undertake to display material that has religious content. So to assert, as we have, that the reindeer garnish in *Lynch v. Donnelly* does not undo the religious message of the Pawtucket crèche is to make a claim about the meaning that members of the Pawtucket community would ascribe to the crèche. The religious valence of a depiction of the birth of Christ is such that we are pretty confident that Pawtucket's crèche carries with it an insistence that Christmas, however secular many of its trappings may have become, ultimately marks one of the most profound events in Christian theology, and that Pawtucket officially joins in a celebration of that event.

It does not follow that nativity scenes are somehow banished material, too culturally hot for public spaces. As we've seen, were there an evenhanded public forum for private displays, a crèche could be erected in such a space; likewise, one could be carried through the streets in an officially licensed parade. Under many circumstances, one could be displayed in a museum as historically or artistically important. And although we are doubtful about Pawtucket's reindeer and teddy bears, we can imagine displays that include a crèche and avoid the problem of endorsement. Fineville might mount a display of "When the Spirit Moves Us," in celebration of much of the range of spiritual commitments of members of the community, including, possibly, music and art. A crèche in such a setting could easily satisfy the obligation that it be framed, or held at arm's length.

Nor is Christmas itself necessarily off-limits. Christmas trees are part of a Christian religious celebration. Yet the tree's role in American culture has become partially secularized, associated as much with Santa Claus, "Happy Holidays," and the "Christmas shopping season" as with the birth of Jesus Christ. Some Jewish families have Christmas trees. We are inclined to think that the Christmas tree has become sufficiently secular that public sponsorship does not amount to a "religious display" in the sense of embracing a religious message. The counterargument is, however, obvious—it is, after all, a "Christmas" tree. The tree is a genuine borderline case, and, as with any such case, reasonable people will differ about where to draw the line.

Context, Close Cases, and a Modicum of Certainty

In the real world, public displays of religious material will serve up many hard cases. As suggested by the examples of the Catholic missions and the City of San Antonio, the preservation of religious materials over time can shift the meaning of their display away from endorsement and toward historical memorialization. So, for example, some cities incorporate crosses and other religious imagery into town seals that appear on the sides of police cruisers and elsewhere. We think that such emblems may be constitutional, even if recently designed and adopted, so long as they incorporate other aspects of local history along with the religious ones. Nothing in the Constitution requires towns to ignore or suppress religion's contributions to their history. Indeed, the inclusion of religious symbols in town insignias (which some people regard as an inappropriate endorsement of religion) is no different from the inclusion of churches in historical preservation programs (which some people regard as an inappropriate infringement upon religion): both are efforts to preserve and memorialize contributions to a town's heritage and character. So long as they are motivated by genuine historical concern and so long as the state does not discriminate for or against religion (or particular sects), both policies are constitutionally permissible.

That said, tradition and historical pedigree will not save sectarian symbols in other contexts. So, for example, a prominent cross in a courtroom would be a problem even if it had been there for a very long time: litigants would quite reasonably regard the cross as a suggestion that Christianity enjoyed favored status in the eyes of the court. (Of course, this point applies *a fortiori* if a judge attempts to introduce a cross into a courthouse that lacked one, as Judge Roy Moore attempted to do with the Ten Commandments in Alabama[14]—but our point here is that, in a courtroom, the passage of time does not drain the symbol of its sectarian meaning.)

Town emblems and courtroom crosses represent extreme cases; between them are a host of more difficult ones. For example, a large cross stands on publicly owned property on Mt. Soledad in San Diego, California. The cross was erected in 1954 to honor America's war dead and became a symbol of the city. In 1989 Philip K. Paulson, a local resident, sued, claiming that the cross violated the Establishment Clause and demanding that it be removed. His suit began a legal battle that continues today. San Diego might want to keep the cross for historical reasons, but it is equally possible—if not probable—that citizens value it for the Christian message of respect it was originally intended to convey. They understand it, in other words, as a continuing endorsement of the religious view its creators expressed. It would be reasonable for other, less sympathetic viewers to interpret the cross in that way.[15]

Context, it should be clear, is critically important to these examples. Insignias, crests, and emblems may incorporate religious imagery without expressing a religious viewpoint. By contrast, if a religious symbol is not specially marked or set off in some way (such as by inclusion alongside other elements in an insignia or other composition), it continues to express a religious message. Government display of a marble cross means something different if the cross appears among other carvings in an exhibition at a public art museum than if the cross appears in isolation on a judge's bench in a courtroom. Competent participants in American culture must be sensitive to these differences in context, and constitutional doctrine must take them into account.

That said, it would not be satisfactory to leave this area in a state of constant uncertainty, with every case a fresh occasion for the delicate assessment of context. If our constitutional approach to religious displays is radically contextual and uncertain, public officials will be poorly guided (and, worse, encouraged to push at the ill-defined limits of what is permitted), and there will be more roiling controversy and expensive litigation. This kind of uncertainty can make us worse off with regard to the project of treating each other with respect and toleration notwithstanding the diversity of our spiritual commitments. Imagine, for example, how things would be if Establishment Clause doctrine regarding public school prayer had announced that some prayers were fine and others were forbidden, so that dogged school officials would craft prayer after prayer to be closely parsed by judges charged with enforcing the Constitution. Some degree of clarity and predictability is a good thing for everyone involved in these controversies.

One way for the Supreme Court to achieve that goal is to be less indulgent of claims that a mere juxtaposition of religious and nonreligious items can provide a "frame"—rather than a mere "fig leaf"—for religious symbols. Usually the social meaning of religious displays will be more or less the same as the meaning of the object displayed. So, for example, the meaning of a Fra Angelico painting does not depend on its inclusion in an art museum alongside secular works. Suppose that Fineville had no art museum, but that a tycoon who had grown up there bequeathed to the municipality a single brilliant painting. It would be constitutional for the town to display the painting in its city hall—the religious elements of the painting are framed, literally as well as figuratively, by their inclusion within the tradition and vocabulary of visual art. Conversely, a crèche in the park is still a crèche in the park, whether or not it is accompanied by plastic bears. The "three plastic animals" rule is the unfortunate result of supposing that mere juxtaposition with secular symbols will change what it means for government to display a religious one.

Of course, sometimes juxtaposition does matter. We have already given the example of a marble cross in a museum, accompanied by other carvings. Here the fact of inclusion within a collection matters more than it did in the case of Fra Angelico's painting—and, unlike the case of the painting, it would be genuinely problematic for the town to display the cross by itself in City Hall. Yet, on closer inspection, this example actually reinforces how rarely inclusion of a symbol within a larger collection can legitimate an otherwise impermissible display. The example trades upon the idea that the cross is not only in a collection but in a *museum*—a cultural space that facilitates critical distance between observers and the artifacts they examine. Hanging other carvings alongside a cross in City Hall would provide a fig leaf, not a frame.

Friezes and Follies: The Ten Commandments Cases

The recent cases about the Ten Commandments nicely illustrate the limits of mere juxtaposition as a framing device. Like crèches, the Ten Commandments are undeniably religious. While they include widely shared moral precepts such as "Thou shalt not kill," they begin with an announcement that "I am the Lord thy God," and the first five commandments continue in this sectarian vein (there are actually several versions of the Commandments, all of which begin with five distinctly religious commandments but which differ from one another in their wording—this fact, of course, creates another problem from the standpoint of religious freedom, since public officials who post the Commandments must necessarily choose among versions of varying theological significance). In 1981, in its first religious display case, *Stone v. Graham,* the Court held that a statute that required posting of the Ten Commandments on Kentucky public school classroom walls was a violation of the Establishment Clause, despite the fact that the money for the project was raised privately and despite the presence of a remarkably transparent fig leaf. At the bottom of each copy of the Commandments, in small type, Kentucky announced that "the secular application of the Ten Commandments is clearly seen in its adoption as the fundamental legal code of Western Civilization and the Common Law of the United States."[16]

Twenty years later, some Kentucky officials decided to try again. This time, two counties placed copies of the Ten Commandments on their courthouse walls, and the school district of a third county had copies posted in classrooms. Once again, the Kentucky counties defended their actions by saying that the Commandments had secular significance by virtue of the role they played in the origins of American law.[17]

There is not much historical evidence for this claim. Indeed, American law is in some respects inconsistent with the Commandments: American law does not require the worship of a particular (or any) god, and it prohibits stealing but not mere coveting. The Commandments and American law do both prohibit murder, theft, and adultery—but the Commandments are not unique in this regard. Nor did the Commandments loom large in debates at the American founding. Of course, one might say that the Commandments played an important role in the development of Western culture, and that they must therefore have had some influence on the formation of American law; and, likewise, one might observe that many of the American founders regarded the Ten Commandments as important to their personal moral views, and so they must have had some effect on their conceptions of law. But these connections are vague and general. If one were to look for particular documents that had specific importance to American law, one would fix upon Blackstone's *Commentaries* long before considering the Ten Commandments.[18] The only reason for singling out the latter is their connection to a favored religious tradition.

The Supreme Court had rightly rejected the blunt "fundamental to American law" argument in *Stone*. Thus, when the American Civil Liberties Union (ACLU) sued, the Kentucky officials tried a version of the "three plastic animals" defense. All three counties surrounded the copies of the Commandments with various documentary fragments: a bit of the Declaration of Independence, a congressional vote declaring 1983 the "Year of the Bible," the motto "In God We Trust," Abraham Lincoln's pronouncement "The Bible is the best gift God has given to man," and so forth.[19] Then, when it became clear that these materials were not going to deflect the courts' view of the social meaning or the constitutional infirmity of the posted Commandments, the counties adopted a new and much enlarged display of the Commandments, which included the full text of the "Star Spangled Banner," the Declaration of Independence, the Mayflower Compact, and the Magna Carta. The new display bore the title "The Foundations of American Law and Government Display" and included assertions concerning the bedrock status of the Ten Commandments in American law.[20]

Kentucky officials undoubtedly had a precedent in mind when they composed these displays. As it happens, the Ten Commandments are represented in the United States Supreme Court's own courtroom. They are part of a frieze that circles the room near its ceiling. The frieze depicts Moses delivering the Ten Commandments; it also depicts many other famous lawgivers. John Paul Stevens had said in an earlier case that the Supreme Court frieze posed no constitutional problem: it conveys a message of "respect not for great proselytizers but for great lawgivers."[21] Kentucky's officials apparently concluded on this basis that if the Ten Commandments were incorporated into a broader display, their presence in schools and courtrooms would pose no problem.

Unfortunately for those officials, considering their display in light of the Supreme Court frieze serves only to highlight their constitutional problem. First, the Supreme Court frieze depicts Moses with tablets but quotes only the secular portion of the Commandments (that is, the last five commandments)—and does so in Hebrew. Even were this carving to appear by itself, it is arguably more like Fra Angelico's paintings than a marble cross—it might, in other words, be regarded and appreciated as an artwork rather than an expression of religious sentiment. Kentucky, by contrast, simply presented the text of the Ten Commandments.

Second, the Supreme Court frieze as a whole is immediately recognizable as a coherent composition; "great lawgivers" is the obvious theme, and the theme makes sense in a courthouse. In Kentucky's collection, everything besides the Ten Commandments was an afterthought, and the linkage among them was obscure, notwithstanding the explanatory caption "The Foundations of American Law and Government Display."

Finally, the other elements in the Supreme Court frieze help put distance between the government and its display of Moses. It would be bizarre for any observer to suppose that the U.S. government had endorsed Confucianism by displaying Confucius in the frieze; the juxtaposition of Confucius with Moses helps to defeat the inference that the government was endorsing Judaism or Christianity. Kentucky, on the other hand, surrounded the Ten Commandments with symbols of American government. That juxtaposition exacerbates rather than diminishes the problem: the problem with government displays of religious symbols is that they connect the status of American citizenship to a particular religious tradition. Ironically, Kentucky's officials looked for a fig leaf and found . . . well, perhaps we had best say a "spotlight."

Whatever else Kentucky's frantic efforts to cover up the naked display of the Ten Commandments can be thought to have achieved, they surely did not improve the social meaning of the Kentucky counties' display. At the end of the day, no competent member of these communities could have failed to understand the social meaning of any of the evolving forms of the display: the display was an endorsement of the Christian tradition and, by implication, a disparagement of those who reject that tradition.

When the Kentucky case reached the Supreme Court, in *McCreary County v. ACLU of Kentucky* (2005), five justices had no trouble recognizing that the Kentucky display was a fig leaf, not a frame. The Court held that the display was unconstitutional; Justice Souter, writing for the majority, commented that a reasonable observer of the Kentucky display would either "throw up his hands" in puzzlement or else "suspect that the Counties were simply reaching for any way to keep a religious document on the walls of courthouses constitutionally required to embody religious neutrality."[22]

Four justices dissented, but not because they mistook Kentucky's flimsy fig leaf for an effective frame. Instead, they embraced the view that the *Stone* Court had rejected—namely, that the Ten Commandments "have a proper place in our civic history" so that "even placing them by themselves can be civically motivated." The display in *Stone*, the dissenters suggested, would have been permissible had it been in a courthouse rather than a school. Three of the dissenters—Scalia, Rehnquist, and Thomas—also defended Kentucky's display on a more radical ground. They said that the Establishment Clause left the government entirely free to endorse religion over nonreligion and, indeed, to endorse monotheism over other forms of religion. That view, which Scalia tried to defend on historical grounds, is of course at radical odds with the principles of Equal Liberty.[23]

The Court ruled the same day on a second Ten Commandments case that most people regarded as more difficult than the Kentucky case. The Ten Commandments monument at issue in *Van Orden v. Perry* is a six-foot-high red granite block that sits on the grounds of the Texas state capitol in Austin. The Ten Commandments are etched on the stone in large letters (the first commandment, "I AM the LORD thy GOD" is engraved in larger letters than the others). A private organization, the Fraternal Order of Eagles, donated the monument to Texas in 1961. Its stated purpose was to discourage juvenile delinquency, and the order made similar gifts to several other states—so, not surprisingly, cases parallel to the Texas one have arisen in other states, including Utah, Colorado, and Indiana. There is also an amusing commercial element to the story of the stone's origins: Cecil B. DeMille helped fund the Eagles' monuments to promote his film *The Ten Commandments.*[24] The monument does not appear to have excited much controversy at the time it was donated, and the stone sat more or less obscurely on the capitol grounds for four decades without provoking any litigation.

Various other monuments dot the capitol grounds in Texas. There are seventeen in total, including ones honoring or commemorating Texas law enforcement; Texans who served in the Korean War, World War I, and Pearl Harbor; pioneer women of early Texas; Texas youth; the Statue of Liberty; and Confederate soldiers (twice). The Texas legislature has characterized the capitol grounds as displaying "statues, memorials, and commemorations of people, ideals, and events that compose Texan identity."[25]

In its legal arguments, Texas analogized the collection of monuments to a museum, pointing out that they were under the care of the Capitol Curator. The U.S. Court of Appeals for the Fifth Circuit, in an opinion by the distinguished judge Patrick E. Higginbotham, stopped short of accepting the museum analogy but nevertheless agreed with Texas that "the manner in which the seventeen monuments are presented on the state grounds" would not lead a "reasonable observer" to see the display as an "endorsement of the Commandments' religious message."[26] As a circuit court judge, Higginbotham was bound to follow *Lynch*'s problematic holding that juxtaposing plastic animals with a crèche display could eliminate the constitutional problems that would otherwise render it unconstitutional. And there is no doubt that Texas's collection of monuments had more integrity than Kentucky's litigation-driven hodgepodge.

That said, we think that the Texas case, like *Lynch* itself, ultimately illustrates again that mere juxtaposition of secular and religious symbols is unlikely to solve constitutional problems that would exist if the religious items were displayed alone. There can be no doubt about the religious content of the Texas monument. Unlike, say, the frieze of Moses in the United States Supreme Court building, the Texan granite block prominently features the text of the Commandments; to study the monument is to read them. Nor do the monuments in Austin amount to a coherent composition that, like the Supreme Court frieze, could put some distance between state authority and the message of the monuments. The granite Decalogue has no special connection to Texas identity—a point made plain, if evidence were needed, by the fact that the Eagles donated identical monuments to Indiana, Utah, and other states. And insofar as the Texas collection is about constituents of Texan identity, it repeats the problem of Kentucky's display. The other elements in the display reinforce, rather than alleviate, the concern that Texas is making full membership in its political community dependent on embracing the precepts or symbols of a particular religious tradition.

The most significant difference between the Texas and Kentucky displays is historical rather than spatial. Kentucky officials inserted the Ten Commandments into schools and courthouses—especially sensitive venues—at a time of national agitation over religious symbols. It is hard to view their decision as anything other than a deliberate act of provocation, and, not surprisingly, it spurred immediate litigation. Texas officials accepted the monument decades ago, and it does not seem to have stirred an immediate response. Indeed, if the granite block has a special connection to Texas history, it acquired it by virtue of sitting so long on the Capitol grounds—so that an observer might look at it and say, "Well, this is an example of how Texas officials once viewed their relationship to the public" (something one might also say, perhaps, about the two memorials commemorating Confederate war dead).

In that respect, the Texas monument is not so different from the Mt. Soledad cross in San Diego—arguably, both have become (literally) part of the local landscape. As with the cross, though, we suspect that most people who value the Texas monument (and most people who object to it) do so because of its religious message, not because of its independent historical significance or its place in Texas culture. If so, the right response would be to remove the monument. We understand, though, why courts, including both the court of appeals and the Supreme Court, have shrunk from that conclusion. It is the same reason that the head of the New York ACLU saw no need to prevent willing children from singing carols in school. The monument sat obscurely in Austin for forty years, and many people would be upset by its removal—is it really so much to put up with? That is more or less what Justice Breyer, who cast the deciding vote in *Van Orden v. Perry*, said: "This display has stood apparently uncontested for nearly two generations. That experience helps us understand that as a practical matter of *degree* this display is unlikely to prove divisive. And this matter of degree is, I believe, critical in a borderline case such as this one."[27]

The Pledge of Allegiance

If judges and commentators could survey the range of religious liberty cases and vote on one as "The Case We Would Most Like to See Go Away," we expect the clear winner—by a large margin and with support from people with otherwise diverse views—would concern the Pledge of Allegiance. Questions about the constitutionality of the Pledge surfaced prominently in 2002, when a U.S. court of appeals panel agreed with Michael Newdow, who had sued, claiming that the inclusion of the phrase "under God" in the Pledge made its public school recitation a religious ceremony like a prayer, and hence subject to the absolute rule of *Engel v. Vitale* (1962) barring such ceremonies in the public schools.[28] Newdow was the noncustodial parent of his daughter, and on this ground the Supreme Court held that he lacked the standing to challenge the Pledge of Allegiance on her behalf. That holding had the effect not just of preventing the Supreme Court from deciding the question, but of erasing the decisions of the lower courts as well.[29] But the court of appeals decision made clear how open a question the constitutional status of the Pledge is, and another round of litigation about it has already commenced.[30]

Patriotism and religion are a potentially combustible mixture, and the constitutional challenge to the Pledge of Allegiance seems particularly fraught. Part of what makes the case seem so dangerous is the sense that it poses an all-or-nothing choice between two bad outcomes: on the one hand, the Pledge could be understood to be the constitutional equivalent of a school-sponsored prayer, in which case it would indeed be unconstitutional, without any further analysis. That view seems to make a great deal of two words in an oath of allegiance that is not really about religion at all, in stark contrast to the Lord's Prayer and other public school prayer exercises.[31] The result would be to deprive significant numbers of Americans of the opportunity to solemnize their allegiance to their country in a fashion that they find congenial and fitting.

On the other hand, the Pledge could be treated not as a religious exercise of any sort, but as . . . well, a pledge; it could be treated, in other words, as the Pledge of Allegiance itself was treated between the time of the Court's decision in *West Virginia State Board of Education v.*

Barnette (1943)[32] and 1954, when Congress added the words "under God" to the Pledge.[33] *Barnette* gave all students the constitutional right not to participate in the Pledge ceremony, but permitted the ceremony to stand as a voluntary exercise designed by Congress and sponsored by public school officials throughout the country. This too seems an unfortunate outcome. As tepid and banal as the Pledge's reference to God is, it nonetheless has two closely related vices: first, its social meaning includes the suggestion that only those comfortable with proclaiming the United States to be a nation "under God" are worthy to formally declare their allegiance; and second, it in fact permits only those who can comfortably participate in such a proclamation to formally declare their allegiance.

As an independent matter, the Pledge in its present form seems to violate at least the spirit of Article VI of the Constitution, which provides that "no religious Test shall ever be required as a Qualification to any Office or public Trust under the United States." We presume that this principle should apply to the ordinary office of "citizen" as well as to special ones (such as "judge" or "governor").[34] A requirement that one utter religious words to declare fidelity to the United States seems to us a kind of "religious test" prohibited by Article VI—even though, of course, Melanie Newdow would not be stripped of citizenship for refusing to pledge allegiance.

We see a constitutional path between banning the Pledge in its present form and putting up with its not inconsiderable constitutional vices, a path that seems more favorable to the concerns of Equal Liberty than does either of these outcomes. That path—overlooked so far by the lawyers, judges, and commentators caught up in the Pledge of Allegiance controversy—becomes clear if we think for a moment about a variety of public ceremonies in which God is fleetingly invoked as a means of solemnizing secular commitments. One of these is the truth-telling oath required of witnesses called to testify in courts of law. Another is the oath to uphold the Constitution and laws taken by lawyers as a condition of admission to the practice of law, as well as by public employees and applicants for citizenship. Yet another is the oath of office taken by many public officials, including national officials, who are required by the Constitution itself to take such an oath.[35] All of these have in common a familiar form of solemnization, namely, the emphatic affirmation of commitment embodied in the closing phrase "so help me God." Some go further, and require the oath-taker to place his or her hand on a Bible when reciting the oath. All these oath ceremonies have one other feature, which we think is of critical importance: every one of them makes available an alternative, secular form of declaration that does not involve the Bible, the invocation of God, or any other religious reference.

Why are we so tolerant of these religiously tinged ceremonies of fidelity to the truth, to the law, and to the obligations of public office? Three features seem critical to their place in a democracy that values Equal Liberty. First, these are, in their essence, ceremonies of secular fidelity; religion enters the picture largely as a familiar means of solemnizing these secular commitments. Second, the religious invocations in these ceremonies tend to be terse, and relatively generic. Third, and most important, these oaths are offered together with an alternative secular form of commitment; the would-be oath-taker can eschew the invocation of God, and instead solemnly promise or affirm that he or she will tell the truth, uphold the law, or discharge the responsibilities of the office to the best of her or his ability. The shorthand for this choice is the opportunity to either "swear" (the religious form) or "affirm" (the secular form) to act in the required way.

For example, the Constitution requires the president to promise to execute his office faithfully, and it assumes that most presidents will make this promise in the form of an oath. The framers recognized that swearing an oath was a religious act in much the same sense as uttering "under God" when saying the Pledge—in their view, "swearing" meant "swearing to God" or "on a Bible." Therefore, in light of the principle set forth in Article VI, the framers carefully stipulated that officeholders, such as the president, had a nonreligious option: they could either "swear (or affirm)" to carry out their responsibilities and uphold the Constitution.[36] Likewise, federal law guarantees that courtroom witnesses may swear or affirm to tell the truth, the whole truth, and nothing but the truth.[37]

By offering a secular form of commitment in these ceremonies of fidelity, governments avoid the constitutional vices that plague the Pledge of Allegiance in its present form. While the Pledge includes the social meaning that only those able to commit themselves to "one Nation, under God," are worthy of the role of committed citizen, these other ceremonies of fidelity leave the choice of religious and secular form to the individual who participates in the ceremony. It is a private, not a governmental choice that invokes God as its means of solemnization. And while the Pledge excludes from its ceremony of fidelity anyone who chooses not to pledge fidelity to "one Nation, under God," all these other ceremonies permit those who choose not to invoke God to participate.

By now the reader will have anticipated our position: in their present form, public school Pledge of Allegiance ceremonies are indeed unconstitutional, but they can be easily fixed, and fixed without depriving those who hold dear the Pledge in its present form of the opportunity to recite it. Like the other ceremonies of fidelity that are a commonplace in American life, the Pledge of Allegiance references God in a terse, generic, and relatively nonsectarian way.[38] And like these other ceremonies, the Pledge is fundamentally about a secular commitment, not a ritual of religious entreaty or obeisance. But unlike these other ceremonies, the Pledge endorses a religious view as Congress's (and the school district's) own; and unlike these other ceremonies, the Pledge requires that every person who wishes to join in the ceremony act as though he or she also endorses that view. These constitutional vices can be cured by giving schoolchildren the same choice as presidents—the choice between pledging their fidelity in religious terms or pledging their fidelity in secular terms.

It is not hard to imagine how this can be arranged. Congress could stipulate an alternative, secular form of the oath. After some reflection, we have our own favorite candidate: "one Nation, under *law*."[39] School districts could then instruct their students that there are two perfectly appropriate forms of the Pledge, neither one of which is better suited than the other to the enterprise of marking allegiance. A simultaneous recital could then follow, with students invited to speak the Pledge in the terms of their choosing. Were this done, we think the constitutional objections to the Pledge and to the language "under God" would be fully met. No one would be denied the opportunity to proclaim America "one Nation, under God," but neither would anyone be forced to make that proclamation upon penalty of being denied the opportunity to pledge his or her allegiance. Congress and public school authorities would leave the question of how to characterize what or whom our nation is "under" to parents and their children. And with that, we hope (no doubt in vain) that perhaps we can all get along.

An Armistice in the Culture Wars?

As America's debate about religion's public role intensifies, the idea that we should "all just get along"—not just about the Pledge of Allegiance, but about religious freedom more generally—starts to appeal to more and more observers. Some judges and scholars, searching for a path to peace, have blamed courts for creating needless disputes. These commentators suggest that when courts limit religious expressions by the government, they create a powerful backlash and hence do more harm than good. If so, then perhaps courts should give the government more latitude to display religious symbols. For example, Justice Breyer made an argument of this kind to explain why he cast the deciding vote in favor of Texas in *Van Orden v. Perry*, the decision that permitted the state to maintain its Ten Commandments monument. If the Court were to force Texas to remove the monument, wrote Justice Breyer, it might thereby "encourage disputes concerning the removal of longstanding depictions of the Ten Commandments from public buildings across the Nation. And it could thereby create the very kind of religiously based divisiveness that the Establishment Clause seeks to avoid."[40]

Breyer's olive branch went unappreciated. Immediately after the decisions in the Kentucky and Texas cases, conservatives promised new efforts to install Ten Commandments monuments, and liberals predicted new lawsuits to stop them. Charles W. Colson, the conservative commentator (and convicted Watergate conspirator), expressed delight that the Kentucky decision was "so outrageous" because it would provoke "people in churches across America" to "get busy and demand the right kind of appointments to this court."[41] He added that "there is no bigger issue on the Christian agenda."[42]

One might conclude that Breyer's hope for peace was unrealistic. But perhaps the problem was that his plan was not bold enough. Breyer made clear that his pragmatic considerations about avoiding divisive decisions applied only in a "borderline case" such as the Texas one;[43] in the Kentucky case, where the state's endorsement of religion was (in Breyer's estimation) more patent, he joined the five-to-four majority that held the displays unconstitutional. Maybe the Court can cool tempers in America's debates about religion only if it gives the government much broader freedom to sponsor and exhibit religious symbols.

Noah Feldman, for example, has recommended that the Court impose fewer constitutional restrictions on government display of religious symbols, but tighter limits on the government's authority to subsidize religious institutions and practices. He describes his proposal as promoting "a shift to symbolic inclusion," and he predicts that after this shift "the fevered pitch of debate should tone down."[44] Other scholars have offered different proposals with similarly pragmatic objectives and orientations. Like Feldman, Steven Smith worries that the Court's Establishment Clause decisions have "provoked both resentment and resistance" from religious groups, hence generating precisely the sort of religious strife that the Court sought to avoid.[45] Unlike Feldman, though, Smith sees no formulaic solution; in his view, "The judicial imposition of *any* set of consistent and explicit principles is likely to undermine the possibilities for compromise and forbearance, and hence to aggravate the dangers of civil strife and alienation." For Smith, the only way to make progress is through pragmatic muddling: "Civil peace . . . must be the product of prudence, not of principle imposed from above."[46]

One prominent political scientist put the argument to us in blunt and simple terms. The Court, he said, ought to husband its resources carefully, saving them for disputes that really matter—about, for example, coercion, discrimination, or large government expenditures. When it comes to purely symbolic disputes about Christmas displays, the Pledge of Allegiance, and religious monuments, he asked, "Why not just let sleeping dogs lie?"

"Well, for openers, the dogs aren't sleeping," we replied. Controversies are raging about government displays of religious symbols. When scholars call for courts to behave more prudently or pragmatically, they seem to assume that these disputes will vanish, or at least subside, when courts defer to legislative majorities. But that assumption is implausible if not demonstrably false. Intense cultural disputes about religion and other topics arise and persist without judicial involvement. For example, the judiciary has never tried to regulate religious speechmaking by officeholders, but President George W. Bush's expressions of religious sentiment have been extremely controversial. Or, to take an example from another domain, the Supreme Court has (thus far) rejected calls to enforce Second Amendment rights, but few issues are so divisive in the United States as gun control.[47]

In fact judicial deference can itself sometimes inflame controversies that were more or less dormant. The decision in the *Peyote Case*, for example, gave legislatures more latitude, not less, but the case provoked a political firestorm that has run for fifteen years. When the Supreme Court decided its first major Establishment Clause case in 1947, it deferred to a local school district's decision about whether to subsidize bus fare for children attending Catholic schools. Controversy grew, rather than diminished, in the wake of the ruling; Protestant leaders denounced it and formed a new national interest group, Protestants United for Separation of Church and State, to oppose the Court's allegedly pro-Catholic jurisprudence (the group has evolved away from its sectarian roots and has become a widely respected civil rights organization, Americans United for Separation of Church and State).[48] The fact is that people on both sides of disputes about religious freedom (and religious symbols in particular) care deeply about the outcome, and they will continue to care (and to argue) regardless of what the courts decide.

Nor does it seem at all sensible to suppose that the law suits about crèches, the Ten Commandments, and the Pledge of Allegiance are the root cause of the social fissures that worry Feldman, Smith, and other observers. American politics manifests religiously inflected divisions on many important issues. Some of these are issues about religious freedom—such as school prayer, public funding for religious schools, and the teaching of evolution; others—such as abortion and gay rights—are not. These controversies have deep roots in American culture, and it is little more than wishful thinking to suppose that the Supreme Court can make religious conflicts "less threatening to our national unity and more easily subjected to being managed"[49] by taking a more permissive attitude toward town Christmas displays.

Why would anyone think otherwise? If we dig down beneath all the pragmatic declarations about strategies for achieving peace, we find, ultimately, a moral judgment: people *ought* not to care so much as they do about public sponsorship of religious symbols. Thus, for example, Feldman says that non-Christians who find a message of exclusion in a governmentally sponsored Christmas display are just making an arbitrary "interpretive choice."[50] Courts ought to respond with tough love: instead of restraining the government's authority to express religious messages, judges should make clear to offended parties that they should react differently—in Feldman's words, "The answer is for them to strengthen their own identities and be proud of who they are."[51]

As a strategy for peace and reconciliation, we think that this recommendation is simply naive. People do feel excluded when the government endorses one or another religion, whether they ought to or not. Feldman's position might nonetheless be tenable as a moral argument—an argument, that is, about what sorts of harms a people committed to religious freedom ought to recognize and redress—but we think that this is a badly flawed moral claim. Indeed, despite his benign intentions, Feldman sounds remarkably like Justice Brown, the nineteenth-century jurist who said that if African-Americans regarded segregation as a "badge of inferiority" it was only because "the colored race chooses to put that construction upon it."[52] As we have already argued, contrary to the view of Justice Brown, African-Americans were right to perceive an insult in segregation. Americans today are likewise correct when they discern a message of exclusion in governmentally sponsored religious displays. It does not follow that they ought always to sue—it is often an act of virtue to ignore insults, however real or hurtful they may be, and undoubtedly we as a country would be better off if Americans (on all sides) could do so more often. It does mean, however, that it is just plain wrong for us to pretend, when people do sue over a display, that no injury has been done them.

Arguments to the effect that those offended by mainstream religious symbols ought not to rock the boat suffer an unfortunate asymmetry. They counsel minorities to buck up and suffer a bit of disparagement in order to avoid producing a nasty backlash. But what would fuel the predicted backlash? The majority's deep attachment to its symbols, of course. This is counsel to the weak to yield to the strong, pure and simple. Our Constitution can do much better than that.

Perhaps this last is a good note upon which to end this chapter. The matters we have taken up here share the quality of stirring passionate controversy. They also seem to inspire a kind of take-no-prisoners mentality, in which one side wants to purge the public space of any-thing remotely religious and the other insists not just on public space but upon the privilege of public endorsement.

There is an important lesson to be learned from the extreme pas-sions these cases provoke: in the realm of our spiritual commitments, symbols matter a lot. When the highest-ranking judge of the State of Alabama wraps himself around the Ten Commandments, candlelight vigils follow; when a federal court of appeals pronounces the Pledge of Allegiance unconstitutional, threats to amend the Constitution en-sue. When Michael Newdow—a physician, not a practicing lawyer— represents himself before the Supreme Court of the United States in his case challenging the Pledge, he speaks with a passion that appears to rock the Court and that stirs even the jaded *New York Times* to com-ment. On a personal note, when we submit a friend-of-the-court brief to the Supreme Court, urging the moderate course with regard to the Pledge that we described above, we receive a rancorous e-mail from a fellow academic, excoriating us for our willingness to appease the sup-porters of the Pledge in its present form. The social meaning of sacred texts and symbols and of religious references more generally is not an abstraction but a reality that burns red hot.

There is another lesson to be taken from our excursion through the controversies surveyed in this chapter. The middle path we find our-selves urging in the Pledge of Allegiance controversy is characteristic of our prescriptions for religious liberty. This is not an accident. Nei-ther is it the product of a pragmatic effort to temper discord, nor an ar-tifact of our moderate academic inclinations. It is instead the natural product of viewing the question of religious freedom from the vantage of Equal Liberty. Early on, we noted that Equal Liberty does not ask whether and when religion is good or bad. Equal Liberty seeks to set out fair terms of cooperation for a religiously diverse people who accept the obligation to treat one another with respect as equal members of our political community. That being our enterprise, it is not surprising that more often than not we find ourselves supporting principles that treat the concerns of both sides of these disputes as having some call on constitutional outcomes.

· V ·

God in the Classroom

THE SCOPES MONKEY trial of 1925 is an iconic event in American legal history. Arranged as a test case, and pitting Clarence Darrow against William Jennings Bryan, it resulted in the conviction of John Scopes, who had been charged with the crime of teaching evolution. The trial was a media sensation when it occurred and later became the basis for a successful drama and film, *Inherit the Wind.*[1] More than eighty years have passed since the Scopes trial, yet the controversy about teaching evolution in the public schools is still raging. In 2005 a Pennsylvania court created a media sensation by prohibiting a school district from teaching "intelligent design" alongside evolution as a theory of human origins, one more acceptable to those who accepted the biblical account of Genesis.[2] During the year preceding the court's decision, both President George W. Bush and Senate Majority Leader Bill Frist endorsed the teaching of intelligent design, the Kansas Board of Education adopted standards designed to accommodate the intelligent design position, and science teachers in some school districts reported that they avoided mentioning evolution in their classrooms out of fear that they might incur the wrath of school officials.[3]

Deep and durable as controversies concerning religion and the public school curriculum have proven to be, questions about school prayer have provoked more intense passions. Prayer exercises are near the core of religious experience for many Americans, and they touch a very sensitive constitutional nerve. The Supreme Court's decisions banning official prayer in public schools have been the focus of sustained and bitter criticism. Together, prayer and religiously inflected curricular prescriptions have made America's public schools the roiled site of sustained constitutional concern and contentious disagreement.[4]

Throughout, the Supreme Court has been remarkably firm and constant. The justices have consistently barred public schools from conducting official prayer exercises, even in such familiar contexts as benedictions at graduation ceremonies and prayers before football games. The Court has taken the view that, under some circumstances, even official provision for a moment of silence in the course of the school day is unconstitutional. The tone of the Court's school prayer decisions persists in a series of decisions involving religiously charged curricular choices. There, the Court has prohibited public schools from teaching religious lessons while permitting the same schools to teach secular lessons even when (as in the case of evolution) those lessons offend some religious parents and even when the state legislature has tried to bar them from the curriculum.

This imposing edifice of Supreme Court doctrine matters a great deal to many people, and, taken as whole, this group of cases is one of the most disputed areas of constitutional law in the United States. These cases have special significance for us because, on the face of the matter, the Supreme Court's decisions regarding religion in the public schools do not seem promising exemplars of Equal Liberty. Consider: teachers may not lead students in a prayer, but they are free to lead them in the Pledge of Allegiance—except, possibly, to the extent that the words "under God" render the Pledge itself religious; public schools may offer classes on democratic principles but not Christian principles; those schools may teach the theory of evolution but not creationism or "creation science." As some commentators have been at pains to point out, religion appears to be the subject of unique prohibitions that have no secular analogues.[5]

While we do not embrace fully each of the Court's constitutional judgments regarding religion in the public schools, we are generally sympathetic with the Court's view of these cases. But can proponents of Equal Liberty embrace this chronic pattern of apparently unequal treatment? The challenge posed by that question makes this area an important testing ground for the equality-centered approach to religious freedom we espouse. In this chapter we show that the principles of Equal Liberty do in fact support the Court's general stance with regard to religious exercises and teachings in the public schools.

School Prayer, Social Meaning, and Disparagement

In its landmark decision in *Engel v. Vitale*, rendered in 1962, the Supreme Court prohibited officially sponsored prayer in public schools.[6] *Engel* and its progeny were immediately unpopular with significant portions of the American public, and they remain so. On the other hand, many church leaders have come to accept *Engel* because they do not want the state deciding how people should pray or forcing prayers on unwilling religious minorities.[7] Indeed, although politicians and the popular press sometimes portray the school prayer cases as a battleground between devout believers and atheists or "secular humanists," that is a serious mischaracterization. For example, the plaintiffs who objected to prayers in two of the Supreme Court's most recent school prayer cases were not atheists or secular humanists; they were religious minorities who did not want to participate in governmentally organized religious rituals.[8]

Engel would be easy to defend if it merely prohibited *compulsory* prayer rituals. The Supreme Court's landmark 1942 decision in *West Virginia State Board of Education v. Barnette* held that students could not be forced to "confess by word or act their faith" in any doctrine of "politics, nationalism, religion, or other matters of opinion."⁹ *Barnette* dealt with a flag salute ceremony, not a religious ritual, but its rule obviously entitles students to abstain from reciting prayers. Yet *Barnette* guarantees students only the right to opt out of rituals in which they do not want to participate. *Engel* goes further. It prohibits school-sponsored prayer entirely; it is not sufficient for schools to excuse students from the ritual if they object to it. Moreover, in two recent decisions, *Lee v. Weisman* (1992) and *Santa Fe Independent School District v. Doe* (2000), the Court extended *Engel*'s rule to bar school-sponsored prayers at extracurricular events, such as graduation ceremonies and football games.¹⁰ As the dissenters in these cases pointed out, attendance at graduation ceremonies and football games is itself optional—students offended by the prospect of a public prayer can stay home.

One line of defense of *Engel*'s strict rule focuses on the social pressure felt by students who choose to opt out. Students who visibly abstain from public prayer rituals may find themselves shunned, teased, or even assaulted by students in the mainstream.¹¹ Were this so, the rituals would have a substantial coercive effect in spite of the opt-out provision—students would have to conform to mainstream practice or pay a heavy price. To be sure, it is not at all clear that flag salutes are any different from prayers in this respect. Indeed, during wartime, opting out of a flag salute or the Pledge of Allegiance might require *more* courage than opting out of a prayer. Calling attention to the possibility of intense social pressure does not, in other words, help to explain why *Engel*'s rule is more absolute than *Barnette*'s. But it would be possible to argue that *Barnette*'s rule, not *Engel*'s, is mistaken.

Either way, this line of argument falls short of justifying *Santa Fe Independent School District*, the case that dealt with a school-sponsored prayer at a football game. Students could opt out of the prayer by staying away from the football game. Such a choice is hardly costless—especially in Texas, where high school football is taken very seriously—

but life is full of tough choices. It seems a bit much to argue that social pressure renders meaningless the option not to attend the game, so that the prayers recited there are, for practical purposes, compulsory.

We believe that *Engel*, its absolutism, and its broad extension to graduation ceremonies and football games are important and correct aspects of modern constitutional doctrine. What they lack is a clear and persuasive rationale. In our view, the concepts of social meaning and disparagement, which we elaborated in the previous chapter, supply the needed principles. Public school prayer rituals are like publicly sponsored crèche displays. Indeed, they are significantly worse, both because schools (like courthouses) are venues where government should be especially sensitive to the need to treat people equally and because prayer rituals (by contrast to, say, Christmas carols) are especially powerful markers of religious identity.

Government-sponsored prayer rituals involve a public embrace of the faithful . . . more precisely, of those whose faiths are consistent with mainstream public prayer. As a result, their social meaning includes this blunt message: *The real members of this community (the school community, and by extension the larger community serviced by the school or school district) are practicing Christians of a certain sort; others dwell among us but lack the status of full membership.*[12] These public rituals create a class of outsiders and thereby disparage those relegated to that status. Such disparagement is a constitutionally cognizable harm, and the harm persists even if students can avoid the prayer ritual—as is almost certainly true of prayers at football games—and so are not coerced to participate in rituals that conflict with their beliefs.

Proponents of school-sponsored prayer will no doubt object that neither they nor school authorities have any intention to disparage anybody; their goal is simply to make prayer rituals available to those who will appreciate them. This claim may sometimes be true. On the other hand, no reasonable person could suppose that it is always (or almost always) true; the history of sectarian divisions in this country, of jealousies and animosities, of so-called culture wars, is too rich to support such optimism. In any event, as we emphasized in the previous chapter, the relevant question is not about the intentions of particular speakers, nor about the perceptions of particular audiences, but rather about the social meanings of rituals, practices, and religions. Those meanings flow not from the thoughts and desires of the officials who sponsor rituals, but from the cultural characteristics of religions in America—their comprehensiveness; their tendency to treat people as either "in" or "out"; their use of symbols and rituals to signal who is "in"; and, finally, the profound stakes they attach to the status of "in" or "out." Everything that we said about the impermissibility of crèche displays applies *a fortiori* to prayer rituals. When the government sponsors religious rituals in schools, it marks young and vulnerable Americans as either "in" or "out" of the circle of community members who enjoy the blessing of official approval.

Crucial to bear in mind at this point is that the constitutional bar to *publicly sponsored prayer* in schools is not the same thing as the exclusion of prayer from the schools. To the contrary, students in public schools have rights of free speech that emphatically include the right to various forms of religious speech, including privately initiated prayer. Students have a right to pray at school, they may gather together to say prayers or read the Bible, and they may distribute religious newspapers.[13]

This constitutionally protected right to speech, inclusive of religious speech, can be exercised in highly public fora, such as graduation ceremonies or the editorial page of the school newspaper. In such circumstances, drawing the line between public sponsorship and individual action requires care and subtlety. For example, if a student is chosen to give his school's valedictory speech, he may choose to include a prayer in the speech. The school principal would act unconstitutionally, however, if she chose a particular student as school valedictorian *because* she believed that he would include a prayer in his speech. If she did that, she would be doing indirectly what the Constitution prohibits her from doing directly: she would be using her power over the valedictory speech to sponsor a prayer at the graduation ceremony. Likewise, the school principal could not authorize the student body to vote on whether or not to have a prayer at graduation. A principal who did that would, in effect, be delegating to the students a power that she does not possess (and hence cannot delegate)—namely, the power to determine that the graduation ceremony should include a prayer. On the other hand, the school principal could permissibly authorize the student body to select the graduation speaker, even if she knows that the student body might select a speaker who will say a prayer. The principal thereby delegates to the students only a power that she might permissibly exercise herself—namely, the power to *choose* a speaker who *might* say a prayer, not the power to *determine that* a prayer will be said.

It is true that a student graduation speaker who offers a prayer may be divisive, may cause bruised feelings, and may set in motion other undesirable consequences. But the Constitution does not, and could not, guarantee that graduation ceremonies will be soothing, unifying, or benign. Indeed, graduation ceremonies are like weddings: they provide clumsy or belligerent speakers with plentiful opportunities to inflame the sensibilities of a tender audience. Ecumenical prayers are not the worst such offenses. What the Constitution does is to prevent *the government*—not private individuals—from committing *certain specific wrongs*, including, as here, the disparagement of those who lack particular religious commitments.

Does Religion Get Second-Class Treatment in the Schools?

Still, some of those who view the school prayer decisions with distaste see them as unfair or partial—as inconsistent, in other words, with the equality norms that form the heart of the approach we recommend. Their complaint has a blunt logic: religious rituals are banned but secular ones are permitted; hence, bias against religion must be at work. We considered a related argument in Chapter 4, when we examined—and rejected—the claim that the prohibition of publicly sponsored religious displays itself disparages religious believers. We believe that such arguments are equally mistaken when applied to religion's role in the public schools, but they seem plausible to many people, and so it behooves us to consider in some detail what "equal treatment" means with respect to religion in public school classrooms.

Let's begin with the following observation: if there were indeed secular rituals that carried the social meaning of disparagement, and were those rituals happily embraced by the Supreme Court, then these critics of the school prayer decisions would indeed have cause for complaint. But there aren't such rituals in fact, and if there were, they would be unconstitutional. Suppose we visit a Fineville very different from the one we have been imagining. In this alternative Fineville, at the start of each day students are invited to recite the following "meditation," prepared by the principal at the suggestion of the board of education:

> We begin the school day conscious of the fact that we each have but a limited time in which to fill our life with meaning by virtue of our contribution to the well-being of the society of which we are a part. We know that there is no transcendental being to thank or blame for our success or failure as individuals or as a people. This is all the more reason to dedicate ourselves to the challenge of discerning what is good and just and pursuing that with all the vigor, commitment, and knowledge we can muster.

A bit inelegant, to be sure, but what can you expect from a make-believe high school principal scripted by two law professors? More importantly, this school-sponsored ritual would plainly be unconstitutional, precisely because it would disparage traditional religious believers.

Our hypothetical, antireligious "meditation" is also far-fetched, and for a good reason: in the real world, it is very hard to find or even imagine secular rituals that can be sensibly compared to public school prayer rituals. This makes it difficult for the claims of secular/religious inequity to gain factual traction. Perhaps the critics of Equal Liberty can get some help from U.S. Court of Appeals Judge Michael McConnell. In an article written long before his appointment to the bench, McConnell claimed that "if a public school football coach (or even a member of the team) offers a prayer or other religious inspiration before the game, he will be stopped; a girls' tennis coach who offers feminist words of inspiration before the game engages in protected speech."[14] Suppose we simplify McConnell's hypothetical by contrasting a tennis coach or player who offers her team "a prayer or other religious inspiration" before a big match with a tennis coach or player who offers her team "feminist words of inspiration" in the same setting. How valid is the complaint that religious speech in such settings is systematically disfavored?

We start with an important point that we have already noted: whatever the constitutional limitations that apply to the tennis coach herself, they do not extend to individual expression by team members, and McConnell is simply wrong to suggest otherwise. Individual students have a constitutional right to express themselves, a right that encompasses matters of religious belief and observance. In *Tinker v. Des Moines Independent School District* (1969), the Supreme Court held that students do not surrender their rights of free expression at the schoolhouse doors. *Tinker* involved two students who wore black armbands in class to protest the Vietnam War. The school forced the students to remove the armbands, and the students sued. The Supreme Court upheld the right of the students to express their views.[15]

The speech at issue in *Tinker* was not religious, but the rule of the case applies to religious speech no less than to political speech. Students are free to express their personal political and religious convictions at school and during school events, so long as they abide by general rules of classroom conduct (the First Amendment does not, for example, license students to interrupt the teacher, talk during "quiet time," or spew expletives at their classmates). To be sure, lower courts in the United States have sometimes got this point wrong. For example, a federal district court once held that a middle school principal could put special restrictions on the distribution of religious newspapers at his school in order to prevent students from mistakenly concluding that the school itself had sponsored religious speech. This ruling, which was vacated on appeal, would have left students with more freedom to publish and disseminate a newspaper when its contents were secular rather than religious.[16]

The Supreme Court, however, has consistently upheld the freedom of students to express their personal religious views.[17] The Court has been right to do so—there is no reason to treat private religious speech, in schools or elsewhere, differently from other controversial speech about political, moral, and ethical matters.

Critics of the Supreme Court sometimes complain that it has excluded religion from the public schools. Framed this broadly, the complaint is simply false. The Court's jurisprudence applies to public sponsorship of religion, not to individual exercise or expression of it. General principles of constitutional liberty guarantee that students need not shed their religious identities at the schoolhouse door. Religion is present within schools through the free exercise of it by individual students.

Of course, matters are different if the tennis coach asks an athlete to lead a prayer, or if she calls upon a specific player to speak only because the coach knows that player is likely to offer a prayer. At that point, the athlete's speech is no longer like the expression protected in *Tinker.* The speech is not simply an expression of the athlete's personal point of view; the athlete has instead become a kind of mouthpiece for the coach and, indirectly, for the government—the public school district—that employs the coach. Under the *Tinker* principle, students are free to express their own personal views, but it does not follow that the government (here, the school district) can use student speakers to get around constitutional restrictions on the speech of its agents.[18]

The interesting question, then, is what our tennis coach herself can say (directly or through a surrogate), not what the players can say. McConnell suggests that the coach cannot offer "a prayer or other religious inspiration" but that she can offer "feminist words of inspiration." We should ask two questions about this claim. The first is whether it is descriptively accurate. And the second is whether, to the extent that it is true, it is defensible in terms of the model of Equal Liberty.

Is McConnell's claim descriptively accurate? It depends what he means by two key phrases: "prayer or other words of religious inspiration" and "feminist words of inspiration." Let's begin with what seems most clear. The coach cannot lead her team in a prayer or encourage the team to pray. On the other hand, she certainly can tell her team, "I believe in you girls; I believe in your capacity to be good athletes, and more than that, to live up to your dreams and do whatever you want to do in this society—even to do things that have been traditionally done by men, such as competing successfully on the tennis court." That speech could count, we suppose, as "feminist words of inspiration." So, on this interpretation of McConnell's claims, he is correct to say that the coach cannot offer a prayer but can offer "feminist words of inspiration."

This disparity is hardly troubling, however. It compares apples and oranges. The prayer, unlike the speech, is a participatory ritual that affirms a particular (in this case, religious) identity. Moreover, even a nonsectarian prayer may be offensive to some members of the team (both to nonreligious players, who will not want to pray, and to some religious players, who want to pray privately or in their own way), whereas the "feminist" speech we have imagined is so bland that it is hard to imagine its offending anybody.

To make "feminist words of inspiration" comparable to a prayer, we would both have to remake them into a ritual—like a pledge—and sharpen the words to the point where somebody could object. Imagine, then, a coach who requests that her players, before they begin play, pledge allegiance to the values of the American feminist movement. It is clear that the coach could not require her players to recite the pledge: the prohibition on compulsory rituals of obeisance was settled sixty years ago in *West Virginia v. Barnette,* which held that students could not be required to salute the flag.[19] But what if the coach permits her players to opt out of saying the feminist pledge if they so desire? Such a partisan political ritual would still be at odds with the more general principle declared in *Barnette:* "if there is any fixed star in our constitutional constellation, it is that no official, high or petty, may prescribe what shall be orthodox in matters of politics . . . or religion."[20] In our view, it might well be unconstitutional to conduct such a feminist pledge as a sustained practice in a public school setting; certainly this would be true if a plausible claim of disparagement could be made.

We have not been able to find any actual instance of a secular ritual comparable to the imaginary tennis coach's feminist pledge. We are aware of at least one instance in which a teacher demanded that students pledge fidelity to a secular precept or lose an important benefit: a biology professor at Texas Tech University refused to provide reference letters for his students unless they affirmed that they believed the theory of evolution.[21] In our view, the professor's requirement was clearly unjust and (because he taught at a public university) unconstitutional. As a biology professor, he could demand that his students *understand* the theory of evolution, but not that they *endorse* it. The fact that partisan requirements of this kind are rare—rare by comparison to, for example, instances of prayer or religious speech in school—is itself significant, and we will return to the point later. For the moment, though, we simply emphasize that when such cases do arise, the Constitution protects schoolchildren from the imposition of orthodoxy, religious or not.

We can further sharpen the comparison between religious and feminist speech. The coach might tell her players, "Today's match will test not only your physical strength but your spiritual strength. When things go badly, I want you to think about the sources of that strength—your beliefs, your family, your religion, your culture—and I want you to muster every drop of courage that you have." (A pretty hokey speech, perhaps, but no worse than "Pray that our Lord and Savior will be on our side when we take on Springfield.") Or the coach might articulate sectarian themes without naming their religious origins. For example: "Be not prideful! Remember that rule. It is a good rule for life and for this game. This game is a team game. Be not prideful!" Though the coach's words never mention God or religion, her allusions would hardly be lost on religious athletes.

This last example is especially important, because it illustrates another misconception that is common in the vitriolic debate about religion's role in the public schools. People on both sides of that argument sometimes seem to assume that if schools cannot organize prayers or provide explicitly theological instruction, then the school will be wholly secular, stripped of any religious influences. We have already noticed one important way in which this view is false: religion will enter through the expression of religious students. Now we can identify a second way, one that extends to the public acts of the school. In the United States, curricular choices will inevitably reflect the moral and ethical content of religious traditions. This fact is perhaps most evident in the domain of sex education, where competing educational strategies—promoting abstinence, discussing contraception, or not mentioning sexuality at all—inevitably reflect competing religious traditions. But the influence of religion's moral teaching is more pervasive. It extends to lessons about war and peace, civic virtues, crime and punishment, American history, and the environment, and it affects how teachers treat the children in their classrooms. Anybody who doubts the point need only examine the power of Norma and Mel Gabler, conservative fundamentalist Christians from Texas who have reviewed public school textbooks and exerted considerable (and widely reported) influence over publishers for decades.[22]

In the United States, then, the influences of religion on the public school curriculum are inevitable and deep. The Constitution does not prohibit these influences; in many important contexts it protects those who seek to exert them. In general, constitutional concerns arise only when teaching incorporates explicitly sectarian or theological elements (we say "in general" because of the difficult problems posed by "moments of silence" and the controversy over creationism and evolution; we take up those cases later in this chapter).

Nevertheless, let's press ahead with this inquiry, and suppose that our coach offers her players explicitly sectarian or theological words of inspiration. Perhaps, for example, she says, "I want you to take inspiration from the following words in the Gospel according to John, . . ." Now we may be getting close to the constitutional line. It is important to note, however, that even the most controversial of the Supreme Court's decisions in this area involve much less subtle and evanescent practices than the one-off choices of inspirational tropes by a tennis coach. The early school prayer decisions involved firm school policies that required teachers to lead their students daily in formal prayers specified by the state. The rationale of these cases was extended more recently to graduation exercises. There again, the inclusion of religious material took the form of a formal religious ritual, and was by design: a member of the clergy was included in the graduation program for the purpose of pronouncing a benediction.[23] Most recently, the Court invalidated an effort by a local school board to continue its longstanding policy of public prayer at high school football games. The prayers in question were a scheduled part of each game, and were conducted through the use of the public address system. (When the school board's longstanding policy of conducting such prayers came under constitutional attack, the board replaced it with a student voting procedure to choose mechanisms of "solemnizing" the games. The

Court believed that both the purpose and effect of this mechanism was to continue the board-sponsored practice of prayer; and that, in any event, a formal policy implicating a public religious ritual adopted under these circumstances was plainly unconstitutional.)[24] All of these cases are a far cry from a handful of words expressed by our impassioned tennis coach.

Equal Liberty offers clear guidance on how to think of such occasional uses of language, and it also indicates why it is hard to have a clear sense—at least without more facts about the tennis coach's practices—of whether she has crossed the line with her invocation of St. John. The question is whether the coach is engaged in conduct that disparages the non-Christians in her environment. We would need to know things like: Does she (and possibly other coaches or instructors at her school) regularly make such references? Are these references part of a sizable portfolio of inspirational bits culled from history and literature (or *Bartlett's*), or is there a sectarian leitmotif? More generally, are there reasons to suppose that her remarks, in context, carry with them a social meaning that could fairly be understood as disparaging of some members of the community? When we understand disparagement to be the issue, we can with considerable confidence conclude that many religious references—like occasional quotations from the Reverend Martin Luther King or the Reverend Billy Graham—are constitutionally benign.

Once we understand disparagement to be the gravamen of the complaint about speech of this sort, we can see reasons to suppose that some nonreligious sources of inspiration are, if anything, more clearly off-limits to public school coaches in their pregame orations. The Constitution almost certainly would prohibit inspirational messages that appealed to or excited deep divisions in American society. A coach who told her players to "go out there and uphold the values of the white race" or "prove that you can play like white girls" would violate the Equal Protection Clause. So, too, would a coach who told her girls to "win this one for the values of European culture" or to prove "that you're real Americans who are better than a bunch of lousy immigrants." Moreover, the same free speech principles that prohibit a coach from demanding that her players swear a feminist oath will also prohibit her from demeaning them on the basis of their political beliefs. So we think, for example, that it would be unconstitutional for a public school coach to tell her players to "go out there and fight like brave Republicans instead of capitulating like sissy Democrats," or to "prove yourselves to be real feminists, like Gloria Steinem and Billie Jean King and Martina Navratilova, not a bunch of worthless housewives."

All this said, there remains something of an asymmetry in the example of our tennis coach, albeit nowhere near as great a one as many are inclined to believe. Courts are and *should* be more sensitive when religious language is deployed by teachers, coaches, and other school personnel who carry with them the authority of the community. A reference to the words of Jesus Christ, no matter how benign the overt content of that reference, will raise questions of constitutionality under circumstances in which a reference to the words of Gloria Steinem will not. The justification for this increased sensitivity is the risk of disparagement that sectarian references carry with them. And the measure of that risk is what should animate Establishment Clause doctrine in this context.

Moments of Silence

As the Court has progressively restricted the authority of schools to sponsor prayer ceremonies, some legislators and school officials have responded by establishing formal "moments of silence" in classrooms. One purpose of these moments is to allow, or perhaps to encourage, students to pray. Not surprisingly, moments of silence are intensely controversial. To their proponents, they are a neutral means of accommodating religion: they provide an opportunity for prayer without officially endorsing it. To opponents, they are thinly veiled prayer ceremonies, unnecessary for purposes of accommodation (because students may pray silently throughout the school day) and likely to be implemented in a way that ostracizes students who visibly depart from mainstream prayer rituals.

There is something to be said for both of these positions. It is true that under the best of conditions making a minute or so of silence available for students to reflect with some degree of solemnity about themselves and their worlds, small and large—and, yes, to engage in private prayer when so motivated—seems benign and attractive. It is also true that, in some circumstances, at least, moments of silence will carry much the same social meaning as public prayer rituals—perhaps with the added energy of a ritual driven underground by an unsympathetic national court—and thus be no less disparaging of nonmainstream believers than such public rituals.

The Supreme Court's one encounter with moment-of-silence legislation reflects these competing perspectives. In 1985 the Court declared that an Alabama moment-of-silence statute was unconstitutional.[25] In so doing, the Court was, however, at pains to emphasize that nothing in its judgment implied that all public school moment-of-silence arrangements were unconstitutional. The Court's reasons for finding Alabama's moment-of-silence provision unconstitutional were narrow and, significantly, largely congenial with our analysis of the central constitutional concern about school prayer, the vice of disparagement. In essence, the Court's problem with the Alabama statute was that an earlier statute had already authorized a moment of silence "for meditation," and the new statute authorized a moment of silence "for meditation or voluntary prayer." A variety of circumstances—including the uncontradicted testimony of the new statute's sponsor—convinced the Court that the new statute was enacted for "the sole purpose of expressing the State's endorsement of prayer activities."[26]

From the vantage of Equal Liberty, disparagement is the pernicious consequence of state endorsements of religion. Our only quarrel with the Alabama case, accordingly, is that the Court acted on the intent of the state to endorse the mainstream religious practice of prayer, while we think that it is the social meaning of the state's enactment of the new statute, not the subjective intent of the state, that should govern. In fact a plethora of circumstances in the Alabama case supported the conclusion that the social meaning of the new statute was indeed the endorsement of prayer, and hence the disparagement of those who do not pray. Justice O'Connor, who concurred in the result in the Alabama case, came somewhat closer to our view; she found the new Alabama statute unconstitutional on the grounds that "government action endorsing religion or a particular religious practice is invalid . . . because it 'sends a message to nonadherents that they are outsiders, not full members of the political community, and an accompanying message to adherents that they are insiders, favored members of the political community.'"[27] She too, however, seems ultimately to have focused on the subjective purpose of public acts rather than on their objective social meaning. On our account, purpose enters the story only indirectly, as a potentially potent element of social meaning. In the case of the Alabama statute, for example, a competent member of the Alabama political community might well have read the enactment of the new statute as an endorsement of prayer precisely because it was hard to resist the view that the state meant to use the moment of silence as a kind of school prayer-in-exile; it was hard to resist this view, both because there was no other apparent purpose for the government to act at all, and because of the pro-prayer rhetoric that accompanied the statute's enactment.[28]

The Supreme Court left the original Alabama provision for a moment of silence—which made no reference to prayer—standing, and did not take up the question of the constitutional status of moment-of-silence provisions when the issue of endorsement is not sharply implicated. And presently, at least twenty-nine states have statutory provisions requiring or permitting moments of silence.[29] Formally neutral moments of silence raise an interesting and important question about the appropriate shape of constitutional doctrine in the area of religious liberty, the problem of the degree to which it is appropriate to suppress legitimate opportunities for religious practice in order to guard against illegitimate occasions of state-sponsored disparagement of nonmainstream believers.

At a formal level, defenders of moments of silence are clearly correct: if the practice is fairly and conscientiously administered—if teachers, administrators, and legislatures avoid creating an environment that encourages prayer at the cost of disparaging those who do not choose to pray—then there is nothing improper about providing for a moment of silence that is available for prayer as well as for other forms of reflection. Persons of many moral and religious persuasions might well benefit from such a moment. Moreover, if any principal, teacher, or coach uses a moment of silence to conduct a covert prayer ceremony, her actions are unconstitutional, and a student or parent could in theory bring an action to stop such rogue behavior, even if the general moment-of-silence policy were permissible. So too, if a school board or state legislature provides for a moment of silence under circumstances that carry a disparaging social meaning, the enactment is for that reason unconstitutional. Accordingly, the constitutional argument against moments of silence more generally must reach for notions of prophylaxis: it must contend that the risk of covert prayer ceremonies is so great, and the difficulty of policing them on a case-by-case basis so onerous, that we ought to prohibit the practice entirely (even though we thereby forfeit the benefits of a practice that is, if appropriately conducted, socially useful and constitutionally unobjectionable).

This prophylactic argument has considerable appeal. We would find it persuasive if it were offered as policymaking advice to teachers, school boards, or legislatures. We think that even if moments of silence are constitutionally permissible under some circumstances, schools would be better off without them. In the past one of us went further and endorsed the prophylactic objection to moments of silence as a matter of judicially enforceable constitutional doctrine.[30] Both of us now believe, however, that this position is probably mistaken. Prophylactic constitutional rules make most sense when there is a clear imbalance of risks (the classic example is "better to let a hundred guilty men go free than convict one who is innocent"). In religious liberty cases, prophylactic constitutional rules should be used sparingly if at all, for the simple reason that the risks, broadly considered, are likely to be closely balanced.[31]

With regard to moments of silence, we do not think that schools have a constitutional obligation to provide for such a practice; indeed, as we have said, we would generally counsel against such a provision, precisely on prudential or prophylactic grounds. But a broad, judicially enforced, prophylactic constitutional rule seems ill advised. Such a rule would necessarily be one-size-fits-all, and would function as a durable bar against a wide range of schools in various places and times even experimenting with moments of silence under circumstances in which they might promise to be benign and useful. And such a rule, emanating from the judiciary—and, presumably, ultimately from the Supreme Court itself—could encourage one of two undesirable perceptions. First, such a rule could encourage an attitude among legislators and school officials that it is safer to suppress religious exercises and expressions of all kinds in the public schools, even those that are genuinely spontaneous and private acts by individual students and groups; such a rule could thus lead to errors in judgment with a constitutional dimension. As we have emphasized, students and student groups have important constitutional rights to engage in religious exercises and to utter religious expressions in the course of their public school experiences, and there is evidence that public school officials, overly zealous to comply with *Engel* and its progeny, have sometimes discriminated against religious speech. Second, a willingness on the part of the judiciary to adopt a prophylactic constitutional rule that prevents private prayer under benign circumstances can be misread by some as judicial indifference or hostility to the interests of religious believers.

We may be wrong about this question of prophylaxis yet again. The question of whether a prophylactic constitutional rule is appropriate is exquisitely sensitive to practical and empirical concerns that are not easy to assess. Of this we are certain: the underlying principle in this area is the antidisparagement principle. And serious and sensible discussions about the appropriate constitutional response to moments of silence and to other issues associated with prayer in the public schools must proceed with reference to this guiding principle. If, at the end of the day, we have underestimated the pervasiveness of the risk of disparagement posed by moments of silence and overestimated the good faith and judgment of school personnel and the ability of courts to police such personnel, then perhaps the desirability of a prophylactic ban should be revisited.

Curriculum

Although school prayers and other religious rituals provoke a great deal of passion and debate, the analytic framework applicable to them turns out to be fairly straightforward. We think that there are sound constitutional reasons to prohibit such practices. Those reasons flow from general principles of Equal Liberty, principles that prohibit government officials (including public school teachers, coaches, and administrators) from using partisan ethnic, social, or political criteria to demean the status of groups and individuals. To the extent that these principles apply differently to religious practices than to political or ideological ones, it is because of the different social meanings associated with those practices—not because religion is subject to an entirely different set of principles.

We now turn to a set of cases that pose more subtle concerns. They deal not with rituals but with religious influences on, or objections to, the public school curriculum. The role of religion in these cases varies, but in all of them it is less direct than in the prayer cases. The controversies fall into three categories: explicitly religious components of school curricula, religiously motivated objections from parents who want to exempt their children from secular instruction, and religiously motivated government decisions about what to include or exclude from the public school curriculum. We consider examples from each category in the pages that follow.

The Bible in the Public School Curriculum

Until the Supreme Court's decision in *School District of Abington Township v. Schempp* (1963), the American public school curriculum routinely included Bible-reading classes.[32] In general, these classes treated the Bible as a sacred text to be revered, memorized, and followed, not critiqued or analyzed as a cultural or literary artifact. Public school classes that read the Bible devotionally are not much different from the prayer rituals we have already discussed. Hence the classes have all the constitutional problems associated with the coach's prayer. More specifically, inspirational Bible-reading classes are not constitutionally distinguishable from classes celebrating the Republican party platform or proselytizing on behalf of the National Organization for Women. Such classes are impermissibly partisan; they put the government's prestige behind a partisan doctrine and a specific social group.

Of course, one need not teach the Bible devotionally; one need not teach it any more reverently, than, say, classics like John Locke's *Second Treatise on Government*. One can treat the Bible as great literature, historically important, and ethically profound without insulating it from critique or arms-length analysis, without denying that it might be profoundly *wrong* about the substance of many subjects. Thus, though the *Schempp* Court prohibited public schools from sponsoring devotional

Bible readings, it recognized the possibility of nondevotional Bible studies in the public schools and expressly found this form of study to be constitutional.[33]

In practice, though, the Bible seems to have all but disappeared from the curriculum of public schools in some parts of the country.[34] Its absence helps to fuel accusations that the Court has inappropriately secularized the public sphere in general and the public schools in particular. No doubt some school districts have misunderstood the Supreme Court's ruling, believing (wrongly) that judges would prohibit them from assigning portions of the Bible for any reason. Misunderstandings of this kind are, of course, inevitable with any legal doctrine. But it is also worth remembering that the Court quite rightly held that schools *may* include the Bible in their curriculum, not that they must do so. They may choose to exclude it on the grounds that there are equally or more important, or equally or more fertile, materials upon which to focus. They may also choose to exclude it on the ground that the Bible's theological content makes it difficult or even impossible for teachers to present it neutrally and effectively. We expect that, in light of this country's multicultural religious environment, many school districts have made some combination of these judgments, and that this is what explains the Bible's absence from their curriculum.

"Secular Humanism"

Religious parents sometimes object to secular public school lessons that are at odds with their religious beliefs. These objections often focus upon hot-button topics such as sex education or the theory of evolution, but in some instances the objections sweep much more broadly. For example, in a much-discussed controversy that arose during the 1980s, Vicki Frost, Robert Mozert, and other fundamentalist Christian parents fought a protracted battle with the Hawkins County, Tennessee, School Board.[35] The conflict centered upon the Holt Basic

Readers, textbooks published by Holt, Rinehart & Winston and recently adopted by the Hawkins County Schools. Frost, Mozert, and others claimed that the stories in the readers embodied a religious viewpoint that they called "secular humanism." Some of their complaints pertained to selections about evolution (the parents objected, for example, to an essay in which Jane Goodall described chimpanzees as "human's closest relative"), but they also applied to a wide variety of fictional stories, including one about Martians, some dealing with witchcraft, and hundreds of others. In a letter signed by Mozert, but apparently written by Jennie Wilson (a Hawkins County protestor who had no children in the schools), the parents even complained about the Holt version of "Goldilocks." They said that the story was objectionable because the Three Bears treated Goldilocks nicely even though she was a trespasser who violated the bears' property rights.[36]

The parents eventually sued the school district, seeking two different forms of relief. First, they contended that the Holt reader series amounted to an unconstitutional establishment of "secular humanism," and they demanded that the district stop using it. Second, they sought to force the district to exempt their children from the particular lessons they found offensive. It is difficult to muster any sympathy for the first of these claims. Nobody—religious or not—is entitled to demand a public school curriculum fully consistent with his or her own ideology. Such an entitlement would, of course, make it impossible for the schools to teach anything at all. As the Hawkins County dispute vividly illustrates, nearly anything—even a story as innocuous as "Goldilocks"—can offend somebody.

Equal Liberty, as we have said before, requires equality, not neutrality. The Hawkins County School Board had no obligation to produce a public school curriculum that is neutral among faiths—nor could it possibly do so, even if that were its ambition. On the other hand, the board had to respect the equal status of the Frosts, the Mozerts, and other fundamentalist Christians who are a part of its community. The board would have violated the Constitution if it adopted a curriculum that mocked fundamentalists or if it required students to pledge their support for evolution, feminism, or other doctrines inconsistent with their fundamentalist religion. Of course, the board was never accused of any such behavior, and there is no evidence that its curriculum was pervasively hostile to fundamentalist Protestantism. On the contrary, in the early 1980s, when the controversy erupted, Bible-reading and teacher-sponsored prayers were still relatively commonplace in Hawkins County classrooms.[37] The Hawkins County protesters accused the board of showing sympathy for views with which they disagreed, not of mocking or disparaging their own beliefs.

The second claim of the Hawkins County parents, seeking exemptions for their own children, raises more difficult questions. It is, of course, a specific case of the more general exemptions issue that we considered in Chapter 3. We argued there that government must show equal regard for personal commitments, be they religious or secular, mainstream or peripheral. If Hawkins County allows parents in general to pull students out of classes that they find objectionable, then the county cannot deny that right to Vicki Frost or Robert Mozert because it deems their views silly or extreme. On the other hand, even if Hawkins County grants some such requests, it might deny the request of Frost and Mozert because their objections sweep too broadly to be accommodated—Frost and Mozert objected to huge slices of the curriculum, and that fact distinguishes their complaints from those of parents who seek to exempt their children from a single course (such as sex education).

Let's suppose, though, that Hawkins County has no policy permitting parents to exempt children from portions of the required curriculum. The parents may seek help from another set of constitutional principles, those that protect the right of parents to guide the education and upbringing of their children. The Supreme Court recognized these principles more than eighty years ago, in *Pierce v. Society of Sisters*

(1925).[38] In that case, the Supreme Court struck down an Oregon statute that required all parents to send their children to public schools. *Pierce* neatly illustrates the third strand of Equal Liberty—broad rights that expand the capacity of all citizens to live according to their conscience and commitments, whether religious or not. Indeed, *Pierce* itself combined two cases: *Pierce v. Society of Sisters*, which involved a Catholic school, and *Pierce v. Hill Military Academy*, which involved a secular military school.

Pierce would entitle Vicki Frost and Robert Mozert to remove their children from the public schools and insert them instead into private schools with a reading list more to their liking. Frost and Mozert, however, sought something different. They did not want to pull their children out of the Hawkins County public schools; they wanted to keep them in those schools, but to exempt them from particular assignments they found objectionable. Do the rights of parental autonomy recognized in *Pierce* provide them with any comfort? Perhaps. Once we agree that the Constitution recognizes the value of parental autonomy, that value may influence not only the question of whether the government can compel children to attend public schools, but also the issue of how the government should treat children within those schools. On the other hand, it would be wildly impractical to demand that schools tailor their pedagogy to fit the conscience of every parent (or every child). It would also be wrong, as a matter of principle, to give ideological outliers so much power to unseat public school practices.

In general, parents who object to the public school curriculum may have to put up with it or else exercise their right, guaranteed by *Pierce*, to school their children elsewhere. That is probably the case for Frost and Mozert: one might argue that the Hawkins County schools should have tried harder to accommodate them, but their objections to the curriculum swept so broadly that accommodation would have imposed significant costs on the district.

More generally, this seems an area in which the role of courts is likely to be very limited. It is easy and sensible to say that school officials should respect the spirit of the *Pierce* decision and make reasonable efforts to accommodate the special concerns and difficulties of parents with regard to the school curriculum and activities. That is so whether or not these concerns emanate from the parents' *religious* commitments. Where possible, schools should eschew reflexive bureaucratic intransigence in favor of flexibility when that can be obtained at relatively little cost. But courts are poorly equipped to supervise or encourage this attitude at the margins.[39]

Evolution, Creation Science, and Intelligent Design

We come now to an especially vexing set of controversies, those dealing with religious efforts to include creationism—or exclude evolution—from the public school curriculum. Creationism—in its strongest form, the belief that "God created human beings pretty much in their present form within the last 10,000 years or so"—is popular in the United States. A 1997 Gallup Poll found that 44 percent of Americans embrace this view.[40] Another 39 percent embrace a milder form of creationism: they believe that "human beings have developed over millions of years from less advanced forms of life, but God has guided this process." Only 10 percent of Americans believe that human beings evolved over millions of years *and* that "God had no part in this process." These numbers, moreover, are reasonably consistent across age cohorts—so, for example, 43 percent of Americans age eighteen to twenty-nine and 47 percent of Americans age fifty to sixty-four are strong creationists.[41] In a poll released in 2005, nearly two-thirds of respondents thought that creationism should be taught alongside evolution in America's schools.[42]

When these numbers are set against the clear verdict of science—which supports the basic theory of evolution as firmly established—

the controversy that has swirled in this area of public school curriculum is hardly surprising. More than eighty years after the famous Scopes trial, a staple of scientific understanding is regarded by a great many Americans as false if not blasphemous. The opponents of evolution have tried many different ways to eliminate it from the curriculum of the public schools or to have it taught alongside creationism as a contested theory. These battles, which have ebbed and flowed for decades, have heated up of late, and news stories describing efforts by local school boards or statewide commissions are again common.

Federal courts have taken a strong line against these anti-evolution efforts. In *Epperson v. Arkansas,* decided in 1968, the Supreme Court confronted an Arkansas statute that prohibited the teaching of evolution—or, more precisely, that part of evolution that pertained to the origins of the human species—in the public schools.[43] Arkansas defended the statute by arguing, among other things, that evolution was simply too controversial to include in the public school curriculum, but the Court struck down the law. Justice Fortas spoke for the Court and concluded that "the overriding fact is that Arkansas law selects from the body of knowledge a particular segment which it proscribes for *the sole reason* that it is deemed to conflict with a particular religious doctrine; that is, with a particular interpretation of the Book of Genesis by a particular religious group."[44]

After *Epperson,* creationists turned their efforts toward including creationism alongside evolution in the school curriculum. The Louisiana Balanced Treatment Act, for example, demanded that public schools give equal treatment to evolution and creation science: if they included a unit on evolution, they also had to include a unit on creation science. Creation science focused on gaps in the fossil record to argue, on secular grounds, that the theory of evolution was mistaken and that human beings had suddenly appeared on earth. The Supreme Court examined the Louisiana statute in a 1987 case, *Edwards v. Aguillard,* and again concluded that the statute was unconstitutional because it had a religious purpose.[45] As Laurence Tribe points out, the Court "did *not* examine the scientific validity of creation science"; instead, it ruled that, regardless of whether the doctrine was scientifically legitimate, the Balanced Treatment Act was tainted by the religious intentions of the legislature that enacted it.[46]

Edwards did not end the controversy. Rebuffed in their attempts to incorporate creation science into the school curriculum, creationists pursued new strategies. Instead of advocating creation science, they threw their support to a slightly different theory called intelligent design.[47] Intelligent design is a "kinder and gentler" version of creation science distinguished by three basic characteristics. First, unlike creation science, intelligent design accepts large portions of the evolution story—including the basic idea of natural selection and the idea that man evolved from the apes and, further back, from single-celled animals.[48] Second, it maintains that there are gaps in the evolutionary story that cannot be explained by the mechanism of natural selection. More specifically, it contends that there are certain sorts of complex structures—such as the wings of birds—that could not have evolved through natural selection, since they depended upon the survival of certain intermediate stages that served no evolutionary purpose of their own.[49] Third, it asserts that these gaps in the evolutionary story suggest the existence of an "intelligent designer." Proponents of the theory are fond of quoting William Paley's observation that, if you find a watch lying in a field, it makes sense to presume the existence of a watchmaker; likewise, they say, if you find a living being with complex features that you cannot explain, it makes sense to assume that the being was created by an intelligent designer.[50] Crudely summarized, then, intelligent design affirms much of the theory of evolution and natural selection, but contends that the process depended upon the guidance and assistance of a beneficent intervenor.[51]

To many people, efforts to limit the teaching of evolution in the public schools—or to supplement it with creation science and intelligent design—seem obvious violations of the Establishment Clause. After all, the consensus in favor of the theory of evolution among leading scientists is overwhelming. Creation science and intelligent design seem to be religious doctrines draped in secular disguises: it is hard to imagine that any significant number of people could endorse them except on religious grounds. Thus, even Stephen Carter, who laments America's "culture of disbelief" and urges more sympathy for creationists, ultimately agrees with the *Epperson* and *Edwards* courts on this issue. In his view, "*Edwards v. Aguillard* is correctly, if perhaps tragically, decided. The decision is correct because of the difficulty of articulating the precise secular purpose for the teaching of creationism: even if dressed up in scientific jargon, it is, at heart, an explanation for the origin of life that is dictated solely by religion."[52]

We sympathize with Carter's assessment. Like him, we believe that the theory of evolution is persuasive and important, and we want it taught in the schools. The theory of evolution is important not only as an answer to questions about the origins of human life, but as a foundational element in all of modern biology. Assessed as scientific theories (rather than theological doctrines), creation science and intelligent design strike us as slickly marketed intellectual snake oil, no more respectable than alchemy or cold fusion. And yet the judicial decisions in this area are somewhat troubling.

Let's begin with *Edwards,* the creation science case. The Supreme Court emphasized the all-but-undeniable purpose of the law, which was to promote the view of the creation presented in the book of Genesis. Without more, this is a problematic reason for the outcome in *Edwards.* Think about states like New Jersey, where a state statute requires that sex education courses stress abstinence as the best way to avoid pregnancy or AIDS.[53] One might plausibly suppose that much of the support for New Jersey's law came from widely held and vigorously pressed religious convictions. Should we be tempted to the view that the New Jersey approach to sex education is unconstitutional?

Certainly Equal Liberty cannot embrace this view, as it would leave secular citizens free to press for public policies on the basis of their most passionate convictions, even if they cannot give a good defense of their convictions (and even if their convictions turn out to be horribly self-interested or partisan), while requiring religious citizens to suppress their convictions when they seek to influence public policy. If the case against the constitutionality of creation science laws turns upon the religious motivations of particular legislators, then the case is a shaky one.

There is, however, an important difference between New Jersey's law about sex education and Louisiana's law about creation science. New Jersey citizens might prefer to see schools emphasize abstinence for any number of reasons, some religious and some not. One cannot say the same thing about Louisiana's law if one knows the details of creation science. Kent Greenawalt, in a thorough study of the evolution controversy, points out that creation science does not merely deny that man descended from the apes; it insists on the literal truth of the biblical creation story.[54] Thus it claims, for example, that the Earth is around 6,000 to 10,000 years old. To produce this result, creation science must make a number of wild claims. Among other things, creation scientists contend that radio-carbon dating is unreliable because natural processes changed radically in the wake of the Flood. They attempt to explain the layering of species in the fossil record by arguing that more advanced species climbed higher before drowning in the Flood.[55] Greenawalt persuasively suggests that this version of "science" is profoundly sectarian. From a scientific perspective, setting the age of the Earth at 10,000 years is ad hoc and arbitrary; the only way to get to the creation scientists' theories is to start with a commitment to the biblical story—Flood and all—and work back to the theories necessary to support that commitment.

To mandate the teaching of creation science as either a supplement to or a replacement for evolution is tantamount to requiring that the book of Genesis be taught as fact. And such a requirement, in turn, is not much different from sponsoring a school prayer ceremony or displaying a crèche in the town square: it affiliates the government with a particular religious view and so violates the Equal Liberty reading of the Establishment Clause.

Intelligent design theory is actually an even easier target, at least insofar as it insists on an intelligent designer. Suppose that there are gaps in the evolutionary story, as the intelligent design school suggests. So what? Science contains plenty of unsolved problems. For scientists, these problems call for new theories and more experiments, not speculation about supernatural intervention by deities, wizards, fairies, or space aliens (from the vantage of intelligent design theory, all these deigners have equal standing—any of them might play the role of watchmaker). The suggestion that there exists an intelligent designer is not a scientific proposition at all; it is a vague kind of religious view— and, if God or gods are identified as possible designers (at the expense of, say, wizards and fairies) the problem is manifestly made worse.[56]

That leaves us with *Epperson,* the case about the Arkansas statute banning the teaching of evolution. *Epperson* is in two respects the most troubling of these cases. First, the damage done by the law is, we think, especially severe: it denies students access to fundamental precepts of modern biology. Second, the constitutional rationale we applied to creation science and intelligent design laws does not explain the result in *Epperson.* The law in *Epperson* does not require that any doctrine, religious or otherwise, be taught.

To be sure, Arkansas banned the teaching of evolution precisely because, and only because, the theory contradicts certain religious views. It is therefore tempting to revisit the motivation-based analysis that we rejected earlier. Is there anything special about the Arkansas statute that might lead us to conclude that the religious motivations of the legislators rendered the law unconstitutional, even if such motivations do not ordinarily have that effect? Perhaps. The circumstances surrounding the legislation convinced the *Epperson* Court that the purpose of the enactment was not merely to avoid the teaching of ideas that might offend some students or sow division within the schools; the purpose, the Court concluded, was to promote the biblical story of creation. These circumstances were not subtle. One was evident on the face of the statute: while the teaching of evolution was made a misdemeanor and grounds for the immediate discharge of the offending teacher, no other theory of the origin and growth of the universe, the diversity of species on Earth, or man was banned.[57] Thus—the Constitution aside—it was perfectly legal to teach creation science or its equivalent. Further, prominent aspects of the political campaign on behalf of the *Epperson* legislation expressly pitted Christian belief against the supposedly malevolent threat of atheism. The *Epperson* legislation was enacted in the shadow of the Scopes trial in the adjacent state of Tennessee, and to the Supreme Court, at least, it was easy to read Arkansas legislators as having come as close to mandating the teaching of the book of Genesis as they dared.[58]

From the vantage of Equal Liberty, the visible effort of officials to act on behalf of what they perceive as religious truth is itself redolent with social meaning. If the social meaning of the *Epperson* enactment included the affirmation of the political community's commitment to the book of Genesis as truth, that circumstance alone is adequate grounds for the Court's decision in *Epperson*.[59]

That said, we believe that the best way to defend *Epperson* does not invoke religious liberty in a direct sense at all. We have already quoted the famous line from *West Virginia v. Barnette*, where Justice Robert Jackson declared that the state had no power to declare what shall be orthodox in matters of opinion. When the state identifies some specific topic, widely recognized as a fit subject for education, and labels it taboo, we may reasonably suspect that the state is attempting to impose an illegitimate kind of orthodoxy.

The public schools have long been seen in our constitutional tradition as the seedbeds of intellectual inquiry and freedom, and as places where concern about government-imposed orthodoxy runs especially high. Suppose, for example, that a state were to prohibit its public schools from teaching some language—say, Arabic—on the ground that studying the language was un-American (Nebraska and Iowa in fact banned the teaching of German during the 1920s).[60] Would that law be constitutional? We think not, and for the reason identified in *Barnette:* the law is, at bottom, an indefensible imposition of orthodoxy.

Of course, public schools do not impose orthodoxy simply by omitting some subject from their curriculum. Many schools, for example, have reluctantly dropped art or music classes because of budgetary shortfalls. Nor does unconstitutional orthodoxy result whenever the state limits the intellectual freedom of children; the state does that all the time, such as by requiring students to learn and apply the rules of English grammar. Nor, finally, does the state impose orthodoxy by prohibiting classes in astrology or other sorts of hokum. But it is a different matter when the state flatly prohibits all public school teachers from communicating a rigorous and respected body of knowledge (such as Arabic, the theory of evolution, or, for that matter, the history of Christianity) that it deems subversive or controversial. When that happens, there is at least a prima facie case that the state has abused its constitutional authority to control the education of children.

Seen as Supreme Court responses to occasions when there was a threat that a state-imposed orthodoxy would displace academic freedom, the outcomes in *Epperson* and *Edwards* are easy to understand. In *Epperson,* a teacher who chose the wrong textbook could be guilty of a misdemeanor and subject to discharge. And any reasonably prudent science teacher would have to be a vigilant self-censor, lest she inadvertently teach the theory of evolution. Suppose, for example, that she was talking about what almost everyone in the scientific community regards as the rough age of the universe; or suppose she was showing a film clip about the first creatures to leave the sea and find their perilous place on land; or suppose she was giving an account of dinosaurs and their neighbors. And what was she to do when a student asked any sort of question that depended on a view of evolution for a sensible answer? If the law were taken seriously, teaching biology and much of science in Arkansas would have been rather like teaching property law or civil liberties in the Soviet Union at its worst. The sense that one could innocently step dangerously out of line would have been an extraordinary inhibition on teachers. The pall in Arkansas public school classrooms would have been palpable and oppressive.

This view of *Epperson* is far from novel. Early on in the litigation, a lower Arkansas court condemned the anti-evolution law on grounds of freedom of speech and thought, noting that it "tends to hinder the quest for knowledge, restrict the freedom to learn, and restrain the freedom to teach."[61] And the Supreme Court itself gestured seriously in this direction:

> Courts do not and cannot intervene in the resolution of conflicts which arise in the daily operation of school systems and which do not directly and sharply implicate basic constitutional values. On the other hand, [t]he vigilant protection of constitutional freedoms is nowhere more vital than in the community of American Schools. As this Court said in Keyishian v. Board of Regents, the First Amendment "does not tolerate laws that cast a pall of orthodoxy over the classroom."[62]

The Court then veered off into its Establishment Clause analysis, apparently prompted by the view that religious liberty offered a somewhat narrower and less complex ground upon which to base its decision.

We thus think that the best understanding of the outcome in *Epperson* is not that the statute was impermissibly religious, but that the statute abused the state's educational power by attempting to impose an orthodoxy (religious or not). Viewed in this way, *Epperson's* doctrinal neighbors are not the school prayer cases like *Engel v. Vitale* and *Lee v. Weisman*, which are best understood as antidisparagement decisions, but a small run of cases about narrow-minded, inquiry-threatening constraints on the public school curriculum. These cases include *Board of Education, Island Trees Union Free School District v. Pico* (1982), in which the Supreme Court prevented a school board from excising controversial books (such as Kurt Vonnegut's *Slaughterhouse Five*) from a high school library; and *Meyer v. Nebraska* (1923), in which the Court struck down a Nebraska statute that prohibited the teaching of German.[63]

We believe that this fortified understanding of *Epperson*, along with the more religion-specific analysis of *Edwards* presented earlier, provides a firm basis for the federal judiciary's commendable efforts to turn back attacks on the theory of evolution. These rationales have their limits, however, and not every challenge to evolution in the public schools will be unconstitutional. Thus the U.S. Court of Appeals for the Fifth Circuit may have gone one step too far in *Freiler v. Tangipahoa Parish Board of Education* (1999).[64] A Louisiana board of education had required that whenever

> the scientific theory of evolution is to be presented, whether from textbook, workbook, pamphlet, other written material, or oral presentation, the following statement shall be quoted immediately before the unit of study begins as a disclaimer from endorsement of such theory.
>
> It is hereby recognized by the Tangipahoa Board of Education, that the lesson to be presented, regarding the origin of life and matter, is known as the Scientific Theory of Evolution and should be presented to inform students of the scientific concept and not intended to influence or dissuade the Biblical version of Creation or any other concept.[65]

On our account, the Tangipahoa disclaimer requirement is very close to an important line that courts in this area will have to draw. On the one hand, if what teachers are required to say to their students is something like "Science is science and religious faith is religious faith. Nothing we are going to say about the scientific evidence and theory of the evolution of animal species should be taken to be a commentary on the value or validity of anyone's religious commitments," then we think such a disclaimer provision is within the constitutional authority of a public school officials.[66] On the other hand, if teachers are required to say (and maintain throughout their discussions) something like "Evolution is merely a theory, and as such is fully on a par with the creation theory; science has no reason for preferring one over the other; it's entirely a matter of faith," then we think concerns about state-imposed orthodoxy again come to the fore. In the latter case, we imagine that teachers will be unable, for example, to present and explain experiments intended to show the short-term ability of some species to evolve in adaptation to new environments, much less indicate their view of the force of these experiments as a scientific matter. And, in the latter case, the bleak picture we painted of the science classroom in a state where the *Epperson* law was in place and taken seriously would in large measure apply.

If benignly interpreted, so that it does not impair the academic freedom of classroom teachers, the Tangipahoa Parish disclaimer is a mild, and fairly innocuous, way to accommodate objections to the theory of evolution. We can also imagine more lamentable attempts to undermine the theory that should nevertheless survive constitutional scrutiny. Suppose that a state goes partway down the path of intelligent design by requiring teachers to present arguments that assert the existence of irremediable gaps in the theory of evolution. The state might prescribe that teachers assign portions of books by Michael Behe, a biochemist at Lehigh University who is a proponent of intelligent design.[67] Most leading biologists believe that Behe's claims are very badly mistaken. Let's suppose, though, that the state does not ask (or permit) teachers to assign the portions of Behe's books in which he argues for the existence of an intelligent designer, and that the state's schools present the evidence in favor of evolution in some detail. Let's suppose, too, that the state leaves teachers free to report the scientific community's widespread disdain for Behe's work. Under those circumstances, we would consider the law regrettable but not unconstitutional. We do not believe that the Constitution prohibits schools from presenting both sides of a scientific argument about, say, evolution or cold fusion, even when one side of the argument seems rather dodgy, provided that the arguments presented are genuinely scientific (and not, as in the case of creation science, theologically driven).

Equal Liberty in the Classroom

For more than forty years, a majority of the Court has bravely—and, we think, rightly—fought to eliminate public sponsorship of religious rituals and doctrines in the schools. These cases carry an intense emotional charge, and the Court's decisions have provoked cries of outrage from those on the losing side. They have decried what they see as judicial efforts to banish religion from America's public schools. These blunt slogans, like others we have encountered throughout this book, are politically effective but terribly misleading. As we have seen, religion is very much present in America's public schools. It is present through the speech, practices, and convictions of individual students and teachers. And it is present through the influence of countless religious parents and interest groups—including activists such as Mel and Norma Gabler—on the public school curriculum. But government cannot, through its teachers or other officials, throw its weight on the side of religion, or on the side of particular religions, any more than it can take a position against religion.

Unlike newspaper pundits, academic commentators are unlikely to say that religion has been banished from the schools. But they sometimes make a more sophisticated version of the same mistake, claiming that religion is subject to special restrictions in the public schools that cannot be explained by Equal Liberty or other views that emphasize equality. In this chapter, we have tried to show that this critique is mistaken. The critique fails partly because the restrictions on religion in the schools are not so unusual as people sometimes suppose, but mainly because it misconstrues Equal Liberty. Equal Liberty does not deny that there exist grounds, at the level of constitutional principle, for treating religion specially; on the contrary, it insists that there is such a ground, namely, the vulnerability of conscience to discrimination, mistreatment, and neglect. Equal Liberty insists on the need for special constitutional solicitude toward religion in the name of equality; what it denies is that religion should suffer special constitutionally rooted disabilities or enjoy special constitutionally rooted advantages as against other deep human concerns and commitments.

Equal Liberty is, moreover, a theory about how religion is (and is not) distinctive *at the level of constitutional principle*. It does not deny, and of course must recognize, empirical features of religious practice that affect the application of constitutional principles to it. In this chapter and the preceding one, we have emphasized one set of such features: the cultural characteristics manifested by American religions that inform the social meaning of government sponsorship of religious symbols, doctrines, and practices. We must take these characteristics into account when we apply Equal Liberty.

· VI ·

Public Dollars, Religious Programs

THE MODERN ESTABLISHMENT Clause was born in 1947. For much of our history before that date, the clause appeared to have lost its relevance: by the second half of the twentieth century there simply was not any serious likelihood that, say, New Jersey would make a particular religious sect the official church of the state. Moreover, there was some question as to whether the Establishment Clause even applied to state and local governments, as opposed to the federal government, which was its original target.[1] Until 1947, Establishment Clause cases had been virtually absent from the Supreme Court's docket.

Everson v. Board of Education changed all that. While the justices in *Everson* disagreed about how to decide the case, they all agreed that the Establishment Clause, like other important parts of the Bill of Rights, is "incorporated" into the Fourteenth Amendment and applies to the states.[2] The justices also agreed that public support for religious activities could violate the Establishment Clause even when that support fell significantly short of formal public sponsorship of a church as the official religion.[3]

Everson itself involved public behavior that was a far cry from public sponsorship of an official religion. The case concerned a New Jersey township that reimbursed parents for the expense of sending their children to school on public buses, and made the travel allowance available to both public and private school students, including students who attended religious schools. But for those in the grip of the separation metaphor, this practice looked like an expenditure of public monies for the benefit of religious schools, and that made the township's program immediately suspect. Justice Black—who wrote for the majority—appeared at the outset to embrace the separationist approach. He spoke of the Constitution's insistence on a "high and impregnable" "wall between church and state."[4] And he suggested that the township's school transportation program brought it to "the verge" of unconstitutionality.[5]

But, having set out to be faithful to the idea of separation, Justice Black found himself checked by common sense. Black noted that providing police and fire protection to churches would not violate the Constitution; that the township was conferring a practical and secular benefit on parents and their school-age children; and that, separation aside, the worst that could be said of the program was that it was evenhanded in its treatment of all those who rode public transportation to school.[6] Moreover, Justice Black observed, the Constitution required that parents be given the right to send their children to religious schools; it would be odd in the extreme, he mused, if the same Constitution required a community to become the fiscal "adversary" of parents who exercised that right.[7] All this led Justice Black and the majority of the Court for whom he wrote to uphold the township's school transportation policy, despite its separation problems.

The justices who dissented in *Everson* understandably saw this toing and froing as deeply inconsistent. Justice Jackson began his dissent with this famously acid comment on Justice Black's opinion: "In fact, the undertones of the opinion, advocating complete and uncompromising separation of Church from State, seem utterly discordant with its conclusion yielding support to their commingling in educational matters. The case which irresistibly comes to mind as the most fitting precedent is that of Julia who, according to Byron's reports, 'whispering "I will ne'er consent,"'—consented."[8]

The real problem in *Everson,* though, was not Justice Black's constancy; the problem was with the very idea of separation with which Justice Black began. As we insisted in Chapter 1, the idea of separating the modern church from the modern state with a high and impregnable wall is silly and incoherent. Justice Black was surely right in observing that extending police and fire protection to churches was entirely consistent with the Constitution. The same could be said of garbage collection, street sweeping, and access to the legal system to enforce contracts and recover for injuries in tort. And Justice Black was surely right as well in thinking that there was no sensible way of drawing a constitutional line between these settled forms of public support and a reasonable, evenhanded program of public transportation for schoolchildren.

The Court's own unsuccessful efforts to draw such a line demonstrate the futility of that project. For many years after *Everson,* the Court embraced a separation-inspired "no aid to religion" principle, and struggled to distinguish between the benefits that no one could imagine denying to churches and religious schools and those that somehow crossed the line into unconstitutional "aid." The result was a shambles, with largely arbitrary lists of those benefits which government was permitted to confer on religion and those which it was not.

Equal Liberty rejects the idea that something has gone wrong anytime government resources benefit a religious institution or practice. There are indeed important constitutional concerns that arise when state programs confer material benefits on religious enterprises. But the shape of and justification for those concerns comes from sources other than the blunt and improbable idea of separation. In this chapter—with the guidance of our conceptual lodestar, Equal Liberty—we reconsider the question of public monies that reach religious pockets.

Equality-Based Limits on Subsidies

Almost everyone agrees that it is an important virtue of our political arrangements that people have a wide range of choices about how to lead their lives. Many of those choices connect in some way with religion. Americans are free to make alliances with each other and to create formal and informal groups; some of those are centered on a commonality of religious faith and worship. So too, Americans are free to develop and express their views about a variety of matters, including religious truth and guidance. And, beyond mere expression, Americans are free to try to inculcate in others—and in particular their children—their values and views, including those inspired by religion.

People can do these things only if they enjoy a broad set of associational rights, free speech rights, property rights, and rights to form and maintain families. In the main, Americans do enjoy these rights. Some are attributable to the religion clauses of the Constitution. Some are attributable to more general guarantees of liberty, like the First Amendment's protection of speech and the Due Process Clause's protection of privacy. And some may be merely a durable feature of our political sensibilities.

For our present purposes, it is not important whether these rights are protected by the Constitution or by ordinary legislation (though, of course, Equal Liberty's third component insists upon a broad set of constitutionally entrenched liberties). Nor is it important to decide the exact scope of these rights. But it is important to realize that this general picture of liberty is part of our identity as a people and, further, that any plausible approach to religious liberty will celebrate and depend on the robust set of liberties that composes this picture.

Seldom in our tradition of liberty does it follow from the existence of a right to act that the government is obliged to fund the action in question. Parents have a constitutional right to elect to send their children to private schools, including religious private schools, but government is not obliged to subsidize parents who choose to exercise that right. Americans are free to publish religious (or antireligious) magazines, and to build temples to their gods or memorials to their secular heroes, but have no right to be subsidized in these endeavors.

Two things follow from this state of affairs. First, while everyone enjoys the right to do these things, some will be far less able to afford to do them than others. Second, if the government chooses to redress inequalities in wealth, some citizens will use the resources they receive from government to send their children to private religious schools, some will publish religious magazines, and some may contribute to the construction of temples. In all those ways, the provision of public funding may benefit religion. But it would be a mistake to think that government has thereby preferred religion or affiliated itself with religion. Instead, what the government has done is to subsidize the exercise of liberty. The benefit to religion is a side effect of the private— and often constitutionally protected—choices of individual citizens.

We can extend this point further if we recognize that the economic structure of society, and hence the capacity of individuals to exercise their liberties, is inevitably the product of government choices and policies. Without government, life would be, as Hobbes said, "nasty, brutish, and short."[9] As we observed in an earlier chapter, it is hard to know what choices people would make under such all-but-unimaginable circumstances, and even if we could divine those choices, there would be no reason to grant them normatively privileged status. The point of government is not to replicate the harsh conditions of prepolitical life but to improve upon them, so that people have the capacity to pursue satisfying lives. Government thus inevitably constitutes the options of a free people; the question is not whether it should affect them, but how it should do so. Insofar as the government is responsible for disparities in the capacity of citizens to exercise their rights, then surely it ought to be within its power to adjust those disparities to promote equality, justice, and the common good. The baseline goal is not, as some scholars of religious freedom have suggested, to replicate the choices that would exist in the absence of government, but to provide people with meaningful choices—including meaningful choices about whether and how to be religious.

Equal Liberty evaluates government support for religious activities and institutions against this critical background of individual choice. From the vantage of Equal Liberty, what generates special constitutional solicitude for religion is the vulnerability of conscience to discrimination or mistreatment. Equal Liberty permits government to offer resources to citizens that they can spend for religious as well as nonreligious purposes. Equal Liberty also permits government to channel resources to citizens through religious providers of aid or services. What Equal Liberty insists is that, in the course of making such resources available, government avoid preferring, endorsing, or affiliating itself with a particular viewpoint about religion.[10]

Accordingly, when government in effect sends resources to religious groups through the choices of private citizens, or sends resources to private citizens through religious groups, it must observe two important conditions. First, when electing to spend public resources or to receive public benefits, citizens must enjoy a meaningful secular alternative to available religious options; government cannot, in effect, condition the flow of benefits to providers or recipients on their religious characteristics or their willingness to participate in religious activities. Second, government must avoid playing favorites among religions: it must be equally welcoming of religions that are equally able to provide the services the government seeks. If these two conditions ("genuine secular alternative" and "nonpreferentialism") are satisfied, citizens who receive services from religious providers do so by their own choice, and there is no affront to Equal Liberty.[11] In this chapter we will see how these principles play out in the context of current controversies over the public funding of private religious choices.

Tuition Vouchers

Public funding for religious education has been the most durable single topic of Establishment Clause controversy. As we have seen, the Supreme Court's first major Establishment Clause ruling was the 1947 decision in *Everson* about the use of public money to pay bus fare for children attending private schools. Political and constitutional agitation about public monies and religious schools goes back to the nineteenth century.[12] As Joseph Viteritti and others have emphasized, anti-Catholic prejudice played a large role in this history.[13] Protestant groups campaigned to suppress Catholic education throughout much of the nineteenth and twentieth centuries. They supported public education partly as a mechanism to assimilate Catholic children, and they vigorously opposed public subsidies for Catholic schools.[14] Catholics, by contrast, sought relief from the costs of private education, and in Supreme Court cases about public support for religious schools, Catholic institutions were the primary beneficiaries of the challenged subsidies.[15]

During the last half-century or so, the social and political complexion of the question of public support for religious education has changed dramatically. Tensions between Protestants and Catholics began to abate after World War II.[16] In recent decades, as John Jeffries and James Ryan point out, the Protestant position on religious education has shifted. The number of Protestant-supported Christian schools has increased substantially since 1970.[17] Further, while African-Americans once perceived publicly subsidized private schools as a threat to desegregation, many now see them as an opportunity to escape from a failing public school system. Accordingly, plans that provide parents with public chits—usually called "vouchers"—that can be used to pay all or part of private school tuition now enjoy substantial support from African-Americans.[18]

All this has combined to make voucher schemes politically viable, and much attention has been devoted to Milwaukee and Cincinnati, where voucher programs that include religious schools have been inaugurated.[19] But such plans are far from uncontroversial.

Today's controversies over tuition vouchers play out against a background of constitutionally secured liberty that entitles parents to send their children to private schools if they wish. In the early part of the twentieth century, Oregon passed a statute, supported by a coalition of progressives and anti-Catholic bigots (including the Ku Klux Klan), that required all children to attend public school.[20] In *Pierce v. Society of Sisters* (1925), the Supreme Court held Oregon's statute unconstitutional.[21] Commentators occasionally treat *Pierce* as a free exercise case because the Society of Sisters ran a Catholic school, but the case name is misleading. The Court actually ruled upon two consolidated cases, *Pierce v. Society of Sisters* and *Pierce v. Hill Military Academy,* and the Court's rationale turned on the idea of parental autonomy, not on the idea of religious freedom. The justices said that Oregon's statute "unreasonably interferes with the liberty of parents and guardians to direct the upbringing and education of children under their control."[22] They emphasized that "the child is not the mere creature of the state; those who nurture him and direct his destiny have the right, coupled with the high duty, to recognize and prepare him for additional obligations."[23]

Pierce is an excellent example of how a broad understanding of constitutional liberty contributes to religious freedom. By protecting the right of parents in general to guide the upbringing of their children, *Pierce* enables religious parents in particular to send their children to religious schools. To be sure, *Pierce* has its critics.[24] They suggest that by giving wealthy parents the right to exit from the public schools, *Pierce* has undermined taxpayer support for the public schools. Critics also contend that the state should be able to mandate attendance at public schools in order to integrate the population and teach tolerance. We, too, wish that public schools were better financed and better integrated, though we doubt whether *Pierce* is the culprit: if all children had to attend public school, residential segregation would still produce socially stratified schools. In any event, the integrity of the parent-child relationship is an important human good deserving constitutional protection. The state may intervene to protect children from parental abuse, mistreatment, neglect, and sufficiently extreme foolishness, of course. The state can also encourage forms of parenting that, in its view, are more likely to promote public values and the common good. But the state can pursue these goals by regulating education and subsidizing favored alternatives (we will have more to say about the scope of its discretion shortly); these objectives do not empower the state to compel all children to enter public schools.[25]

The separation model of religious liberty combines with *Pierce* in unhappy ways. In practice, parents can make use of their right to choose private schools for their children only if they can afford tuition at those schools. Many rights have this structure, of course. Rich people and poor people have the same right to publish newspapers or to hire legal counsel, but rich people can exercise these rights far more easily and effectively. These disparities in the value of rights are common, but they are not necessarily just or desirable. Governmental interventions that serve to ameliorate the impact of inequalities of wealth ought to be welcome in general, but separation makes all such interventions unconstitutional when religious projects are at stake. Separationists would require the government to allow parents to send their children to private schools, including religious schools, but would prohibit it from equalizing the power of poor parents and rich parents to do so.[26]

Worse, the separation model insists that when governments confer benefits on private school children or their families, they must ensure that these benefits reach only secular schools. The model, in effect, requires the state to discriminate against religious schools. One of the things that deflected Justice Black from his separation-inspired trajectory in the *Everson* case was his realization that separation obliged governments to deny otherwise available benefits to parents who exercised their right to send their child to religious schools.

Equal Liberty recommends that we analyze the constitutionality of voucher programs differently, by asking whether they are consistent with the state's obligation to value all its members equally, regardless of their convictions about religion. As we have already noted in passing, this general requirement yields two more specific obligations. First, because the state must not condition the availability of public benefits upon participation in a religious practice or institution, it must ensure the existence of a genuine secular alternative so that parents and children have a meaningful choice about whether to use vouchers at religious schools. Second, the government must not play favorites among perspectives on religion—that is, it must not prefer religion over nonreligion (or vice versa), and it must not prefer one religious sect over another.

A voucher program might run afoul of these requirements either on the supply side or on the consumer side. It might impermissibly prefer providers from some religions over others (or over nonreligious providers). Or it might impermissibly favor students and parents from some religions over students and parents from others (or who are nonreligious). Such impermissible favoritism might result from blunt hostility toward minority religions. One could imagine, for example, a school district that explicitly prohibited the use of its vouchers in schools run by unpopular religious groups—for example, in Islamic schools or in schools that promote the ritual sacrifice of animals.[27]

Constitutional violations, however, can result without overt hostility. Suppose, for example, that a small, Christian town with a tiny Jewish minority adopts a generous voucher system, and that all the

Christian parents—nearly the entire population of the town—use their vouchers to send their children to a private, intensely Christian academy. The remaining Jewish children are not sufficiently numerous to provide the bodies or the resources for an ordinary school, secular or religious (we can imagine the group to be as small as you like—perhaps the children from a single family, or even a lone child). Under these circumstances, the district's voucher plan would leave the parents with a set of unsatisfactory options: send the children to the Christian academy (if it would take them), send their children away to school elsewhere (if the parents could afford to do so), enroll the children in a public one-room schoolhouse (if we assume the district offers this option along with its voucher plan), or home-school the children (if the parents have the time). Because the state financing plan provides the parents with no meaningful choice but to send their children to the Christian academy, it would be unconstitutional under the principles of Equal Liberty.

Doubts about the Importance of a Genuine Secular Alternative

One might imagine at least two objections to this application of Equal Liberty. The first observes that the Jewish minority might be as badly (or worse) off if the town abolished public education entirely. The Christian parents might be able to use their saved tax dollars to organize and pay for a Christian school, and the Jewish children might have nowhere to go.[28] Yet the Supreme Court has refused to recognize a constitutional right to a public education,[29] and it would presumably not force the state to create a public school system where none existed. So why should it be worse for the state to create a voucher system?

The most basic answer is that Equal Liberty, like many other constitutional doctrines, obliges the state to treat citizens equally *if* it chooses to act: the state need not create a public school system, but it must respect the principles of equal liberty if it does. Ideas of this kind are familiar. For example, nothing in the Constitution obliges the state to provide public swimming pools, but if it chooses to do so, it must not discriminate on the basis of race[30] (and it would be no answer for a town to say that in the absence of public facilities only—or mainly— wealthy white people would have access to pools, even if that statement were factually accurate).

That answer might suffice, but to complete the story we should mention another one. Schools, we believe, are different from swimming pools: in our view, the Constitution does impose on government an obligation to make an adequate public education available to all children. We believe that judges are poorly positioned to enforce this right; it is, in our view, a right that is "judicially underenforced."[31] We will have more to say about the concept of judicial underenforcement later in this chapter, and it will occupy center stage in Chapter 7. For the moment, we note only that if one believes there is a constitutional right to a public education, then it matters less whether the Jewish family is without a secular option because of a voucher plan or because public financing is lacking altogether: in either case, the family has suffered a constitutionally cognizable harm, though it may not have a judicially enforceable remedy in the latter case.

The second objection begins by observing that the current system for financing public schools might leave some religious parents in the same predicament faced by the Jewish parents in our hypothetical. When the state funds a secular public school system, parents who want religious education for their children may find themselves with no satisfactory option. They may find that no religious schools exist locally or that the schools are unaffordable. If only the state did not subsidize secular schools, religious schools might be more numerous; if only the state provided vouchers, they might be more affordable. So, according to this argument, there is no escaping the fact that systems of school finance will burden one group or another; we should not make the mistake of thinking that voucher systems are inegalitarian simply because they leave some (religious) group less well off.

The last sentence of this argument is, of course, quite correct. As we noted earlier, it is unreasonable—indeed, incoherent—to demand that policies leave all religious groups equally well off. But as a response to our hypothetical about the Jewish families in a Christian town, the argument fails for a critical reason: it assumes that religious families who find state-subsidized secular schools unacceptable are in precisely the same position, for constitutional purposes, as religious (or nonreligious families) who find state-subsidized religious schools unacceptable. It assumes, in other words, that secularism is more or less equivalent to a religion, so that secular public schools are, more or less, just another variety of religious school.[32]

That is a mistake. To be sure, secular institutions are not neutral, in the sense of being acceptable from the standpoint of all religions. But neither is secularity simply another religious viewpoint. Secular institutions and principles are self-consciously incomplete; indeed, they often strive to be incomplete. They aspire to constitute a practical realm in which various competing and contradictory philosophical and religious views may coexist and constructively interact. Secular institutions and principles are even partially embracing of philosophical or religious views that are themselves hostile to the idea of such a secular domain. They insist, for example, on the right to express antisecular views, even while limiting the freedom to translate such views into private and (especially) public actions. Religions, by contrast, are typically comprehensive; they speak to ultimate questions about life's meaning, origins, and value. Religious schools, in turn, typically make curricular choices, and deploy various symbols, rituals, and practices, which, in combination, can function to mark believers as "insiders" and nonbelievers as "outsiders."

This difference is critical to the constitutional project of religious liberty. That project, like secular institutions more generally, aspires to define a realm within which citizens with diverse faiths and convictions can cooperate as equals. This commitment, we noted earlier, will not be equally congenial to all religions. To take the starkest example:

any faith that demands theocratic government will find the constitutional version of religious liberty unacceptable in principle.

In light of this basic constitutional commitment, a child who demands a secular school stands in a different position from the one who demands a school that expresses his own, particular religion. The state can provide everyone with secular schools, and, indeed, the constitutional goal of cooperation in circumstances of religious diversity requires the creation of public spaces within which people of different faiths can interact. From the vantage of Equal Liberty, it is patently inappropriate for the government to deliver education, or any other social service, exclusively through institutions that treat nonbelievers as "outsiders."

Of course, it may be possible for the state to sponsor a menu of religious and secular schools, so that everyone has a secular option and many children have a religious option consistent (more or less) with their own (family's) religious views. That raises the question whether such a possibility might be constitutionally mandatory when it exists. We turn to that question in a later section; for the time being, we consider in more detail what sorts of options suffice to provide citizens with meaningful choices about whether to participate in publicly subsidized religious institutions.

Meaningful Choices about Vouchers

Voucher plans are most likely to conform to the requirements of Equal Liberty if implemented in urban or heavily populated areas, where schoolchildren are sufficiently numerous and diverse to support a varied menu of educational offerings. In such circumstances, voucher plans might, if appropriately tailored, empower parents to choose among religious and secular options, rather than compel them to send their children to a religious school that dominates the market by virtue (in part) of state sponsorship.

Population density does not, however, guarantee meaningful choice. As a historical matter, state subsidies for private education that appear neutral on their face have often benefited only one kind of school—usually Catholic schools—in practice. One of the Supreme Court's most famous Establishment Clause cases, *Lemon v. Kurtzman* (1971),[33] addressed Rhode Island and Pennsylvania programs that supplemented the salaries of certain teachers in private schools. The statutes specified financial criteria for determining which schools and teachers would receive state monies. In Rhode Island, for example, teachers were eligible only if they taught at nonpublic schools at which the average per-pupil expenditures on the secular portions of the curriculum were lower than at the public schools. That criterion seems religion-neutral and, perhaps, benign: it simply provides aid, one might think, to the least well-off schools. In fact, though, when *Lemon* was decided, the Rhode Island statute had benefited only teachers employed by Catholic schools, and more than 96 percent of the pupils benefited by the Pennsylvania statute attended mostly Catholic schools.[34]

Zelman v. Simmons-Harris,[35] the Cleveland school district voucher case from 2002, provides a more recent illustration. Though the terms of the voucher program drew no explicit distinctions between religious and nonreligious private schools, forty-six of the fifty-six private schools participating in it were religious schools, and 96 percent of the students receiving vouchers enrolled in religious schools.[36] These facts provoked substantial debate among the justices. Chief Justice Rehnquist, speaking for a majority of the Court, thought the fact immaterial because "Cleveland schoolchildren enjoy a range of educational choices: They may remain in public school as before, remain in public school with publicly funded tutoring aid, obtain a scholarship and choose a religious school, obtain a scholarship and choose a nonreligious private school, enroll in a community school, or enroll in a magnet school."[37] Justice Souter, writing in dissent, argued that the majority should have focused on whether parents had real choices about how to direct vouchers, not whether they had real choices among state-subsidized educational offerings. Souter would have answered this question in the negative, since, on his reading of the facts, only religious schools were accepting the vouchers—so that the real choice open to most parents was between using vouchers for religious education or sending their children to the public schools. He contended that "if . . . we ask the right question about genuine choice to use the vouchers, the answer shows that something is influencing choices in a way that aims the money in a religious direction."[38] He contended that the "$2500 cap on tuition for participating low income pupils has the effect of curtailing participation of nonreligious schools," since such schools in Cleveland typically charged a tuition far in excess of that cap, whereas their religious competitors charged well below it.[39] Justice O'Connor, whose vote was essential to the Court's five-to-four decision, authored a concurring opinion that responded to Justice Souter in some detail. She emphasized her agreement with Rehnquist that, in determining whether state dollars were flowing to religious schools by consequence of "true private choice" by parents, courts should focus on "all reasonable educational alternatives to religious schools that are available to parents," not just on the range of schools that accept vouchers.[40]

What should we make of this debate? First, and most important, we should notice that the debate focuses on the right question. It asks whether the voucher plan treats parents and children with different religious convictions equally, rather than whether it breaches some mythical "wall of separation" by sending state dollars through parents' hands to religious institutions.[41] Second, we think that O'Connor and Rehnquist were right about how to pursue this inquiry. We should demand equality of the school finance scheme taken as a whole, not of the voucher plan in isolation from other elements. After all, if the state is running its own splendid, secular school system, the availability of that public option would explain the absence of private secular schools. Parents who wanted secular education would gladly send their children to the public schools, and only religious parents would have any incentive to participate in a voucher plan. Under such circumstances, it would be hard to see how parents could be disadvantaged by the absence of a private secular alternative.

That said, Cleveland's public schools were anything but superb. Those schools, like many other inner-city American public schools, were failing miserably. Indeed, Cleveland's schools were performing so poorly that a federal court, which had jurisdiction pursuant to a desegregation order, had stripped the local district of authority and placed the schools under control of the state government.[42] Once we focus on that fact, Souter's argument becomes much stronger: Cleveland's parents found themselves confronted with a choice between lousy public schools on the one hand and better religious schools on the other. Perhaps for that reason, almost two-thirds of the families participating in the Cleveland program enrolled their children in schools that taught a religion different from their own.[43] One might suppose that such children found themselves the target of unwanted, state-subsidized proselytizing. If so, that is a matter of serious constitutional concern: the state's financing scheme would have put students and parents to a choice between forgoing state-sponsored educational benefits or accepting unwanted, state-sponsored religious indoctrination.

Some people might suspect that Cleveland's voucher program had been gerrymandered to benefit religious schools. Such deliberate favoritism would be an obvious violation of Equal Liberty. There was, however, no direct evidence of discriminatory intent, and there are nondiscriminatory explanations for the dominance of religious schools under the plan. Religious schools may have lower labor costs (because people are willing to accept lower wages to work on behalf of their faith or because the schools enjoy an exemption from some otherwise applicable labor laws),[44] and they may have greater access than do private competitors to donations and other funding that might supplement tuition revenues.[45] These explanations are not wholly neutral: one might restate them, tendentiously, by saying that religious suppliers will provide education at lower cost in exchange for the opportunity to proselytize, and that Cleveland's voucher plan capitalizes on that fact. Still, if religious schools are cheaper than other schools, then that difference—rather than an overt preference for religious education—may explain the pattern that so troubled Justice Souter. The pattern, however, is disturbing nonetheless: if children are being put to a choice between either forgoing state-sponsored educational benefits or accepting unwanted religious education, the demands of Equal Liberty have not been met. Whether the district intended to favor religious education or not, its program did so.

We accordingly believe that the Cleveland voucher plan presents a far more difficult constitutional question than any of the justices acknowledged. The majority assumed too easily that Cleveland's weak public schools provided parents with a meaningful choice about whether to send their children to a religious school. The dissenters identified that problem, but they, too, assumed that the quality of the choice was ultimately irrelevant; for the dissenters, the mere fact that state dollars were subsidizing religious teaching rendered the voucher plan unconstitutional, whether or not there was a valid secular option.

Under the principles of Equal Liberty, by contrast, the existence of a genuine secular alternative is the heart of the issue. The choices provided by Cleveland are richer than those in the small town we imagined in our hypothetical—Cleveland does, after all, have a public school system. The system, though, is bad enough that sensible parents will pay considerable costs—including, we expect, subjecting their children to unwanted proselytizing—to exit from it. It would undoubtedly be better, from a constitutional perspective as well as from a policy perspective, if the choices available to Cleveland families were richer.

Ira C. Lupu and Robert Tuttle have provided a sensitive examination of the resulting issues. Lupu and Tuttle analyze voucher plans pursuant to principles consistent with our own. They recognize that "when government uses vouchers to make available an essential good or service, it is constitutionally irresponsible for it to remain indifferent to the possibility that the voucher program may generate significant factual pressure on recipients to undergo religious experience."[46] In their view, and in ours, the government "must be sensitive to [market] pressures, and it must make an affirmative, good faith effort to ensure that recipients have a substantively meaningful choice between secular and sectarian providers."[47]

Has Cleveland made the constitutionally required efforts? Lupu and Tuttle observe that Cleveland's efforts are suboptimal in at least three respects. First, "the state did not require participating schools to offer voucher-financed children the opportunity to opt-out of religious education."[48] Lupu and Tuttle recommend an opt-out that would "extend to attendance at worship services, and to classes devoted entirely to the subject of religion."[49] Second, Ohio did not compel suburban schools to accept voucher-financed Cleveland children.[50] Third, Ohio made the voucher payment too low to encourage secular providers to participate.[51] Despite these deficiencies, Lupu and Tuttle allow that Ohio might defend its plan if Cleveland's community schools and magnet schools are sufficiently desirable to provide parents with meaningful options. For Lupu and Tuttle, there is an unresolved factual question about the quality of the education provided in such schools, and they would put the burden of proof on the state. They accordingly argue that the Supreme Court should have remanded the cases for further factual development on this point, rather than upholding the plans unconditionally, as the justices in fact did.

One might quibble with the details of this analysis, but we think that Lupu and Tuttle have the basic issues right. If the Cleveland plan meets the constitutional minimum, it only barely does so. On the other hand, as Lupu and Tuttle note, the Ohio program "has laudable and important goals,"[52] and it seems better to expand than to contract the options of inner-city parents who must cope with failing public schools (and many other problems). Lupu and Tuttle tack between the contending choices as carefully as is possible; we, and they, would be much more comfortable had Ohio done more to ensure the availability of a satisfactory secular alternative.

The Scope of Government Discretion

We have thus far argued that it is constitutionally permissible for government to subsidize religious education through voucher plans, but only if the school finance scheme gives parents a genuine choice among secular and religious schools. That conclusion suggests additional questions. Suppose it is possible for the state to design a voucher plan that meets constitutional standards. How much discretion does the state have with regard to its financing scheme? For example, is it required to offer a voucher plan, so that parents who want to send their children to religious schools can do so? Can the state attach "strings" to its funding in order to encourage participating schools (including religious schools) to promote public values? May the state allow parents to use its vouchers at schools that discriminate on the basis of religion?

These questions provoke divergent answers from leading commentators. William Galston, Stephen Gilles, and Michael McConnell all contend that the state should promote the capacity of parents to choose religious schools if they want them.[53] Indeed, both Gilles and McConnell contend that the state has a moral, if not a constitutional, obligation to offer vouchers if it funds public education at all; in their view, a wholly secular public school system treats religious parents unequally.[54] Stephen Macedo, by contrast, allows that voucher plans are constitutional, but urges that states put conditions on vouchers to reshape participating schools, including religious schools, so that they conform more closely to public morality.[55] Indeed, for Macedo, one point in favor of voucher systems is that they may provide the state with a lever to induce religious communities to conform more fully to the public mainstream.

Equal Liberty allows the state substantial discretion to choose among financing schemes. The government, we have said, must not condition public benefits on one's religious identity or on participation in religious rituals or practices. As such, it must provide recipients with a secular option, and it must not play favorites among religious providers or recipients. Subject to those crucial limitations, however, the government is at liberty to spend public money to advance the common good, even if its conception of the common good is controversial (as we expect it will be) and even if its financing scheme has a disparate impact upon different religious groups (as it inevitably will).

States may, for example, choose to fund public schools without also funding private religious ones. At least two nondiscriminatory reasons could justify that choice. First, if states operate schools themselves, they retain greater control and evaluate how money is spent. They can monitor teachers, supervise the curriculum, and select the programs they deem best suited to advance the state's educational objectives. Of course, there is plenty of evidence that some public schools are performing badly. That evidence may give the state a reason to try vouchers. But it does not diminish the fact that the state has a valid, nondiscriminatory reason for wishing to retain control over how public funds are spent. Second, the state may legitimately seek to create, and encourage widespread participation in, nonsectarian and nonpartisan public institutions, including schools. The state may wish to avoid balkanization of the citizenry into segregated communities that distrust one another. Schools are not the only such public institutions (parks, museums, libraries, and workplaces are others), but the state might deem them to be important ones, and, if so, that judgment provides the state with another valid, nondiscriminatory reason for preferring public secular schools over private ones, including private religious ones.

Of course, one might believe that public schools do a poor job spending the state's money, or that a mix of religious schools and non-religious schools can develop young citizens better than a system of secular public schools. But these are policy considerations appropriately addressed to legislators or school boards. They do not provide any ground for concluding that the state is treating religious citizens with hostility or neglect. Nor can one infer hostility or neglect from the fact that the state's refusal to supply vouchers will leave some religious parents and students worse off than if vouchers were provided. As we have noted many times already, no policy can be neutral among religions, and the fact that some religions fare worse under a particular plan is not even a prima facie basis for believing that the plan might be unconstitutional.[56]

The reasons we have considered thus far justify a state in avoiding a voucher plan altogether. What if a state opts in favor of vouchers but allows parents to use them only at private schools that are inclusively secular—secular, that is, in the sense that we have been using that word, and secular in the way that we justifiably expect public schools to be? The state might, for example, believe that competition among private providers will encourage higher-quality schools and more efficient use of resources, but also wish to avoid schools likely to encourage division among students into religious, ethnic, or ideological groups. If that is the state's rationale, then presumably the state will exclude from the voucher plan not only religious schools but, more generally, any schools that privilege particular ethnic, cultural, or ideological subgroups. So long as the state's exclusion is general in that way, then we believe that it is constitutionally permissible for the state to include religious schools among the set that is ineligible to receive vouchers, though we admit that the case is closer than if the state avoids vouchers altogether.

Nevertheless, two sorts of circumstances could put a voucher plan that excluded religious schools in constitutional jeopardy. One would be a request for inclusion of a school which was in some unduckable way religious (by virtue, say, of its ongoing affiliation with a particular sect or church) but which could demonstrate that it enjoys all the inclusive virtues of any secular or public school (for example, a Quaker Friends School). Such a possibility suggests that the sweeping exclusion of religious schools might be unjustifiable. That worry would be stronger still, of course, if a voucher plan were to exclude only religious schools. We consider this last possibility below, in the course of discussing *Locke v. Davey*.

Our position about vouchers entails that, if the state does supply parents with vouchers that they may use at religious schools, it is free to attach conditions that limit the educational program at participating schools (including religious schools). So, for example, the state might prohibit such schools from discriminating against applicants on the basis of religion, or it might require them to teach certain subjects (such as sex education), or it might demand that they give participating students the right to opt out of theology classes or religious rituals. Such conditions are permissible so long as they serve legitimate public interests and do not discriminate against religion or among religions. This conclusion should hardly be surprising. After all, states routinely regulate many elements of private education, including religious education, even when schools do not accept vouchers. The state's authority to impose conditions on the use of public money is greater still, both because the state is entitled to insist that publicly financed education promote public purposes and because private schools that object to the conditions are free to turn down the money.

On the other hand, the state is equally free to move in the opposite direction, toward a conception of maximal parental choice, as Galston, Gilles, and McConnell would have it do. The state may even allow the use of vouchers at schools that discriminate on the basis of religion—for example, at Orthodox Jewish schools that admit only Orthodox Jewish students. Some readers will no doubt think it odd that the state could use public money to subsidize a discriminatory enterprise: after all, the state not only cannot discriminate itself but has (in our view, and in the view of many others) an obligation to limit discrimination in the private sector.[57] We sympathize with these sentiments, but we nevertheless believe that the issue resides within the legislature's legitimate discretion. We have two reasons for that conclusion. First, so long as the government makes available a meaningful secular alternative, the voucher program subsidizes not discrimination but parental liberty. Some parents—not the government—are choosing to exercise their liberty by sending children to schools that discriminate on religious grounds. Second, the freedom to attend a religiously segregated school is a valuable, if double-edged, one. Some religious parents and teachers might reasonably believe that it is hard to teach their religion in the presence of outsiders; in some faiths, it may actually be regarded as immoral or sinful for students to attend school with members of other faiths.

We do not mean that the state is bound to approve of or support such exclusivity. On the contrary, we have already said that the state may, if it wishes, fund only secular schools. And if it provides vouchers that may be used at religious schools, it is free to insist that participating schools not discriminate or to impose conditions on the kind of education they (and other participating schools) can offer. Our point is only that religious distinctions have a different moral valence from, for example, racial ones.[58] We would be better off if racial distinctions ceased to matter; the role of religious distinctions, and hence of religiously segregated institutions, is more complex. As a result, when legislators decide how to subsidize education, they must make hard, contestable judgments about how much to promote religious integration, religious tolerance, and other public values and how much to facilitate individual choice. Constitutional principles help to describe the factors relevant to the decision, but they leave the government with discretion about how best to strike the balance.[59]

Locke v. Davey and Discriminatory Subsidies

Thus far we have been addressing the state's discretion to implement school finance schemes that, though they may have a disparate impact on religion, do not single religion out for special treatment; instead, they all treat religion or religious education as one instance of some broader category. What if a voucher plan excludes *only* religious education? As we suggest above, such a scheme seems not only to approach, but quite possibly to cross, the constitutional boundary that limits the government's discretion to fashion school finance schemes.

While the Supreme Court has never considered the constitutionality of a voucher plan that includes all private schools except religious ones, it has recently decided a case that may be inconsistent with our view. *Locke v. Davey* (2004)[60] involved a Washington State program that provided college students with scholarships that they could use to study for any career except the ministry. Washington's scholarships—called "Promise Scholarships" and designed to encourage talented Washington youngsters to attend in-state colleges—thus discriminated against a particular form of religious education. The program's prohibition was limited and highly selective: students were allowed to use the scholarship at any accredited Washington college, including religious colleges; they could use the scholarship to pay for religious education at such colleges; and they could even take courses in devotional theology—that is, they could take courses designed to prepare students for the clergy. They could not, however, *major* in devotional theology or other fields designed to prepare them for a career in the ministry.[61] By imposing this restriction on the use of the scholarships, Washington avoided a conflict with its state constitution, which explicitly prohibits the use of any state funds to subsidize the training of ministers.[62]

Joshua Davey, who wanted to use his Promise Scholarship to prepare for the ministry, challenged the constitutionality of the rule that prohibited him from doing so (ironically, Davey later enrolled in the Harvard Law School). The case reached the Supreme Court. Davey's claim might seem an easy winner under both Equal Liberty and the Supreme Court's jurisprudence. After all, Washington's law targets one form of religious education for special disadvantage. Scholarship recipients can major in anything except theology and retain state funding. In Justice Scalia's words, "when the state withholds [a] benefit from some individuals solely on the basis of religion, it violates the Free Exercise Clause no less than if it had imposed a special tax."[63]

But Scalia wrote those words in dissent. The Supreme Court not only upheld the Washington law, but did so by what is, in this field, an overwhelming majority: the vote was seven to two. Chief Justice Rehnquist, writing for the Court, emphasized that Washington had legitimate "antiestablishment interests" in refusing to allow students to use their scholarships for theological training.[64] Rehnquist acknowledged, as he had to, that nothing in the federal Constitution's Establishment Clause would have prevented Washington from allowing Davey to use his scholarship for theological training—the Supreme Court had reached that conclusion unanimously eighteen years earlier in *Witters* (the case about the blind seminarian, which we discussed in Chapter 1).[65] Rehnquist said, however, that states were free to pursue disestablishment more aggressively than the federal Constitution did.

In general, of course, states are free to pursue constitutional values beyond the point that is constitutionally mandatory. A state can be more solicitous of speech than the Constitution requires, or more concerned with equality, and so forth. And it is surely true that states can avoid Establishment Clause vices even more energetically than the Clause itself requires. But Justice Rehnquist's claim is too facile on two counts. First, it would help to know what interests of this sort can fairly be attributed to the State of Washington's funding exclusion. Second, it is not sufficient simply to find such an interest. We also have to be persuaded that pursuit of this interest—which is by hypothesis *not* constitutionally required—somehow justifies singling out religious studies for radically adverse treatment at the hands of the state.

Justice Rehnquist, who wrote for the majority in *Davey*, was not very helpful on these critical points. Rehnquist focused entirely on history. He noted that "since the founding of our country, there have been popular uprisings against procuring state funds to support church leaders" and that many states "placed in their constitutions formal prohibitions against using state funds to support the ministry."[66] Yet Washington's program, unlike the ones that Rehnquist cited, was not a scheme to support or train ministers; it was a generally available scholarship program. If Joshua Davey were allowed to use his scholarship to study theology, money would flow to religious training by virtue of *his* decision, not the State of Washington's. It would be peculiar in the extreme to think that Washington had somehow preferred Davey's religion—much less given it an official blessing—by virtue of Davey's personal choice. If it were true that some "establishment"-connected vice occurred whenever the benefits of a state program reached a religious enterprise, then the State of Washington would have "antiestablishment interests," of course. But as we have seen, that blunt and broad separationist view is unsustainable; for the *Davey* Court to be persuasive on this point, it needed to identify some narrower and more satisfactory interest of the state.

One line of argument that might redeem the majority view in this regard would capitalize on the narrow form of the Washington state scholarship exclusion, which runs solely to programs and degrees aimed directly at the ministry. Both federal and state governments in the United States steer as far clear of intervening in the ministry as is feasible. As we noted at some length in Chapter 2, churches are free to choose their ministers on the basis of criteria that are considered deeply unjust and have been made illegal in the employment market generally, criteria like gender and race. Further, no government licenses ministers, or applies minimum-wage or overtime provisions or rules governing collective bargaining to ministers. If this hands-off posture of government can be explained, the resulting account might point us to reasons that Washington could use to justify the exclusion of ministerial trainees from its scholarship program.

In Chapter 2 we considered two different ways in which Equal Liberty might come to justify (or possibly even require) special treatment for religious activities. With regard to the ministerial exemption from equal opportunity employment laws, we suggested that the personal relationship between a pastor and his or her flock gives rise to an interest in freedom of association described in modern constitutional doctrine as "the right to privacy." And, with regard to the widely shared squeamishness that many may feel about a National Institution for Religion, we suggested that the choice of meritorious religious projects would so overlap the choice of meritorious religions as to implicate government in the worst sort of preferential treatment. Both of these concerns—a general concern for liberty that plays out in a special way when ministers are at issue, and a concern for nonpreferentialism that is especially acute where religion is involved—are arguably present when a state grants scholarships to participants in educational programs that are part of a ministerial career path. Unless the state is willing to offer scholarships to absolutely anyone enrolled in any ministerial program—think here of an apparently sincere but expensive and quite flaky correspondence course—there is a genuine risk that the state will find itself making decisions about what constitutes a sound preparation for the ministry, and that is a position the state has a substantial interest in avoiding.

This risk not only provides the State of Washington with a reason for steering clear of funding those preparing for careers as ministers; it helps to explain the rather strange and narrow nature of the funding exclusion. Washington permits scholarship recipients to use the subsidy to purchase education from pervasively religious institutions; it even permits them to take classes designed to prepare students for the ministry, so long as they do not actually pursue a degree in devotional theology. The state might see this policy as a way to ensure that it can use various respected criteria of institutional excellence to assess educational programs and to avoid questions of what constitutes satisfactory preparation to become a minister.

All this makes sense from the vantage of Equal Liberty. But there is little if anything in Justice Rehnquist's opinion for the majority that suggests that the outcome in *Davey* turned on precisely this rationale. We may nevertheless hope that the justices will converge on such an explanation in the future. When it works well, the process of case-by-case adjudication enables courts to realize with increasing clarity the normative foundations of their past decisions. Future decisions may thus draw the Court toward a rationale for *Davey* that is expressly consistent with the requirements of Equal Liberty.

Is there any other rationale that can account for the *Davey* outcome, which, after all, attracted seven justices with rather different views about religious freedom to join Justice Rehnquist's opinion?[67] We suspect that the key resides in Rehnquist's suggestion that there must be "play in the joints" between the Free Exercise and Establishment Clauses.[68] Scalia mocks the idea of "play in the joints" as unprincipled,[69] and Rehnquist's exposition of it is sketchy at best, functioning more as a conclusion than as an explanation. We believe, however, that the phrase may reflect an important institutional idea: in particular, it may express a judgment that, when it comes to certain questions about public subsidies, the judiciary should defer to Congress and state legislatures rather than stringently impose its view of the demands of religious freedom.

Deference is common in constitutional cases about subsidies outside the domain of religious freedom. The Court treats regulation and spending differently, for example, in cases about free speech, federalism, and abortion.[70] In the domain of religious liberty, deference would enable the Court to avoid potentially difficult line-drawing problems. For example, Scalia suggested that Washington could avoid constitutional difficulties if, instead of specifically prohibiting religious courses of study, it made its scholarships "redeemable . . . only for select courses of study" that happened to be nonreligious.[71] If so, the Court would have to devise a doctrine that distinguished between a list of *approved* majors that omitted devotional studies (which would be a constitutionally permissible plan under Scalia's view) and a list of *excluded* majors that singled religion out (which would be constitutionally impermissible). What if the list of approved majors included everything except devotional theology? What if it included every major except devotional theology and one or two others?

More generally, if the Court found Washington's plan discriminatory, it would be sure to see a wave of cases about the constitutionality of school financing plans that excluded religious options. Primary and secondary school financing—with voucher schemes front and center—was the "800-pound gorilla" lurking in the courtroom when *Davey* was decided, and the justices were very much aware of the issues that would soon confront them if they held Washington's scholarship plan unconstitutional. One can see why the justices would want to avoid that line of decision, and they put a quick stop to it in *Davey*. Viewed this way, the justices in *Davey* made a pragmatic judgment that the harms from discriminatory subsidy programs were unlikely to be sufficiently great to justify the costs of judicial intervention, except when the state acted on the basis of hostility to religion (or to particular religions).

The Problems of Prophylaxis

This explanation for the decision in *Davey*, if correct, raises a more general question about the role of pragmatic judgments in religious liberty jurisprudence. In *Davey*, a pragmatic judgment about the costs of judicial review may have led the Court to defer to the legislature. Similarly pragmatic judgments might tempt some judges in exactly the opposite direction: on the grounds that effective judicial oversight of religious subsidy schemes is difficult and costly, they might hold all subsidy schemes unconstitutional rather than attempt to distinguish between those that are discriminatory and those that are not.

Lawyers refer to doctrines of this kind as prophylactic or precautionary rules. Such rules draw bright lines that prohibit conduct whether or not it is harmful, on the theory that respecting the bright line is the most effective way for courts to eliminate conduct that is truly harmful. Requiring police officers to give *Miranda* warnings ("You have the right to remain silent . . .") is a classic example.[72] The point of such warnings is to avoid coerced confessions, but the failure to give the warning is always a constitutional violation, whether or not it results in coercion. If judges had to identify instances of coercion on a case-by-case basis, they might miss many of them. By requiring police to give warnings in every case, they implement a bright-line rule that is easy to enforce and that reduces the likelihood of coercion (or so they hope).

Prophylactic rationales can be like jurisprudential kudzu. Once they take hold, they threaten to cover the legal terrain and crowd out more refined analysis. They can justify a wide variety of rules with divergent—even contradictory—implications. So, for example, a prophylactic rationale might recommend holding all voucher plans unconstitutional, since otherwise judges might miss the discriminatory elements of plans that treat some people unequally. Another such rationale might recommend holding unconstitutional the state's failure to finance religious schools along with secular ones, since otherwise judges might overlook discrimination against families who desire religious education. One might recommend (to return to the cases discussed in Chapter 3) that judges exempt religious conduct from generally applicable laws whenever possible, since judges might otherwise miss cases in which the state's failure to grant an exemption is discriminatory. Or, conversely, one might recommend that judges treat statutory exemptions benefiting religion as presumptively invalid, since judges might otherwise overlook instances in which such exemptions unconstitutionally prefer one set of religious beliefs over another.

Rationales of this kind make everything turn on a series of probability analyses. How likely is it that discrimination will occur? How likely that judges will miss it? How costly is it to litigate the validity of statutes one by one? And so on. Because the answers to these questions are usually speculative and impossible to verify, they are highly manipulable. You can arrive at the rule you want by invoking the appropriate, unverifiable empirical speculation to support it.

Nevertheless, prophylactic rationales provide, we think, the most cogent justification for the common view that the Constitution prohibits the use of state funds for religious education under any circumstances. As we have seen, that position cannot be justified by blunt claims that the state should never aid religion, since the state inevitably and legitimately aids religion in many ways. Nor can one plausibly claim that every subsidy for religious education is discriminatory. One might, however, argue that judges should prohibit vouchers in order to avoid the *risk* of unconstitutional discrimination. We observed earlier, for example, that the voucher plan in Cleveland funneled money almost exclusively to religious schools, and that there were accordingly serious questions about whether it complied with the requirements of Equal Liberty. We also noted, more specifically, that it was hard for judges to tell whether parents in fact had a meaningful secular alternative, given the poor quality of the Cleveland schools. If one believes that problems of this kind will frequently infect voucher plans, one might recommend a constitutional rule banning such plans altogether in order to avoid the risk that an unconstitutionally discriminatory plan will go unchecked. That prophylactic rationale effectively imports the content of the separation doctrine into the model of Equal Liberty: it justifies the "no aid" rule as a precaution against undetectable (or at least unprovable) discrimination.

What, if anything, is wrong with these arguments? Some scholars have contended that judges should enforce only the letter of the Constitution and never create or implement prophylactic rules. We cannot embrace that broad criticism. As David Strauss has pointed out, prophylactic rules are ubiquitous in constitutional jurisprudence.[73] More generally, judges invariably make strategic judgments when crafting legal rules to implement constitutional rules; in constitutional jurisprudence, there is no getting away from pragmatic considerations like the ones included in prophylactic rationales.[74]

Yet, while we do not regard prophylactic rules as illegitimate per se, we believe that they will rarely be appropriate solutions to problems of religious liberty. That is because prophylactic rules depend upon a special asymmetry between two courses of action for their justification: they presuppose that it is better to err in one direction, rather than another, to avoid serious constitutional harms. Prophylactic rules effectively *overenforce* a particular constitutional right on the assumption that doing so will maximize the security of that right without damaging other interests of comparable constitutional stature. So, for example, criminal defendants have a constitutional right to remain silent; police officers do not have any competing right to obtain confessions from them. The rule requiring *Miranda* warnings trades on this asymmetry. It also assumes that the constitutional harm from a coerced confession is sufficiently great to justify a rule that will sometimes permit guilty defendants to go free in cases in which their confessions were not coerced.[75]

No comparable asymmetry exists in the domain of religious freedom, at least as conceived by Equal Liberty. Precisely because ideas about equal status and equal membership are at Equal Liberty's core, there are usually constitutional interests on both sides of any dispute. Overenforcing the rights of those who want secular education may infringe upon the rights of those who want religious education, and vice versa. Put more generally, the idea of overenforcing a right to equality does not really make much sense in those cases—of which religion is the preeminent example—in which every contending group is in some sense a minority and when society does not easily divide into dominant and disadvantaged groups. (It might, by contrast, make sense to overenforce the equality rights of disadvantaged racial minorities in the United States.)

Overenforcement of an equality principle creates risks much different from the sort of *under*enforcement that, in our view, best justifies the result in the *Davey* case. Underenforcement, as we saw, involves deference to the legislature. Rather than deciding the constitutional question itself, the court trusts the legislature to adjust the critical factors correctly. Overenforcement, by contrast, is the opposite of deference. It rests on a distrust of other branches: it rests, more specifically, on a judgment that unless the courts overenforce a constitutional right, the legislature (or the executive) is likely to infringe the right in ways that will go uncorrected. Overenforcement therefore bears a higher burden of justification than underenforcement. If overenforcement gets matters wrong—if, for example, it compromises one constitutional right in order to protect another—there is no opportunity for another branch to correct the problem; the whole point of overenforcement is to deprive those other branches of power.

We accordingly regard prophylactic rationales as unattractive responses to problems of religious liberty. We must concede, however, that our objections are not wholly decisive. In principle, it would be possible to marshal sociological premises to bolster a prophylactic rationale—premises, for example, about what sorts of groups are likely to dominate legislatures and what sorts of groups are likely to be harmed by voucher plans (or other laws), and about which sorts of violations courts are likely to catch and which they are likely to miss. We suspect, for example, that at least some partisans of "strict separation" regard the United States as divided into a Christian majority and a Jewish-Islamic-agnostic-atheist-and-other assemblage of minorities (we believe this sociology is too crude: the category "Christian" encompasses a huge number of different groups with discrepant interests, and, as we noted earlier, the political history of aid to parochial education is largely a story about battles *within* Christianity).

With the right set of assumptions in place, one could justify over-enforcing equality rights in the domain of religious liberty to protect some allegedly vulnerable minority (just as it might be desirable, in the domain of racial equality, to overenforce rights on behalf of disadvantaged racial minorities). The sociological generalizations needed to back up these arguments would, however, be highly speculative and controversial, and we fear that they might reflect prejudices, or normative disagreements with Equal Liberty, rather than sober empirical judgments. But we cannot be sure, and so we cannot deny that prophylactic rationales might, in principle, validate separationist doctrines (and, for that matter, many other doctrines) of the sort that we have criticized throughout this book. All that said, we continue to disfavor such rationales.

Other Social Services

Though cases about aid to parochial schools have loomed large on the Supreme Court's docket for more than half a century, the controversy about public funding for faith-based social services is much broader. When George W. Bush ran for president in 2000, he made "faith-based social services" a centerpiece of his program of "compassionate conservatism." Bush's initiative sought to expand the role of religious organizations in providing a range of publicly funded services, including, for example, mental health counseling, substance-abuse treatment, and family planning.[76]

To Bush and other proponents of faith-based social services, the case in favor of a partnership between government and religion is overdetermined. In their eyes, faith-based programs have at least three distinct advantages over those administered by the government. First, for conservatives, it counts as an advantage that these programs are in the private sector. In their view, because private suppliers of social services compete with one another, they acquire incentives to avoid inefficiencies that characterize government bureaucracies. Second, churches and other faith-based providers can capitalize on their connections to communities in which they are embedded. African-American churches, for example, might be better placed than government functionaries to understand the needs of impoverished inner-city neighborhoods. And, finally, the religious content of faith-based programs is another advantage: supporters of such programs believe that schools for children and remedial programs for adults do a better, more effective job when they include a devotional element.[77]

These ideas tend to be more popular with conservatives than with liberals, but they are by no means unique to the Bush administration and its supporters. Frustrated by the failures of public programs and inspired by social science scholarship about the importance of civil society, some liberals and progressives have embraced the promise of faith-based social services.[78] Indeed, as we noted in a previous chapter, the Bush proposals were less novel than most people supposed. As Stephen Monsma and others have documented, religious charities have long benefited from substantial public funding, and in the 1990s Congress, with the support of President Clinton, took steps that invited more religious organizations to provide social services on behalf of the government.[79]

Nevertheless, the Bush proposals sparked a political furor. Whether for that reason or others,[80] Bush's legislative campaign on behalf of faith-based services was largely unsuccessful. Bush, however, promulgated and implemented an executive order that included many of the reforms he failed to get through Congress.[81] There is disagreement about whether or not Bush has in fact delivered major changes to the relationship between government and faith-based charities,[82] but the debate about his policy remains lively and important.

One question is whether faith-based social services in fact have the practical advantages that Bush and others have attributed to them. Sociologists Mark Chaves and Robert Wuthnow have, in two recent books, questioned whether religious congregations have the desire or the capacity to provide social services on the scale presupposed by the Bush administration's proposals. Chaves, after analyzing the first nationwide systematic study of religious congregations, concludes that "most congregations engage only minimally in social services, and typically the few that do engage more deeply rely heavily on paid staff, involve relatively few congregational volunteers, and conduct their efforts in collaboration . . . with secular and government agencies."[83] He suggests that "for the vast majority of congregations, social services constitute a minor and peripheral aspect of their organizational activities" and that "we fundamentally misunderstand congregations if we imagine this sort of activity is now, was ever, or will ever be central to their activities."[84] Wuthnow, drawing partly upon research by Chaves, contends that politicians, journalists, and others have failed to distinguish between congregations and religious organizations more generally. He argues that insofar as religious organizations have provided social services, they have done so not at the local, congregational level (which is where, by and large, the community-based characteristics lauded by the Bush administration reside) but through large-scale religiously sponsored charities, which, Wuthnow says, look and behave very similarly to their secular counterparts.[85]

The arguments of Chaves and Wuthnow are about policy consequences. Our focus here is on constitutional principles. Suppose that government officials—whether rightly or wrongly—believe that faith-based initiatives can facilitate the delivery of social services. How do the principles of Equal Liberty constrain the government's discretion to subsidize religious providers of social services?

At a general level, of course, the principles that govern education also apply to other social services. Thus, if the government chooses to deliver social services through religious providers, it must ensure the availability of a wholly secular alternative, and it must not play favorites among perspectives on religion. Yet, though the principles are unchanged, applying them to services other than education may produce distinct challenges. For example, it is probably obvious to parents that their children will be getting religious training if they attend Catholic schools; it may be less obvious to a substance abuser that she can expect a religious encounter when she enrolls in a publicly subsidized twelve-step program. And, as Martha Minow reminds us, it may be unreasonable to expect distressed persons, suffering from mental health or substance-abuse problems, to shop around and compare competing programs.[86] Ought not disadvantaged people to be entitled to expect help that is free from religious pressure or proselytizing when they turn for assistance to a state-sponsored provider?

Lupu and Tuttle have suggested that special constitutional problems arise if the government subsidizes programs in which religious exercises or practices are essential to the treatment provided.[87] For example, some counseling or substance-abuse programs may rely on intense religious experiences as a means to address personal problems (again, Chaves, Wuthnow, and other sociologists question how often faith-based providers rely upon such transformative techniques, but they do not deny that such approaches are sometimes used).[88] In such programs it would be hard, if not simply impossible, for the provider to excise the religious content of the program when clients do not want it—whereas, by contrast, it might be possible to excuse some publicly subsidized students from devotional exercises at religious schools.

We agree that these features of a program might yield some practical problems. So, for example, it might be hard to determine what counts as a satisfactory secular alternative to a state-subsidized, thoroughly religious mental health program. Such difficulties may be especially severe if the religious practice has a much higher success rate than its secular competition. That differential success rate might be an indication that the state is failing to fund a sufficiently robust secular alternative, and raise concerns much like those we canvassed when considering the constitutional status of Cleveland's regime of educational vouchers. Or the differing success rates might simply show that, for some subset of the population, the faith-based program's thoroughly religious approach was more effective (that is, that subset wanted or benefited from a distinctively religious approach).[89] But these points are only further refinements of the idea that if government dollars flow to religious providers, they must flow there by virtue of genuine private choices, not as a result of the government's own preference. If the dollars reach providers only on that basis, we see no constitutional reason to object if their treatment is pervasively and intensely religious.[90]

Some of the controversy about faith-based social services has concerned discrimination not against recipients of the services but against employees, actual and potential, of the providers. Although state and local antidiscrimination laws apply to faith-based organizations, those laws sometimes contain exemptions allowing religious organizations to discriminate on the basis of religion.[91] Hence faith-based organizations may engage in discriminatory hiring that would be unlawful if practiced by the government. Some commentators have suggested that it is unconstitutional for the government to delegate social service functions to discriminatory organizations.

If the critique were framed at the level of policy rather than at the level of constitutionality, we would embrace it wholeheartedly: we think it both unwise and unjust for the government to subsidize organizations that discriminate in ways the government itself could not. But if the question on the table is the constitutionality of funding such organizations, then it more or less replays the debate between Galston, who celebrates the distinctively religious character of some private schools, and Macedo, who wants to ensure that any school receiving public money embraces public values. We said, with regard to that debate, that the government had discretion to choose between these two visions. And here, too, it is up to the government to decide whether it should put "strings" on its vouchers to force faith-based organizations to embrace public values in their hiring practices, or whether it should give recipients the option to seek services from pervasively religious employers who, because of their religious orientation, discriminate in their hiring practices. So long as the government provides a genuine secular alternative, and so long as the government does not play favorites, the demands of Equal Liberty are met.

Prison Chaplains

When we present the ideas of this chapter to audiences, people regularly ask us about prison and military chaplains. They correctly point out that the government hires chaplains to minister to prisoners and soldiers. The government decides from which sects it will hire, and, because the chaplain is its employee, officials can exercise considerable control over what the chaplain will say. Public dollars thus flow to a particular religion by virtue of government choices rather than private ones. Indeed, the government selects what religious message it would like to convey, and it conveys that message through its own employees. Such chaplaincies are familiar, and few people would suggest that they be abolished, but they seem worrisome from the vantage of Equal Liberty, since the government is quite clearly preferring some religious viewpoints over others.

We have no quarrel with any of these observations. In our view, it illustrates how Equal Liberty (and, for that matter, any other plausible conception of religious liberty) presupposes a sphere of general liberty within which people can make meaningful decisions about religious exercise. In ordinary civilian life, people are free to make choices about which religious services to attend or visit, which religious associations to join, which religious organizations to support financially, which religious exercises to undertake, and so on. They can travel long distances, if they wish, to find religious communities more congenial to their values and commitments. Religious believers enjoy these options not because they possess some special privilege to attend meetings, join organizations, control property, or travel, but rather because they share equally in liberties valuable to all persons, religious or not.

Of course, we do not mean to say that these choices are unaffected by government. As we have said before, that would be an impossible goal: all choices have costs, and government policies affect what those costs are. But the choices are meaningful nonetheless, and their existence is crucial to the idea of Equal Liberty.

When the government exercises comprehensive control over life, as it does in prisons and the military, the basic liberty that all of us normally enjoy is gone. This deprivation of liberty is a substantial loss, and everyone recognizes it as such. In prisons, the loss is a penalty, one of the harshest our society imposes. In the military, the loss is a sacrifice, one that all of us recognize as significant. It is hardly surprising that under such conditions, ordinary notions of liberty, including ordinary notions of religious liberty, become less apt or useful. Usually we think that Americans ought to be free to build and attend the churches they want for themselves. This idea makes little sense in prisons or the military, not only under Equal Liberty but under any other plausible theory of religious freedom (the idea of "separation of church and state," for example, obviously offers little hope for explaining why the state should be able to hire clerics to preach to prisoners and soldiers).

That said, Equal Liberty at least points in the right direction for identifying the constitutional constraints on prison chaplains and military chaplains. If the government decides to make chaplains available to soldiers and prisoners, it must do so evenhandedly. If, for example, it affords a minister to Protestant troops whenever a certain number are present in a regiment, then it must be equally accommodating of Jews, Muslims, Mormons, or Catholics. And if there were some secular analogue to religion—it is hard to see what would count for these purposes, but perhaps we can imagine a cultural group that wants guidance from certain "elders"—it ought to be treated equally. Such an approach does not require the government to choose chaplains on purely numerical grounds. It may select them on the basis of, among other things, their consistency with the purposes of the prisons or military services in which they are supposed to serve—so that, for example, the government may prefer humanist Muslims over militant Muslims even if prison populations have a different preference.[92] Here, as with school vouchers and faith-based social service, the government has a lot of discretion about what sorts of strings to attach to its funding—and because the absence of general liberty creates an extraordinarily intimate relationship between government and religion, the strings bind more powerfully. But the strings must be justified in terms of the government's secular purposes, and once those purposes are exhausted, the requirements of Equal Liberty apply fully.

We accordingly think that there is no reason to be concerned about the tension between Equal Liberty and common intuitions about prison and military chaplaincies. It is probably enough to say that these chaplaincies are made necessary because the basic conditions for religious liberty are missing—but, in fact, it is possible to say more, since Equal Liberty provides a useful guide to government action even in these exceptional circumstances. Perhaps advocates of separation and its cousins could derive similar guidance from their preferred models, but it is hard to see how. Separation is even more manifestly incapable of describing the government role in prisons and armies than it is of explaining government's role in society more generally.

Legislative Responsibility
for Religious Freedom

IN CHAPTERS 1 AND 3 we encountered Simcha Goldman, an Air Force physician and an Orthodox Jew. His faith required him to wear a yarmulke, but the Air Force forbade him to do so while in uniform. On its face, the Air Force's position seems unreasonable: allowing Orthodox Jewish doctors to wear yarmulkes would not appear to compromise the military's ability to function in any way. Given the measures the military takes to accommodate the religious needs of the men and women who serve in the armed forces—for example, by providing chaplains and opportunities to attend formal religious observances—it is hard to believe that the Air Force was taking Goldman's religious needs seriously.

Goldman sued, and his case eventually reached the Supreme Court. The Court ruled against Goldman.[1] The justices cited the military's need to have common uniforms; the military's superior competence to judge when exceptions to its rules might prove disruptive; and, finally, the difficulty of drawing lines. A yarmulke might not prove disturbing, but what about a turban? Large beaded necklaces? Flowing saffron robes?[2] But while Goldman lost his court case, he prevailed in another forum. Responding to the Court's decision and the plight of Goldman and others like him, Congress passed a statute requiring the military to permit reasonable, religiously motivated departures from its standard uniform.[3]

Congress, of course, had certain advantages over the Supreme Court in this case. In particular, Congress was free to make its legislative demand for reasonable accommodation and then step back and see how its prescription would work in practice; if compliance unduly encumbered military operations, Congress could rescind or modify its demand. Congress thus could afford to be less obeisant to military judgment and less concerned that its implementation of constitutional principles would burden the armed forces with impractical obligations.

Goldman's story illustrates the important role that Congress can and regularly does play in enforcing the requirements of Equal Liberty. To this point in our consideration of religious freedom, we have focused mainly on judges, especially the justices of the Supreme Court. As the primary source of constitutional doctrine, the Supreme Court is indeed very important: Supreme Court doctrine directly guides the lower federal courts and state courts when they take up cases concerning religion; and this doctrine may also guide the way public officials think and act when issues of religious liberty present themselves. But, as Simcha Goldman's example demonstrates, judges are not the only critical actors with regard to religious freedom. Full enforcement of Equal Liberty's norms will depend upon the active engagement of legislatures, including Congress, and other political actors, such as executive branch officials.

Legislative Oversight of Practices That Threaten Equal Regard

In Chapter 3 we stressed an important implication of Equal Liberty: Equal Liberty begins with the idea that religious liberty requires that persons not be treated unequally on account of the spiritual foundations of their deep commitments; Equal Liberty thus calls on government to exempt religious observers from burdens that are not shared fairly with others. In many situations, courts will be capable of determining when breaches of this basic principle have occurred. This is true, for example, of the case we considered in which high school basketball players committed to the tenets of Judaism were prohibited from wearing yarmulkes while playing, while others were permitted to wear properly secured eyeglasses; and it is true as well in the case in which Sunni Muslim police officers were required to shave their beards, while officers suffering from an adverse skin condition were not. In cases like these, where officials have made accommodations for some important interests but neglected nonmainstream religious interests, there is a patent failure of what we have called the principle of equal regard.

In other cases, failures of equal regard may be more elusive because no obvious benchmarks of accommodation exist. Goldman's case is one example. Even if the justices had been willing to set aside their tendency to defer to military judgment, assessing Goldman's claim would have required them to compare the Air Force's prohibition of yarmulkes to the military's general stance with regard to mainstream religious needs. So far as we know, there were no examples of military accommodation that provide a simple one-to-one comparison.

The *Peyote Case* is another interesting example.[4] Oregon's legislature had made special provision for the sacramental use of wine, even in counties that had declared themselves to be "dry." Oregon's failure to make a similar provision for the sacramental use of peyote may have reflected a failure of equal regard. Oregon could, however, offer a plausible response to that concern—namely, that peyote is more dangerous than alcohol, and peyote rituals would be substantially more damaging to state interests than Christian communion ceremonies.

Another hard case from Chapter 3 concerned the Forest Service's decision to locate a road on federal land that included a sacred Native American religious site.[5] Particularistic decisions like this one, about how to use a unique piece of land, rarely benefit from the existence of obvious comparative benchmarks, but it is nevertheless clear that the interests of the Native American religion were not taken seriously. We suggested in Chapter 3 that there was an implicit counterfactual question at stake: "If the location of the road threatened a well-recognized conservationist interest (by killing off some of the last great redwood trees, say) or was a site sacred to a small but well-acknowledged group of Catholics or Orthodox Jews, would the Forest Service have pushed ahead with its plans?"

Simcha Goldman's case, the *Peyote Case,* and the Forest Service case are hard cases, especially for courts. In the absence of obvious benchmarks, questions inevitably arise about the nature of the harm to social interests threatened by peyote rituals relative to the use of wine in Christian communion ceremonies, or the weight of the Forest Service concerns that prompted the particular location of the road. Legislatures are better situated than courts to answer questions of this sort, since they involve not just judgments about the factual circumstances and constitutional principles surrounding the case, but about the weight of public policy concerns in the eyes of the political community. Accordingly, superintending compliance with the principle of equal regard in hard cases like these is an important legislative responsibility in a well-functioning regime of Equal Liberty.

The suggestion that legislatures in general and Congress in particular have an important role to play in assuring Equal Liberty may seem like asking the fox to guard the henhouse. In fact, however, Congress has been remarkably alert to the interests of religious minorities, especially in the sorts of cases in which courts have had difficulty in enforcing the principle of equal regard. After the Supreme Court issued its decision in the *Peyote Case,* for example, Congress enacted a law requiring states like Oregon to provide a comparable exemption in their controlled-substance laws.[6] When the Supreme Court declined to intervene in the Forest Service decision to run its road through a Native

American religious site, Congress promptly defunded the road.[7] And when Simcha Goldman sought relief from the uniform regulations that prohibited him from wearing a yarmulke, Congress crafted an exemption after the Supreme Court denied one.[8]

These victories are no accident. The United States is a very religious country, denominational rivalries in America have waned in recent years,[9] and even the largest faiths are minorities. As a result, religious leaders and organizations work together across denominational lines to secure the rights of religious believers, and legislators tend to take a sympathetic view of religiosity and spirituality in general. Of course, some nonmainstream faiths may fare better than others: legislators and bureaucrats have granted exemptions to benefit faiths that seem quaint, charming, or benign to many Americans—such as the Native American Church and the Amish—but they may be more reluctant to intervene on behalf of members of religions that strike them as more threatening—such as Santerians, who sacrifice animals, or fundamentalist Muslims, whom some may suspect of sympathizing with terrorists.[10]

But some not so very sympathetic religions have received help from the political branches as well. For example, in 1967 the Internal Revenue Service revoked the tax-exempt status of the Church of Scientology. The IRS contended that the practice of "auditing," in which church members paid church officials to purge them of negative thoughts, was a for-profit business; the church characterized it as a sacrament. When the Scientologists took their claim for tax-exempt status to the Supreme Court, the justices refused to help.[11] The IRS nonetheless changed its position a few years later.[12] Scientology is not what most people would regard as a "warm and fuzzy" religion—and it has been the target of considerable animosity from European governments.[13]

In any event, to the extent that legislatures or administrative agencies treat specific faiths worse than others, judicial enforcement of Equal Liberty reenters the picture. If the legislature grants exemptions for religions it finds benign, judges have constitutional ground to fashion comparable exemptions for religions treated with hostility and neglect. This remedy will not be perfect, but it will be significant.

Moreover, the diversity of religious faiths in the United States will often give legislatures an incentive to craft provisions broad enough to protect unpopular faiths along with popular ones. For example, the statute allowing conscientious objection to military service during the Vietnam War benefited pacifists who acted on the basis of "religious training and belief." Some successful objectors belonged to faiths not widely practiced in the United States.[14] Title VII, a federal antidiscrimination law, prohibits employment discrimination on the basis of religion, but it makes an exception for churches and other religious organizations.[15] This exemption applies to all churches, including very unpopular ones. Likewise, zoning and tax laws often make exemptions for religious institutions (usually in combination with other institutions, such as charities or schools—a significant fact to which we will return shortly).

There is another way in which legislatures can enforce to full measure the constitutional guarantee of Equal Liberty. Equal Liberty demands not only that religions be protected from hostility and neglect, but that citizens in general enjoy broad space within which to pursue and act upon their most valued commitments and projects, whether these be religious or not. To some extent, we can expect judges to secure this space by enforcing constitutional rights related to speech, property, association, privacy, travel, and other constitutional values. But legislatures have an important role to play. For example, if legislatures enact statutes that authorize persons to create "living wills," those laws will increase the freedom of persons—religious or not—to live their last days in a way consistent with their own convictions about life's meaning and value. If legislatures create public fora—such as parks, meeting rooms, and arenas—where organizations can gather and spread their message, their action will increase the freedom of religious organizations and persons along with other organizations and persons. If legislatures limit the authority of the police to spy upon organizations in general, they will thereby protect religious organizations along with other organizations.

The Limits of Legislative Authority: Equal Liberty

But while Equal Liberty depends in significant ways on the assistance of Congress and state and local legislative bodies, it also places important limitations on the kinds of help that such bodies can offer religion. Equal Liberty's demand that persons not be treated unequally on account of the spiritual foundations of their deep commitments not only entails the requirement that religious observers be free from burdens not shared fairly with others; it also insists that such observers bear their fair share of the burdens and limitations that go along with membership in organized society. This combination of principles seems not only to limit, but indeed to all but *eliminate* the legislative role in assuring that the principle of equal regard is respected. We have just finished congratulating Congress for making Oregon safe for the sacramental use of peyote, for curbing the Forest Service, and for permitting yarmulkes to be worn in the Armed Services. But every one of these enactments—at first blush—seems to give religious believers a special privilege, and seems for just that reason to be unconstitutional. This line of thought has persuaded some scholars that legislatively crafted, religion-specific accommodations are nearly always unconstitutional and that only judges should create such exemptions.[16] How does it come to pass that we find ourselves celebrating rather than condemning legislation of this sort?

Our answer depends on three principles, principles that in combination circumscribe the area in which legislative accommodation of the needs of religion may proceed. First, we agree that, in general, legislatures ought to accommodate religion along with other, analogous activities or commitments. For example, Section 501(c)(3) of the tax code grants tax-exempt status to charitable and educational organizations along with religious ones.[17] That sort of a provision—which extends not only to religious practices but to other, comparable activities—will usually be the most constitutionally desirable form of accommodation for religion. Sometimes, however, a legislature may have good cause to exempt a particular practice—such as a peyote ritual—that is unique to a particular religion or to religion in general. Religion-specific obligations must answer to the second principle: such religion-specific accommodations are permissible if and only if they are reasonable efforts to guarantee (rather than undermine or depart from) the equal distribution of liberty. And, third, even if the legislature has acted in a good-faith effort to promote equal liberty, the courts should broaden the exemption (through either constitutional review or statutory interpretation) to include religious or secular groups with equally compelling claims of conscience. That is what the Court did, for example, when Daniel Seeger complained that conscientious-objector status was unavailable to atheists. If it is impossible to broaden the exemption so that it applies equally, the courts are obliged to hold it unconstitutional.

We believe that the Supreme Court has more or less tracked these three basic principles in its major cases about legislatively enacted accommodations for religion. We have already mentioned Seeger's case, in which the Supreme Court demanded that an apparently religion-specific exemption be expanded to accommodate comparable secular claims of conscience.[18] Though technically decided on statutory rather than constitutional grounds, *Seeger* and the other conscientious objector cases exemplify the third of the three principles we have just mentioned.

There are four other major Supreme Court precedents about constitutional limits on the legislature's power to fashion religion-specific accommodations. The most recent case is *Cutter v. Wilkinson,* a unanimous decision upholding a statute that required prison wardens to accommodate the religious practices of inmates when feasible. The Court rejected the view that religion-specific accommodations were never permissible, and it identified several factors that, in combination, led it to approve the accommodation for prison inmates. First, the Court said that the statute remedied "exceptional, government-created burdens on private religious exercise" (the Court called this the "foremost" reason for its decision). Second, the Court found that the statute was "measured so that it [did] not override other significant interests," including the interests of nonbeneficiaries. Third, the statute did not "differentiate among bona fide faiths."[19]

Though the *Cutter* Court did not explicitly say that legislative accommodations should aim at equality, its reasoning was entirely consistent with that view. By requiring that religion-specific accommodations address burdens that are "exceptional" and "government-created," the *Cutter* Court helped to ensure that such accommodations will result in equal treatment rather than special privilege. The Court's description of the statute's history and purpose reinforced this point. The Court found that Congress had "documented, in hearings spanning three years, that 'frivolous or arbitrary' barriers impeded institutionalized persons' religious exercise." The Court appended a footnote with examples from the hearings, including an Ohio prison policy that provided Jewish prisoners with kosher food but denied halal food to Muslims, and a Michigan prison policy that permitted prisoners to light votive candles but not Chanukah candles.[20] These examples involve manifest failures of equal regard; they are exactly the sort of problems that justify legislative intervention from the standpoint of Equal Liberty. The *Cutter* Court's final two considerations express a concern with equality even more directly: they demand that the interest in accommodating religious practice not overburden other interests, and that the accommodation be administered fairly.

Cutter left in place three earlier decisions. In two of them, *Estate of*

Thornton v. Caldor (1985)[21] and *Texas Monthly v. Bullock* (1989),[22] the Supreme Court examined religion-specific accommodations and found them unconstitutional. *Thornton* involved a Connecticut statute that prohibited employers from compelling employees to work on their Sabbath. The Connecticut statute provided a benefit to employees who had a religious reason for preferring to take a particular day off from work, but not to employees with a secular reason for doing so (such as the need to care for a child or an ailing relative). The Court held, by an eight-to-one vote, that the statute impermissibly favored religion.[23] *Texas Monthly* dealt with a Texas law that exempted religious publications from a sales tax applicable to other publications. The Court struck the law down by a six-to-three vote. Five of the justices thought that the law preferred religion over nonreligion, and so violated the Establishment Clause; Justice White concurred on the ground that the law favored some viewpoints over others, and so violated the Free Press clause.[24]

On the other hand, in *Corporation of the Presiding Bishop of the Church of Jesus Christ of Latter-day Saints v. Amos* (1987),[25] the Court upheld a very broad exemption that benefited only religion. *Amos* dealt with the provision from Title VII, the federal antidiscrimination law, that we mentioned a few paragraphs ago. In general, Title VII prohibits employers from discriminating on the basis of race, sex, or religion, but it provides an exemption that permits religious organizations—and only religious organizations—to discriminate on the basis of religion. One can easily see that religious organizations have a unique justification for discriminating on the basis of religion. It makes perfectly good sense for the Catholic church to insist that its priests be Catholic, but there is no comparable reason for, say, McDonald's to scrutinize the religious beliefs of its short-order cooks.

If Title VII's exemption applied only to clergy and other employees who participated in religious acts or ceremonies, it would be an example of how religion-specific accommodations can promote Equal Liberty: the statute would provide religious organizations with a benefit uniquely appropriate to them. That said, the exemption would also be redundant, because it duplicates a more general right provided by the Constitution itself on terms that are not religion-specific. As we indicated in Chapter 2, we believe that the Constitution itself guarantees churches (and other associations, both secular and religious) the freedom to select leaders and officers on the basis of their constitutive principles. In some respects this freedom is broader than Title VII's exemption, since it may permit churches to discriminate on the basis of race or sex, in addition to religion, if their faith so requires—so, for example, the Catholic church may discriminate not only against non-Catholics, but against women, when it hires priests. If Title VII simply spelled out one implication of this general freedom—namely, that religious organizations were free to discriminate on the basis of religion when appointing persons to lead them or perform religious functions—it might help to clarify the law and avoid mistaken rulings, but it would not otherwise add to the rights that churches already have.

Title VII's actual language is more interesting. It authorizes religious organizations to discriminate with respect to all their employees, even ones who have no connection to the religious functions of the church. The *Amos* case, for example, arose after the Mormon church fired a "building engineer"—a maintenance worker—at a church-run gymnasium that was open to the public. It is possible, of course, that in some religions, believers might be required to exercise only in places maintained by the faithful—so that, in effect, gymnasia were sacred spaces and building engineers had religious responsibilities. Yet Title VII's broad exemption applies without regard to such details. Churches are permitted to discriminate against workers without showing that their work has any religious significance or that it in any way affects the ability of believers to practice their religion. In *Amos*, the Supreme Court upheld this very broad exemption.

We have said that religion-specific exemptions are permissible if and only if they are reasonable efforts to guarantee the equal distribution of liberty. Does Title VII's exemption meet that standard? At first, it might seem that the answer is clearly no: Title VII gives religious organizations, and only religious organizations, complete freedom to discriminate on the basis of religion, whether they do so from good motives or ill. No other organization enjoys such a broad exemption from the nation's antidiscrimination laws. One can, however, make a case in favor of Title VII if one focuses on the possibility that the judicial process will make factual errors in suits against religious organizations—especially unpopular religious organizations. One might fear two kinds of errors from the judicial process. First, one might believe that judges and juries would be prone to exaggerate the likelihood that a church had discriminated against outsiders. They might, in other words, assume that the Mormon church had fired Amos because he was not Mormon, even if, in fact, the church dismissed him because he was a poor worker. Second, one might worry that judges and juries would inappropriately minimize the associational interests of nonmainstream churches. For example, if a religious organization claimed that its gymnasia were sacred spaces and that believers could exercise only with other believers, jurors might find these ideas implausible or silly, and so resolve cases adversely to the organization. Congress might have determined that the expansive exemption from Title VII's prohibition on religious discrimination was necessary to protect churches from these sorts of mistakes—mistakes to which churches and other religious organizations are uniquely vulnerable. If so, Congress's goal would have been consistent with Equal Liberty.

In our view, Title VII's exemption pushes to the perimeter of the constitutional power to craft religion-specific accommodations. Reasonable people committed to the principles of Equal Liberty might differ about whether judges should uphold Title VII's exemption provision. For present purposes, the critical point is not the provision's ultimate constitutionality or unconstitutionality, but the features that make it a close case. First, the Title VII exemption arguably protects religious organizations from two harms to which they may be uniquely vulnerable: prejudicial determinations that they mistreated employees who did not share their faith, and interference with employment relationships that are essential to their associational autonomy. Second, Congress might have made a thoughtful judgment about how to respond to precisely those harms. More precisely, Congress might have concluded, on the basis of an assessment of religious practices and judicial institutions, that these risks required a "safe harbor" to protect religious organizations from unintended applications of Title VII's prohibition on religious discrimination. It is this combination—of congressional judgment or expertise applied to a domain of distinctive religious vulnerability—that renders Title VII's exemption arguably consistent with Equal Liberty.

Enumerated Powers and Underenforcement

The limitations on legislative accommodation of religious interests that we have been discussing so far are in service of Equal Liberty's call for treating the deep commitments of members of our political community equally, without regard to the spiritual foundations of those commitments. As such, they apply to all legislative efforts, whether federal, state, or local; and as such, they come from within Equal Liberty itself. We now need to take up a problem that is distinct to *federal*—that is, *congressional* or *national*—accommodations of religion and is a consequence of the general structure of legislative authority in the United States.

Constitutional lawyers generally agree that Congress has only those powers that are expressly given it (the term of art is "enumerated") in the Constitution, along with the power to do those things that are sensibly understood to be in furtherance of its stated powers. This well-established idea is called "the doctrine of enumerated powers," and it is understood to be a principle of federalism, that is, a principle that effectuates a division of authority between the state and the national government by limiting the reach of national power. For our purposes here, the most important consequence of the doctrine of enumerated powers is this: any national legislation that attempts to tell the states what they must do or not do—like Congress's statute requiring Oregon to create an exemption for Native American peyote rituals—must connect to some power given Congress in the Constitution.

If Congress seeks authority to require Oregon to create an exemption for Native American peyote rituals, the most natural place for it to look is Section 5 of the Fourteenth Amendment. Section 5 gives Congress power to enforce rights guaranteed elsewhere in the Fourteenth Amendment.[26] It is generally accepted that these Fourteenth Amendment rights incorporate the religious liberty provisions of the First Amendment. Since Equal Liberty endorses congressional efforts to remedy failures of equal regard, and since Oregon's refusal to treat peyote rituals as it treats Christian communion ceremonies was at least arguably a failure of equal regard, it would seem to follow that Congress had the authority to require Oregon to create an exemption for Native American peyote rituals.

But here's the rub: As we have had occasion to discuss many times, in the *Peyote Case* the Supreme Court ruled that Oregon could ban the use of peyote in all settings without violating any provision of the Constitution, including the First Amendment's provisions guaranteeing religious liberty. How can Congress, in the name of enforcing those same provisions, turn around and give members of the Native American Church the statutory right to disobey Oregon's ban?

We have already gone a long way toward answering that puzzling question, by observing that courts—including the Supreme Court—may have a hard time identifying failures of equal regard in cases like the *Peyote Case* and *Lyng* (the Forest Service road location case) and, further, that Congress has become an important partner in helping to police equal regard in these sorts of cases. With these observations in place, we can see an important reason for thinking that courts should not always be the only authoritative interpreters of the Constitution. This is an important revision of a view common among many citizens and practicing lawyers, according to which judges have the final and decisive say about what the Constitution means, and the discretion of legislatures to enact various measures exists only within the constitutional boundaries set by the courts.

Though common in ordinary political debate, the idea of a judicial monopoly over constitutional interpretation no longer attracts much support from constitutional scholars. Even those who believe in judicial supremacy—that is, those who believe that judges should have the last word about constitutional meaning—generally agree that other political actors (such as Congress and the president) have an important role to play in defining and enforcing the guarantees of the Constitution, so long as their efforts do not place them in the position of starkly contradicting the Court. Many scholars go further and see other political actors—including ordinary citizens—as entitled to contest judicial conceptions of constitutional meaning. Scholars who take this view agree that judges do not always have final authority over constitutional meaning, but they disagree about what mechanisms are legitimate vehicles for confronting the Court. They disagree, in particular, about such matters as whether the president may ever ignore judicial mandates, and about whether Congress may correct the Court only through constitutional amendments and the judicial appointments process, or whether Congress may also pursue more aggressive measures.

Underenforcement is a concept developed by one of us in the 1970s and now used by constitutional scholars to describe one important way in which nonjudicial actors participate in constitutional law.[27] The critical idea behind underenforcement is this: sometimes judges refuse to grant constitutional relief not because they deny the existence of a constitutional right, but because they recognize institutional limits on the judiciary's capacity to enforce it. For example, they might believe that the Constitution secures all children the right to a decent education, but they might recognize that securing this right depends upon raising revenue to pay for schools, and they might believe that judges lack the competence and authority to allocate tax burdens fairly. Under such circumstances, we would say that there is a constitutional right to a decent education, but that it is judicially underenforced. If a right is judicially underenforced, its enforcement will depend on the behavior of other political actors.

The idea of underenforced rights has three important consequences. First, and most obviously, it entails that other branches of government, or perhaps the people as a whole, have the constitutional responsibility to render such rights meaningful. Second, it implies that such rights should affect the way in which judges construe the scope of congressional power. Several constitutional provisions—including Section 5 of the Fourteenth Amendment—give Congress the authority to enforce constitutional rights.[28] If judges enforced all rights fully, then Congress could never use these provisions to enforce any rights except ones that the judiciary itself had enforced. But if some rights are judicially underenforced, then Congress may legitimately use the Constitution's "enforcement provisions" to go beyond the scope of judicially enforced rights. More precisely, Congress would have the authority and the responsibility to enforce the full measure of constitutional rights that the judiciary, because of its institutional limitations, underenforced.

Third, and most subtly, the concept of underenforcement helps to justify some judicially enforceable rights. For example, in a 1982 decision, *Plyler v. Doe,*[29] the Supreme Court held that it was unconstitutional for states to prohibit undocumented aliens from attending public schools. That was a surprising result. Undocumented aliens are not a group that usually enjoys judicial protection: because they are undocumented, they are subject to deportation and a host of other penalties and deprivations. And the Supreme Court had previously refused to find a judicially enforceable right to an education in the Constitution.[30] So why did the Court uphold the claim in *Plyler?* The justices were unable to agree on a single rationale, and their opinions were unclear. We think that the best explanation builds on the idea of an underenforced constitutional right to a decent education.[31] Normally, judges cannot enforce that right, because they are not well positioned to make the judgments necessary to fund it. But when the state designs and funds such a system, and then excludes one group from it, the situation is different: the Court can easily supply a remedy for that group by demanding that it have access to the system available to others. *Plyler* thus illustrates how judicially underenforced rights may occasionally manifest themselves in judicially enforceable forms.

As should now be obvious, cases like the peyote and Forest Service cases provide good examples of judicial underenforcement of the Constitution. These cases are hard precisely because they involve judgments of social value that seem more naturally to belong to the legislature. In the *Peyote Case*, the sticking point was how to assess the difference in social cost of permitting Native American peyote rituals on the one hand, and Christian communion ceremonies on the other. In the Forest Service case it was the question of just how compelling were the Forest Service's reasons for locating the road just where it did. These questions are uncomfortable for courts, but much less so for legislatures. And so we might well hope for just what we find: when the Court in these cases declined to intervene under circumstances that may well have included failures of equal regard, Congress was moved to take action.

In cases in which the courts—often for the best of reasons—underenforce constitutional principles such as Equal Liberty, other actors have a particular responsibility to act in their stead. That is just what Congress has done in the cases we surveyed early in this chapter. And in such cases, grants of congressional power like that contained in Section 5 of the Fourteenth Amendment should be construed broadly, precisely to permit the more complete recognition of important constitutional principles like the First Amendment's protection of religious liberty. And that, of course, is our solution to the puzzle of Congress's authority to insist that members of the Native American Church be permitted to use peyote in their sacraments.

Lessons from the Religious Freedom Restoration Act Debacle

We have painted an attractive picture of Congress and the Supreme Court as partners in the enterprise of Equal Liberty, and together making a pretty good job of it. Underlying this cooperative enterprise is a conceptual structure that makes good sense of our constitutional framework and of productive divisions of labor within that framework. It would be nice if we could just leave things on this happy note and push on to the conclusion of our exploration of religious freedom.

Unfortunately, there is a rather large and ungainly blot on this happy picture, centering on a piece of legislation called the Religious Freedom Restoration Act[32]—known to insiders as RFRA. The story of RFRA is rather tangled, and it does not reflect altogether favorably upon the politics of religious liberty in the United States. RFRA was a legislative response to the Supreme Court's decision in the *Peyote Case*. As we have seen, the Court in that case abandoned its strict scrutiny test, which required the government to show that every substantial burden on religious exercise served a compelling state interest. In our view, the *Peyote Case* changed remarkably little about free exercise law. The compelling state interest test had always talked tough but performed feebly. Despite its stringent language, federal appellate courts rejected nearly all free exercise challenges to generally applicable laws. Nevertheless, churches, civil liberties groups, and many academics were very upset about the *Peyote Case*. They made wild claims about it. As we noted in an earlier chapter, Oliver Thomas, an attorney for the National Council of Churches, went so far as to compare *Smith* to the *Dred Scott* decision, a pre–Civil War case that is almost uniformly reviled as the most abominable in the Court's history.[33] Some of the groups and their lawyers asserted that the *Peyote Case* had effectively rendered the Free Exercise Clause meaningless. They took their case to Capitol Hill and asked Congress to reinstate the legal rights that existed before the decision in the *Peyote Case*. RFRA was the fruit of their labor. It purported to "restore the compelling interest test as set forth in Sherbert v. Verner . . . and Wisconsin v. Yoder . . . and to guarantee its application in all cases where free exercise of religion is substantially burdened."[34]

RFRA's proponents formed a powerful lobby. Interest groups that normally opposed one another, such as conservative churches and the ACLU, worked in tandem to support the bill. This coalition of groups played its hand well. For example, "Religious Freedom Restoration Act" was a clever name. Who could be against helping "religious freedom," much less "restoring" it? Since the bill (allegedly) did nothing more than revive a venerable jurisprudential test, representatives and senators could assure themselves that it would do no great harm. After all, free exercise jurisprudence before the *Peyote Case* was not like the Establishment Clause cases about school prayer or town Christmas displays: the free exercise cases were unknown to most of the electorate and had generated no political earthquakes.

To be sure, this tranquil political history concealed serious jurisprudential problems and moral issues. As we saw in Chapters 1 and 3, free exercise doctrine before the *Peyote Case* was fraught with inconsistencies, and if the Court had ever put teeth into the compelling state interest test, it would have had explosive consequences. But these concerns depended upon detailed knowledge of the case law, and RFRA's proponents told Congress a simpler, somewhat sanitized story. Douglas Laycock, a leader of the coalition that drafted RFRA, wrote

some years later that, after the decision in *Boerne,* "RFRA's supporters
. . . portrayed the problem in its worst possible light to maximize the
need for legislative action."[35] To accomplish their goals, "RFRA's supporters . . . said that nearly all laws were neutral and generally applicable and that [the *Peyote Case*] had all but repealed the Free Exercise
Clause."[36] Laycock believes that his "own testimony avoided the worst
of this rhetoric," but he admits that he "did not contradict the general
impression."[37] Thomas Berg, another proponent of the statute, conceded in a law review article that "Congress never fully faced up to the
inconsistent currents in pre-*Smith* law." As a result, Congress never recognized that it simply was "not logically possible to give effect to all
[pre-*Smith*] cases or to construe the compelling interest test '[no] more
stringently or leniently than it [ever] was prior to *Smith.*'"[38] Ira C. Lupu
sympathized with RFRA's aims but had doubts about its constitutionality. He testified during the hearings on RFRA but found his message
unwelcome. "At the time I gave the testimony, I had the distinct impression that Subcommittee Chairman Don Edwards (D-Cal.) had not
heard that side of the story, and the even deeper sense that the interest
groups backing RFRA did not want that side aired," wrote Lupu several years later.[39]

As a result, the complexities of free exercise jurisprudence were
largely unexplored as RFRA slid through Congress; nobody had much
of an incentive to oppose an alliance that included both conservative churches and liberal civil rights groups.[40] RFRA eventually passed
unanimously in the House and attracted only three votes in opposition
in the Senate. President Clinton signed it with great fanfare.

The groups that backed RFRA knew they would face a tougher time
of it in the courts.[41] RFRA looked like a direct challenge to the Supreme Court's decision in the *Peyote Case;* and indeed, when President
Clinton signed RFRA into law, he characterized it as an exercise of
Congress's "extraordinary" power to "reverse by legislation a decision
of the United States Supreme Court."[42] Congress is not generally free

to reverse Supreme Court decisions about the Constitution. Congress can, however, supplement constitutional rights with statutory ones. That is what RFRA's supporters proposed to do, but they faced a problem: they wanted the new statute to create rights not only against the federal government, but also against states and localities, just as the Constitution itself does. To protect federalism, the Constitution limits the purposes for which Congress can impose restrictions on the states. Congress's power is very broad, but RFRA's provisions were very sweeping; they would extend to every aspect of state and local governance.

RFRA's supporters turned to Section 5 of the Fourteenth Amendment, just as we did earlier in this chapter, and they made arguments that were very similar to those we made under the banner of the underenforcement theory. The statute's proponents noted that Justice Scalia, speaking on behalf of the Court in the *Peyote Case,* had said that it would be impossible for judges to develop fair and consistent standards by which to evaluate exemption claims.[43] They took this statement as an indication that the Court's decision was based upon its view about what judges could do, rather than about the limits of the constitutional right itself. They also pointed out that Scalia and the Court appeared to invite legislative intervention: Scalia said that the Court was "leaving accommodation to the political process." He suggested that "a society that believes in the . . . protection accorded to religious belief can be expected to be solicitous of that value in its legislation."[44] Hence, according to RFRA's proponents, this was an area in which Congress could play an important role in more fully enforcing what we have called judicially underenforced rights.

The proponents of RFRA thus made arguments that we would see as attractive and persuasive *if they were offered on behalf of legislation that promoted the principles of Equal Liberty.* But this was far from the case with RFRA. Congress's approach in RFRA was strange and unfortunate. It flowed quite directly from the theories that motivated the coalition that drafted RFRA. Though RFRA's proponents claimed that the *Peyote Case* underenforced the free exercise right, they were not pleased with the decision. They believed that the case was wrongly decided, and they wanted free exercise rights fully enforced *by judges*. They accordingly drafted a statute that reinstated the test that existed before the *Peyote Case* and thus returned the task of devising and approving exemptions to the courts. Specifically, RFRA declared that the Court's free exercise jurisprudence before the *Peyote Case* had applied a "workable" test,[45] and it directed courts to exempt claimants from any local, state, or federal law that substantially burdened religious conduct unless denial of the exemption was the "least restrictive means" to accomplish a "compelling governmental interest."[46]

RFRA thus involved a peculiar Alfonse-and-Gaston routine. The Supreme Court looked back over its free exercise jurisprudence and found it inconsistent and unprincipled. Few could disagree. The justices went further, however, and declared that it was impossible for courts to devise any principled test that might yield exemptions from neutral and generally applicable laws. That job, they said, was for legislators. Congress, at the behest of the various groups backing RFRA, took up that challenge and found not only that judges were quite capable of devising a satisfactory exemptions doctrine, but that, contrary to the judges' own assessment, they had successfully done so in the past! Congress accordingly handed the job of finding exemptions back to the judges. What's more, RFRA's supporters told Congress, and Congress itself found, that legislators could not be trusted to protect the rights of minority believers! So, in short, the Supreme Court justices found their own jurisprudence wanting and claimed that legislators were better suited than judges to craft such exemptions; Congress responded by finding that judges were better suited to the task than were legislators, and it also made the jurisprudential finding that the Court was wrong to think its own past precedents unworkable.

In 1997 the Supreme Court took the next step in this strange dance.

Six justices held RFRA unconstitutional in *City of Boerne v. Flores*.[47] The case involved a Catholic church in Boerne, Texas. The church was growing and wanted to expand its facilities. Because the church was located inside the city's historic district, local zoning laws restricted its ability to construct an addition. The church claimed that RFRA entitled it to an exemption from these requirements, which, it alleged, "substantially burdened" its exercise of religion. In response, Boerne made several arguments, including the argument that RFRA was unconstitutional because Congress had no power to impose such sweeping restrictions on states and localities.

The Court ruled in Boerne's favor. That result should not have been surprising. After all, what RFRA aimed to "restore" was a legal regime that purported to give religiously motivated persons a presumptive right to disobey laws that got in their way. During the twenty-seven years that this presumption survived as a nominal rule in constitutional jurisprudence, it generated a crazy quilt of decisions that did little to protect religious freedom but made plain how unjust and destructive to sound governance a special privilege for religious practice might be. The Court had an abundance of reasons for resisting the revival of a rule with which it had never been able to live.

The Supreme Court rested its decision on the claim that Congress had exceeded its enumerated powers. RFRA's supporters were outraged and accused the Court of unprincipled judicial activism. The Court's opinion, unfortunately, helped these critics by making an indefensibly broad claim: the justices said that if Congress had the authority to enforce constitutional rights beyond those identified by the Court, then the entire power of judicial review would be in jeopardy.[48] That is not true: the underenforcement theory justifies independent congressional interpretation of the Constitution in appropriate cases, and there are other theories that do so, too. RFRA's friends had a field day with this mistake.

They also argued that *Boerne* was, at best, a misuse of judicial resources, since RFRA increased religious freedom in general even if it went beyond the scope of any rights specifically guaranteed by the Free Exercise Clause. They accordingly maintained that no judicially cognizable constitutional interests were put in jeopardy by RFRA; the justices' objections to it, they implied, were more or less akin to prudential concerns about policy and should be left to the legislature's discretion.[49] This is a legalized version of the argument used to push RFRA through Congress: namely, that RFRA had the virtue of increasing religious freedom, and any harm it might do was insignificant by comparison to that lofty goal.

At the core of this argument was a fundamental mistake about religious freedom, one that should by now be familiar. The argument for RFRA plays upon a simple idea—that any law that enhances the ability of religious believers to practice their religion thereby promotes religious freedom. On this view, such a law is good for religious freedom, even if it may be bad for other reasons. The intuitive appeal of this idea is obvious—but so, we hope, are its flaws. It ignores entirely the concerns that motivate the Establishment Clause, which rests on the insight that helping religious believers may provide them with unfair advantages. As we have emphasized throughout this book, religious freedom has a crucial distributional element. It requires that people have substantial liberty to form and act upon convictions about religion (including atheistic and agnostic convictions), but it also requires that this liberty be distributed fairly. The only coherent and defensible conception of religious freedom flows from the state's obligation to treat people equally, regardless of their convictions about religion. Promoting religious freedom is therefore different from providing benefits or doing favors for religious believers, and the fact that RFRA facilitates religious practices does not create even a prima facie argument that it increases religious freedom. Some laws that facilitate religious practice—for example, a law that pays for religious schooling but not other schooling—would actually detract from religious freedom.

We believe that RFRA itself suffered from an Establishment Clause problem of this kind. It relieved religious organizations and persons of burdens shared by others. RFRA was thus quite different from the religion-specific exemption for prison inmates that the Court would later uphold in *Cutter*. That exemption was narrowly tailored to address only "exceptional, government-created" burdens on religious practice. RFRA, by contrast, applied to every law that burdened any religious practice. Instead of promoting equality, it created special privileges. For example, a Catholic school located in a historic district might invoke RFRA to seek exemption from zoning restrictions, but a secular private school could not. The religious Mrs. Campbell whom we met in the Introduction could operate her soup kitchen in defiance of local zoning ordinances, but her counterpart across the street, who is motivated by compassion for the poor and the hungry, could not. Justice Stevens pointed out this discrepancy in a concurring opinion in the *Boerne* case, and he concluded that RFRA therefore violated the Establishment Clause.[50]

Stevens, however, wrote only for himself. The majority's opinion did not address the Establishment Clause issue; it rested instead on the judgment that RFRA was not a proper exercise of Congress's power to enforce the Free Exercise Clause and the Fourteenth Amendment. We believe that religious freedom's distributional element was nevertheless critical to the majority's argument, just as it was to Stevens's different rationale. The Free Exercise Clause, no less than the Establishment Clause, expresses and implements a principle of Equal Liberty: it insists that the needs of minority religious believers not be treated with hostility or neglect. To count as an effort to enforce the Free Exercise Clause, RFRA must aim at vindicating this equality-based principle. As we have said, promoting religious freedom is not the same thing as benefiting religious practices or religious believers. The mere fact that RFRA facilitated religious practices was no reason to suppose that it enhanced or restored religious freedom, or that it enforced the Free

Exercise Clause—and that was so regardless of whether RFRA discriminated flagrantly enough to violate the Establishment Clause.

If we read the *Boerne* opinion sympathetically, and put aside the Court's overblown rhetoric about RFRA's threat to the power of judicial review, we find the justices making exactly the point we have stressed: that while RFRA provided benefits to religious believers, there is no reason to suppose that it aimed at Equal Liberty, and hence no reason to regard it as an effort to enforce the Free Exercise Clause. Justice Kennedy, who authored the majority opinion, said that "the stringent test RFRA demands of state laws reflects a lack of proportionality or congruence between the means adopted and the legitimate end to be achieved."[51] RFRA did not focus upon state and local laws that were "motivated by religious bigotry," nor did it even incorporate "a discriminatory effects or disparate impact test" that might identify cases of unconstitutional neglect.[52] Instead, RFRA sought to alleviate burdens on religious believers without regard to whether those burdens were shared equally by others. For that reason RFRA was not a valid exercise of congressional power to enforce the Free Exercise Clause: "When the exercise of religion has been burdened in an incidental way by a law of general application, it does not follow that the persons affected have been burdened any more than other citizens, let alone burdened because of their religious beliefs."[53]

The *Boerne* Court's conclusion about the scope of congressional power did not render RFRA altogether void. *Boerne*'s enumerated powers argument struck down RFRA's restrictions on state and local conduct, but RFRA also imposed restrictions on the federal government. These restrictions, which were not at issue in *Boerne*, first reached the Supreme Court in *Gonzales v. O Centro Esperita Beneficente Uniao Do Vegetal* (2006). That case provided a fitting debut for RFRA's federal applications: the fact pattern in *O Centro* was a not-quite-identical twin to the one in the *Peyote Case*, which had provoked Congress to enact RFRA.[54] *O Centro* involved a Christian spiritualist sect, referred to as the

UDV (for Uniao do Vegetal), that is based in Brazil and has a small branch in the United States. Members of the sect ingest a hallucinogenic tea called hoasca as part of their communion sacrament. Federal officials had seized a shipment of hoasca intended for sacramental use and threatened to prosecute members of the UDV under the Controlled Substances Act, which bans use of the tea. *O Centro* produced a unanimous decision. All nine justices found that members of the UDV had a RFRA-based right to the sacramental use of hoasca.

Justice Stevens joined the *O Centro* opinion even though he had said in *Boerne* that RFRA violated the Establishment Clause because it favored religious over nonreligious interests. The Establishment Clause objection to RFRA, unlike the enumerated powers objection, applies to RFRA's federal applications as well as its restrictions upon state and local law. How, then, could Justice Stevens join his colleagues? This question matters a great deal from the standpoint of Equal Liberty, which endorses Justice Stevens's concern about favoritism for religion.

Two features of *O Centro* provide the answer. First, neither party to the case challenged the constitutionality of RFRA's federal application. Their lack of interest in such arguments is easy to explain: on one side was the federal government, which was committed in principle to RFRA's constitutionality, and on the other side was a church group that wanted to use RFRA to protect its right to ingest hoasca. Second—and, from the vantage of Equal Liberty, most important—the Court's analysis in *O Centro* was dominated by concerns that could easily be rephrased in the language of equality.

Under RFRA, the *O Centro* Court had to determine whether the federal government had a compelling interest in barring the sacramental use of hoasca; absent such an interest, RFRA requires the federal government to create exemptions on behalf of important religious interests, including the sacramental ingestion of hoasca by members of the O Centro faith. In an almost literary twist of fortune, the close parallel between the hoasca ceremonies and peyote ceremonies enabled the

Supreme Court to conclude that no compelling interest justified the federal ban on the hallucinogenic tea. Long before the *Peyote Case* arose, the attorney general of the United States had exercised his authority to create exemptions from the Controlled Substances Act to permit members of the Native American Church to engage in the sacramental use of peyote.[55] In 1994 Congress broadened the peyote exemption to include all members of Indian tribes recognized by the United States government.[56] For the *O Centro* Court, the parallels between the peyote and hoasca ceremonies made it clear that no powerful governmental interests justified refusing to grant the members of the O Centro faith the exemption they sought. After all, for thirty-five years the federal government had lived comfortably with the more or less identical exemption in place for peyote.[57]

This rationale did not depend upon RFRA. Having granted members of the Native American Church—and, later, members of all recognized Indian tribes—an exemption to use peyote as part of their sacrament, the federal government violated the Constitution itself when it refused to grant an exemption for hoasca use by members of the UDV. As applied in *O Centro*, RFRA vindicates rather than contradicts the counsel of Equal Liberty. That, in our view, is what made *O Centro* an easy case.

The Establishment Clause objection to RFRA's federal applications thus remains unresolved. In a case in which the constitutionality of RFRA was put on the table, and in which RFRA operated to confer a benefit upon religion that other important human commitments did not enjoy, Equal Liberty would insist that RFRA was unconstitutional.

RFRA's Aftermath

When the Supreme Court handed down its decision in *Boerne*, religious interest groups immediately went to Congress and demanded a response. Their rhetoric was extreme, just as it had been after the

Peyote Case.[58] The political context was now, however, more complicated than it had been after the *Peyote Case*. Decisions rendered under RFRA—including some that had suggested that religiously motivated discrimination might be exempt from civil rights laws—had alarmed some interest groups.[59] Moreover, the Court's decision in *Boerne* made clear that any new statute would have be carefully crafted in order to withstand judicial scrutiny.

After three years of hearings, Congress produced a statute that was, we think, significantly better than RFRA but still problematic. Titled the Religious Land Use and Institutionalized Persons Act of 2000 (referred to by insiders as RLUIPA),[60] the statute again attempted to apply the compelling state interest test to state and local government action burdening religious exercise, but only in two domains: restrictions on religious exercise by prisoners and other institutionalized persons, and restrictions imposed on land use (the "institutionalized persons" component of this statute was the subject of the Court's decision in *Cutter v. Wilkinson*).

"Institutionalized persons" and "land use" bear no conceptual relation to one another, but the combination did not surprise anybody familiar with RFRA's political history. Though testimony in congressional hearings about RFRA focused on horror stories about, for example, state coroners who performed unwanted and unnecessary autopsies on Hmong immigrants in disregard of religiously motivated objections from relatives,[61] such outrages were rare in practice. Disputes about zoning and prisoners' rights made up the bulk of the cases litigated under RFRA.[62]

In an effort to avoid the enumerated powers objections that felled RFRA, Congress packed RLUIPA with provisions designed to invoke multiple enumerated powers—more specifically, they relied explicitly on the Constitution's Commerce Clause and Spending Clause as well as Section 5 of the Fourteenth Amendment.[63] For purposes of our argument, RLUIPA's Fourteenth Amendment components are its most interesting provisions, and we will confine our attention to them. RLUIPA's sponsors sought to get around the *Boerne* decision by compiling evidence that prisoners and religiously motivated landowners were targets of discrimination that frequently went unredressed by courts. Hence, they said, RLUIPA really was an effort to redress exactly the sorts of free exercise harms that the Supreme Court recognized in the *Peyote Case* and *Church of the Lukumi Babalu Aye*—namely, discriminations on the basis of religion. RLUIPA was necessary, they argued, to remedy discrimination that was hard to prove in court and would accordingly go unredressed absent legislative intervention.

This argument was a self-conscious effort to justify RLUIPA in terms of something like the underenforcement rationale we described earlier. If the claims backing up this rationale were true—that is, if religious prisoners and land uses were targets of widespread, unremedied hostility and neglect—then RLUIPA would be an excellent example of the kind of partnership between courts and legislatures that we recommend.

In the case of prisoners, we believe that the case for RLUIPA is plausible. Courts are reluctant to challenge the judgments of prison wardens, who are predictably unsympathetic to requests from prisoners for special accommodations. The Court's opinion in *Cutter,* which rejected an Establishment Clause challenge to the "institutionalized persons" component of RFRA, recited compelling examples (culled from congressional hearings) of prison policies that were clearly inconsistent with the demands of Equal Liberty (such as the Michigan policy that permitted prisoners to light votive candles but prohibited them from lighting Chanukah candles). Of course, religious liberty claims are not the only prisoners' rights neglected by wardens, and we doubt, as usual, that the blunt compelling state interest test is the best instrument for resolving the problem. Nevertheless, the institutionalized persons part of RLUIPA can be defended within the terms of Equal Liberty (in *Cutter,* the Court addressed only Establishment Clause issues and did not discuss the federalism-based enumerated powers objections that are now our focus, but we think that the Court would also reject federalism-based challenges to that portion of the statute, and that it would be right to do so). If RLUIPA included only its prisoners' rights provisions—if, in other words, it was "RIPA" rather than "RLUIPA"—we could welcome it as a good example of legislative and judicial partnership, and we could commend Congress for salvaging a desirable statute from the otherwise unhappy saga of RFRA.

We are not so optimistic, however, about RLUIPA's land use provisions, which we believe suffer from both Establishment Clause and federalism-based problems. Congress heard and relied upon two kinds of evidence to back up those provisions. Some testimony was more or less anecdotal, describing instances in which zoning authorities had refused to allow new or unpopular churches to build in particular communities. These episodes have been frequent in American history, and there is no doubt that they continue to occur. Whether federal legislation was needed is a different question. State law remedies are available, and in some states, at least, those remedies are very effective. New York, for example, flatly prohibits communities from excluding either churches or schools from residential neighborhoods.[64] In any event, concern about exclusive communities could not possibly justify RLUIPA's broad sweep, which gives *every* church (powerful, mainstream ones along with upstart outsiders) a presumptive exemption from *every* land use restriction—not just ones that exclude churches from entire communities, but ones that limit churches' ability to expand parking lots, build on wetlands or in green belts, erect broadcasting antennas, and so on.[65]

RLUIPA is thus stunningly expansive—it quite literally transforms any local zoning dispute about church behavior into a federal case. In the area of land use and zoning, RLUIPA effectively gives churches and religiously motivated persons a presumptive right to disobey laws that get in their way—and thereby creates the kind of unfairnesses that we described when considering the two Ms. Campbells. RLUIPA's proponents contended that this astonishingly broad law was necessary because discrimination against churches permeated the land use process. To support that claim, they presented Congress with a 1997 study, done by a law firm in conjunction with a law professor, which, they said, documented the existence of widespread discrimination against minority churches. The study, however, looked only at litigated zoning disputes; it found that small faiths brought a disproportionate number of such cases. From this finding the study's authors inferred that small faiths must be subject to frequent mistreatment—why else would they bring such a high fraction of suits?[66]

But of course this inference is a non sequitur. The proportion of zoning complaints brought by nonmainstream churches tells us nothing about how often churches are mistreated in the zoning process; if it tells us anything at all, it tells us that *when* churches are mistreated (whether rarely or frequently), the victims of this mistreatment are likely to be nonmainstream churches rather than mainstream ones. That result should not surprise anyone—common sense tells us that powerful, mainstream churches are less likely to be the victims of discrimination.

The relevant question is not which churches complain most frequently about zoning processes, but how often churches are actually mistreated in such processes. That question is much harder to investigate; one cannot analyze it simply by counting published court decisions, as was done in the study upon which Congress relied. In a much more probative study, two sociologists, Mark Chaves and William Tsitsos, used a survey of churches to assess their experience with zoning processes. Chaves and Tsitsos reported that "the nearly universal experience of American congregations seeking government authorization to do something they want to do is one of facilitation rather than roadblock."[67] The Chaves and Tsitsos study was available to Congress, but Congress ignored it.

It is hard to take seriously the suggestion that RLUIPA is designed to combat discrimination against religious land uses. In many ways, zoning law is remarkably favorable to religious land uses—for example, by permitting churches to construct large structures and parking lots in residential neighborhoods, something that virtually no other organization can do. Moreover, many churches are powerful players in local politics, including the politics of land use, because they can muster the support of their congregations at the polls. When land use laws burden religious practices, they often do so as part of a reasonable effort to share burdens fairly among land owners and usages, rather than because of hostility toward or neglect of religion. We do not mean to deny that zoning boards sometimes mistreat religious land owners and that existing state and federal law may sometimes fail to provide effective remedies for such mistreatment. But to address that problem, Congress should identify the characteristics of such troubling cases with some precision, and then craft a law that responds to these failings. That is not what RLUIPA does. It provides a presumptive exemption to *every* religious landowner, no matter how powerful or privileged, from *every* land use law burdening its practice, no matter how fairly the burden is shared with other landowners, unless the state can demonstrate the burden is necessary to further a compelling state interest.

Thus RLUIPA's land use provisions—unlike its prisoners' rights provisions or Title VII's exemption allowing churches to discriminate on the basis of religion—cannot reasonably be regarded as a congressional effort to secure equal treatment for religion. Nor are those provisions in any other respect a good illustration of the partnership between courts and legislatures that we recommend. Instead of bringing congressional powers of investigation to bear upon problems that the judiciary was poorly equipped to tackle, Congress turned a blind eye to the nuances of regulation and imposed upon the judiciary a blunt test ill suited to the challenges of land use regulation.

Little RFRAs

In addition to seeking (and eventually securing) passage of RLUIPA, RFRA's defenders pursued a second strategy in response to the Supreme Court decision striking down RFRA: they went to state legislatures and asked them to enact state-level versions of RFRA. The "little RFRA" strategy was, of course, time-consuming and difficult. To have a national impact, RFRA's proponents had to make their case to fifty state legislatures. On the other hand, the strategy had an important advantage. State laws, unlike federal ones, are immune from the enumerated powers challenge that felled the national RFRA. The enumerated powers doctrine applies to Congress, not to state legislatures. Little RFRAs are still subject to Establishment Clause challenges, but there is no need to connect them to Section 5 of the Fourteenth Amendment or to any other enumerated power of Congress.

The advocates for little RFRAs had considerable success. One of those advocates, Douglas Laycock, reported that, as of 2004, thirteen states had enacted little RFRAs of one kind or another (fourteen others also have applied state-law versions of the compelling state interest test to exemption claims under their state constitutions).[68] Several other states considered RFRAs but refused to enact them.[69]

We have already indicated that we believe that the federal RFRA statute violated the Establishment Clause, and, of course, we have the same concern about the little RFRAs, which parrot the compelling state interest test used by the original RFRA. Nevertheless, the meaning of that test in each statute is a question of state law: it is, in other words, up to the Arizona courts to decide what compelling state interest means in Arizona's RFRA, and up to the Connecticut courts to decide what the phrase means in the Connecticut little RFRA, and so on. Arizona and Connecticut might interpret the phrase differently from one another, and both might interpret it differently from the way the federal courts interpret it in RFRA or RLUIPA.

"So," someone might say, "suppose that a state were to say that a governmental interest is compelling if and only if it is consistent with the principles of Equal Liberty. If that were so, then wouldn't these statutes be consistent with your own view?" Eugene Volokh has defended state RFRAs in more or less these terms. He suggests that the compelling state interest standard simply invites courts to engage in a case-by-case effort to figure out how much protection religious claimants deserve.[70] The courts, on this view, would have the capacity to interpret the compelling state interest standard over time in a way that aligned with whatever they deemed to be the right standard for assessing exemption claims—including, for example, the standard of equal regard that we have recommended. Does this project merely duplicate what state courts have already been doing under the religious freedom clauses of their state constitutions? No, suggests Volokh, because little RFRAs might liberate courts from some of the incentives that might otherwise lead them to underenforce free exercise rights. In particular, since the legislature can correct misinterpretations of the little RFRA through ordinary legislation, courts are free to enforce the requirements of Equal Liberty (or any other conception of religious freedom) aggressively, knowing that the legislature can intervene if the judges get it wrong.[71]

What should we make of Volokh's argument? If a state were to interpret its little RFRA pursuant to the principles of Equal Liberty, then, obviously, we would have no reason to worry that the little RFRA violated the Establishment Clause. The Supreme Court decisions in *Cutter* and *O Centro,* in which the Supreme Court applied the compelling state interest test in a way that conformed to the requirements of Equal Liberty, suggest that such an interpretive practice is indeed possible. That said, we are not optimistic that the effects of the little RFRAs will be so benign. As descendants of RFRA, with its references to *Sherbert* and *Yoder* and its embrace of the compelling state interest test, the little RFRAs come drenched in the language of extraordinary special privilege, not in the language of equality. Their proponents recommended them on the basis of the misguided separation model that treats religion as a constitutional anomaly that ought not to be touched by the state. Legislatures enacted them on the basis of confused accounts of the law which exaggerated the prospects for success of free exercise claims before the *Peyote Case* and which ignored existing accommodations for religion in land use regulations and other state and local laws.

We have great faith in the capacity of courts, through the process of case-by-case adjudication, to work their way toward sensible results. Perhaps they can do so in the case of the little RFRAs, but we have our doubts. The little RFRAs are at best a severely compromised version of the kind of partnership that courts and legislatures ought to practice. The state legislatures did little to gather fresh evidence about whether religious individuals and organizations faced special obstacles under their state's land use laws or other regulations. And if state legislators were concerned about removing discriminatory burdens on religious exercise (rather than about granting religion special privileges), the language they crafted (or, more precisely, copied from RFRA and *Sherbert*) was singularly ill suited to their purpose. None of the legislature's policymaking strengths were brought to bear on the problem of religious freedom. If the little RFRAs eventually sponsor a defensible jurisprudence of religious freedom, it will be the result of luck rather than design.[72]

Partner or Adversary?

Equal Liberty invites and benefits deeply from active legislative involvement. In particular, we should understand the Supreme Court and Congress as partners in the enterprise of securing Equal Liberty. Equal Liberty also imposes unsurprising but important limits on legislators. A willy-nilly effort to make the world better for the religiously committed, without regard to the fair distribution of both the liberties and the burdens of citizenship, is constitutionally barred, both on Equal Liberty and enumerated powers grounds. But reasonable, good-faith efforts to enforce the principle of equal regard suffer no such disabilities. Thus Equal Liberty gives us reasons to welcome and applaud Congress's efforts to permit Native American Church members to use peyote as part of their sacrament, to prevent the Forest Service from a catastrophic siting of a road, and to permit members of the military to wear yarmulkes.

As these legislative successes indicate, there is no shortage of congressional willingness to act on behalf of religious freedom. But as the RFRA debacle indicates, there may on occasion be a shortage of congressional judgment. For its part, the Supreme Court should welcome reasonable, good-faith efforts by Congress to assume its role as partner in the effort to protect religious liberty. If we set aside the overreaching rhetoric of the *Boerne* case, the Court has on the whole done just that. The actual decision in *Boerne* seems clearly correct. In RFRA, Congress allowed itself to be stampeded into a position not of a partner but of an adversary of the Court; indeed, in RFRA Congress unwittingly made itself the adversary of Equal Liberty and therefore of religious freedom itself.

Conclusion

DESPITE REMARKABLE SUCCESS in the effort to discover and abide by principles of fair cooperation for a religiously diverse people, Americans now seem increasingly inclined to allow their religious differences to stoke political divisions, and in turn to allow political divisions to overwhelm their commitment to religious freedom. To oppose this tendency and return Americans to the project of religious freedom, we have introduced the idea of Equal Liberty and applied it to a variety of heated issues involving the interaction of church and state in modern American life. It is now time to take stock. How well does Equal Liberty serve the constitutional project of religious freedom?

We can distill from the many cases we have considered a distinctive virtue that integrates Equal Liberty's diverse applications: it repeatedly identifies shared principles and intermediate solutions where other perspectives, riven by the politics of religious division, see only incompatible extremes. Equal Liberty's treatment of the roiling disagreement surrounding the Pledge of Allegiance provides an especially clear illustration. The two sides in that controversy draw the battle lines in all-or-nothing terms. One side insists that the words "under God" make the Pledge equivalent to a sectarian prayer exercise and that the

Constitution requires that those words be struck. This position makes a great deal turn on two words, and it would prevent many Americans from solemnizing their allegiance in the fashion they find most meaningful. The other side treats the Pledge as though it were utterly benign, despite its clear suggestion that only those committed to the view that the United States is "one Nation, under God" are worthy of public allegiance, and despite its actual exclusion of those who cannot comfortably proclaim their allegiance in these terms.

Equal Liberty recommends a path between these extremes. The path begins with the insight that oaths of fidelity are common in our public life. Public officials take them upon assuming office; witnesses take them before giving testimony in court; lawyers take them when they join the bar. All these oaths have a religious form, typically ending with the emphatic "so help me God!" But all these oaths also have an alternative, secular form, in which the oath-taker solemnly commits without any religious reference whatsoever. The Constitution itself stipulates that officeholders like the president can either "swear" or "affirm" to carry out their responsibilities.

We have argued that the Pledge of Allegiance should be fashioned on the pattern of these other oaths of fidelity. Public schools should offer students two forms of the Pledge. One can retain the words "under God." The other must be secular; we suggest the simple substitution of "under law." School officials should make it clear that both forms are equally satisfactory, and students should choose which form to recite as they take the Pledge simultaneously.

The moderate character of this solution expresses the spirit of Equal Liberty. Equal Liberty directs Americans away from abstract speculations about the ideal relationship of church and state—questions about, for example, whether we have too much or too little religion in our public life, or about whether religion is good or bad for us, or about which forms of spirituality are best. It focuses instead upon how to structure cooperation in circumstances of diversity, and as a result its principles reliably and consistently steer between extremes in search of what is fair.

Consider Equal Liberty's relationship to the two conventional positions about the state's obligation to accommodate the strong religious commitments of its citizens. One view maintains that persons motivated by the demands of their religious beliefs should enjoy a presumptive right to disobey laws that get in their way. The opposing view holds that religiously motivated persons should enjoy no special constitutional solicitude whatsoever and must take democratically enacted laws as they find them. Once again, these positions have a ruthless, all-or-nothing quality: either religious projects are the object of an extreme favoritism that is both unfair and subversive of democratically chosen social goals, or they are made vulnerable to the hostility and indifference that sometimes greets the idiosyncratic needs of minority religious belief.

And once again, Equal Liberty chooses a course that rejects each of these extremes. Equal liberty leaves to democratic government the job of striking the appropriate balance between collective regulatory concerns and individual interest, and makes no blanket demands for special concessions to religious needs and interests. But Equal Liberty insists that government treat the hardships and commitments of all of its citizens fairly, and thus is vigilant against the danger that government may be hostile or insensitive to the needs or interests of minority faiths. The result is a jurisprudence that examines what government has done—or clearly would do—on behalf of mainstream concerns, and then requires that government treat minority religious concerns with the same generosity. Hence the conclusion that the City of Newark had to permit Muslim police officers to wear beards on grounds of religious necessity, just as it had already permitted other officers to do on medical grounds; and hence the conclusion that a high school basketball association that permitted players to wear eyeglasses was obliged to make a comparable concession to Orthodox Jews whose religion required that they wear yarmulkes.

While Equal Liberty's treatment of the accommodation issue is conceptually moderate, it is neither a compromise nor a half-measure. In practice, we expect that Equal Liberty will provide minority believers with more robust protection than they have received under either of the two conventional views. For twenty-seven years, the Supreme Court was nominally committed to the idea that religiously motivated persons have a presumptive right to disobey the laws that everyone must follow. But throughout that period the Court repeatedly found excuses to avoid the consequences of this nominal commitment. The Court's evasions are not at all surprising: the idea of a presumptive right to disobey the law is so undermining of sound democratic governance in the modern state, and so crazily inconsistent with the constitutional impulse to treat people as equals without regard to their spiritual commitments, that sensible judges were bound to find ways to avoid its directive. In contrast, Equal Liberty provides a fair and workable approach to the issue of accommodation. Common sense, compassion, and political accountability will encourage legislators and administrators to accommodate the needs of mainstream groups whose lives they affect. Equal Liberty insists that the special needs of spiritual minorities be treated with the same generosity.

This combination of principled moderation and practical results is pervasive in applications of Equal Liberty, though not always quite so obvious. Consider, for example, controversies over the public school curriculum, such as the newly revived debate over evolution, creation science, and intelligent design. One view of this controversy insists that curricular decisions are invalid if they rest upon a religious purpose or motive. Equal Liberty rejects this view, which would selectively disable religiously motivated members of the community from pursuing their political ends. On the other hand, Equal Liberty also rejects the competing, and equally extreme view, which holds that religiously motivated curricular decisions are constitutional so long as their content is not explicitly religious or theological. Equal Liberty directs us to examine whether the social meaning of curricular decisions, when considered in light of their full context, makes them an impermissible endorsement of religion—as was the case, we argued, with the 1960s Arkansas law that prohibited schools from teaching about evolution. Equal Liberty also requires us to ask whether curricular decisions of this sort cast a constitutionally unacceptable pall of orthodoxy over the public schools—unacceptable on grounds of free expression and educational autonomy, not on grounds of religious freedom per se. Equal Liberty insists on a robust regime of rights not specifically directed at religion, and this is an instance of the importance of such a regime.

Rationales matter, and Equal Liberty's approach to religiously charged curriculum decisions has tangible consequences. Consider the heated controversy concerning the mandated teaching of intelligent design. Intelligent design encompasses two propositions: (1) there are gaps in the scientific record for which evolution cannot account, and (2) it follows that we must be the beneficiaries of interventions by an intelligent superbeing who might well answer to the description of God. The second proposition, favoring God over fairies, transcendental pasta, or the possibility of a science unknown, is constitutionally unacceptable for the same reason that prayer exercises are unconstitutional: it is tantamount to a governmental profession of religious faith, and carries the correlative social meaning of denigrating those who do not share that faith. But the same cannot be said of the first proposition, which critiques evolutionary theory. A state law mandating the teaching of the existence and details of that critique—while scientifically lamentable—would be constitutional, provided that teachers were entitled to express their own views of the scientific validity of the critical claim.

Equal Liberty's principled moderation is likewise manifest in its approach to programs that use public funds to support tuition vouchers for parochial schools and faith-based social services. Controversies over these programs again run to startling extremes. Separationists see the passing of dollars from public coffers to religious pockets as a quintessential violation of religious liberty. For those who hold this view, the blunt fact of public expenditures' making their way to religiously inspired charitable programs or schools is enough to sound the constitutional alarm. The rival position is equally stark. It contends that subsidies to religious programs pose no threat of any kind to religious freedom and that, on the contrary, denying such subsidies to religiously based programs starves them by comparison to their secular counterparts and so does great injustice.

Here too, Equal Liberty rejects both positions. Equal Liberty permits the distribution of public services through private providers, including religious groups; and Equal Liberty permits school voucher programs for which religious schools are eligible. But Equal Liberty insists that, at the end of the day, these programs must offer their beneficiaries a meaningful secular alternative from which to receive public services. And further, of course, Equal Liberty insists that these programs avoid playing favorites among religions.

This approach lacks what the extremes in the debate seem to offer, namely, simple, bright-line principles that cleanly resolve questions involving public funds and religion. But the promise of the extreme views is illusory. From the moment of its inception in the *Everson* case, the separation-inspired "no aid" principle has sown confusion and incoherence. Justice Black, who authored the Court's opinion in *Everson*, could not abide by the very principle that he introduced, and the Court's subsequent record in this area is a shambles. Nobody of whom we are aware has ever believed that churches should be denied all public benefits—including police and fire protection and access to legal process to enforce rights of contract and the like. Judicial efforts to shape a "no aid" doctrine in the face of the stubborn reality of life in the modern state have proven arbitrary and unpredictable. The opposite tack, which would give a green light to the channeling of public benefits through religious providers, would be unacceptably dangerous to religious freedom if it tolerated circumstances in which the only access to public services was shrouded in religious content. Both extremes are so normatively flawed as to completely unseat their theoretical clarity under the pressure of actual judicial practice.

The conceptual touchstone of Equal Liberty is that members of our political community are entitled to equal regard, whatever the nature of their spiritual commitments. What is remarkable about the extreme claims that Equal Liberty rejects is not just that they are insensitive to equality-centered concerns, but that they stubbornly insist on deviations from equal regard. In free exercise cases, religious freedom is somehow taken to insist that recognizably religious persons have the extraordinary prerogative to disobey laws that other persons with interests and commitments no less important to them must obey. In Establishment Clause cases, religious freedom is somehow taken to insist that otherwise perfectly well-qualified religious groups must be starved of public funds for which other groups with similar enterprises are eligible. The injustice that lies on the surface of these propositions has not gone unnoticed. But too often critics veer to the opposite extreme, ignoring the equality-centered concerns that made these otherwise bizarre ideas plausible in the first place. Our view is that the underlying concerns that once made these strange turns in Free Exercise and Establishment Clause doctrine seem attractive were always those of equal regard, and that Equal Liberty is the means to return our understanding of religious freedom to its deep and compelling normative roots.

It is not at all surprising that Equal Liberty rejects perspectives on free exercise and establishment that insist on deviations from the norm of equality. Nor is it surprising that Equal Liberty likewise rejects reactions to those perspectives that ignore the powerful equality-centered concerns that made them plausible in the first place. Hence Equal Liberty's durable commitment to the principled middle, working to excavate and develop the impulse toward equality that underlies not just religious freedom, but the whole of our constitutional tradition.

We have tried to demonstrate that a commitment to equality lies at the heart of religious freedom. But even if we have succeeded, it does not follow that there is anything obvious, or easy, or uncontroversial, about the project of moving from this insight to the concrete implementation of equal regard in constitutional law. In our discussion of the various contemporary controversies inspired by the interactions of Americans as a religiously diverse people, we have tried to avoid simplistic formulations, to explore what are sometimes quite difficult and complex problems, and to be as fair as possible to competing views. It is unlikely that any reader will agree with us at every step, and it is not our ambition to sweep the field of doubt or disagreement. We will be quite content if we have persuaded the reader that the project of finding fair principles of cooperation for a religiously diverse people is vital to our well-being as a people who value justice, that equal regard lies at the heart of the project, and that justice lies in the equality-driven middle ground between systematically advantaging or disadvantaging religion on the one hand, and ignoring the vulnerability of nonmainstream spirituality to hostility or neglect on the other.

This is not to say that the appeal of this middle ground will be universal or that a call to the enterprise of fairness will in a stroke calm the clamorous discord of our time. It is in the nature of a religiously diverse society that some groups and individuals will perceive their well-being as less than fully served by fair terms of cooperation. Consider again, for example, our proposal regarding the Pledge of Allegiance. Recognizing an alternative, secular form of the Pledge would acknowledge the equal stature of all members of our political community, and it might enable Americans to avert a painful showdown. Those for whom the "under God" form of the Pledge is important can employ that form, with official approval. Those for whom that language is problematic also can participate in the Pledge ceremony without giving false voice. This would seem to go a long way toward a solution with which both sides of this controversy could be satisfied.

Yet it is easy to anticipate objections from each. Some of those for whom "under God" is congenial will complain that nothing even modestly spiritual is safe, that they are being deprived of an environment in which public affirmation of principles that link millions of Americans is encouraged. Some of those for whom the contested phrase is anathema will complain that schoolchildren are being asked to make what may well be an unpopular choice in a public setting where that choice may be observed and stigma may result, and that the pressure to conform will for many be irresistible.

Neither of these complaints is groundless, and there surely is a tangible sense in which many persons in each of these opposing camps would be better off—more secure in their values and better protected from an assault on those values—if their view of constitutional justice were to prevail. But for a religiously diverse people living side by side in a modern state, fair terms of cooperation will often be like this. No group can reasonably expect that the world around them will be shaped in perfect conformity to their spiritual commitments, and no group can reasonably expect that they will be the beneficiaries of a perfect public prophylaxis against private ill will.

But this is a soup in which we all find ourselves. For many Americans spiritual commitment and metaphysical truth matter enormously. Surely we should be able to understand that the things that matter so deeply to us have their analogue in the very different beliefs, commitments, and projects of others. Justice and empathy alike ought to draw us toward fair terms of cooperation. That is the project of religious freedom; that is what the Constitution commands; that is what we as a people have often been able to salute with understandable pride; and that is what we have tried to offer in these pages.

Notes

Introduction

1. See, e.g., Lance Banning, "James Madison, the Statute for Religious Freedom, and the Crisis of Republican Convictions," in Merrill D. Peterson and Robert C. Vaughn, eds., *The Virginia Statute for Religious Freedom: Its Evolution and Consequences in American History* 109–138 (1988).

2. "God and Christianity are nowhere to be found in the American Constitution, a reality that infuriated many at the time [it was drafted] . . . the Constitution was bitterly attacked for its failure to mention God or Christianity." Isaac Kramnick and R. Laurence Moore, *The Godless Constitution: A Moral Defense of the Secular State* 27–28 (2d ed. 2005).

3. U.S. Const., art. VI and amend. I.

4. Sarah Barringer Gordon, *The Mormon Question: Polygamy and Constitutional Conflict in Nineteenth-Century America* (2002).

5. "Excerpts from President's Remarks on the War on Terrorism," *New York Times*, Oct. 12, 2001, p. B4.

6. Church of the Lukumi Babalu Aye, Inc. v. City of Hialeah, 508 U.S. 520 (1993).

7. Stephen L. Carter, *The Culture of Disbelief: How American Law and Politics Trivialize Religious Devotion* (1993).

8. Ron Suskind, "Without a Doubt," *New York Times Sunday Magazine*, Oct. 17, 2004, p. 44.

9. For a sympathetic account of "separation," see Kramnick and Moore, *The Godless Constitution;* for a historical critique, see Philip A. Hamburger, *Separation of Church and State* (2002).

10. Robert A. Wuthnow, *The Restructuring of American Religion: Society and Faith since World War II* 218–222 and passim (1988); idem, *The Struggle for America's Soul: Evangelicals, Liberals, and Secularism* 19–38 (1989).

11. See, e.g., Amy E. Black, Douglas L. Koopman, and David K. Ryden, *Of Little Faith: The Politics of George W. Bush's Faith-Based Proposals* (2004).

12. For example, in 1993 "65 percent of Catholic Charities' revenues came from government sources, as did 75 percent of the Jewish Board of Family and Children's Services revenues, and 92 percent of Lutheran Social Ministries' revenues." Stephen Monsma, *When Sacred and Secular Mix: Religious Nonprofit Organizations and Public Money* 1, 69–70 (1996).

13. Carrie Johnson, "Fan Church Group Plans an Appeal: Meal Program for Homeless to Fight Zoning-Violation Notice," *Richmond Times Dispatch*, Sept. 17, 1996, p. B1.

14. "Love Thy Neighbor," ibid., Sept. 21, 1996, p. A8.

15. Gordon Hickey, "Regulations on Homeless Are Altered: Rules Affect Shelters, Food Programs," ibid., July 29, 1997, p. B1.

16. Idem, "Council Ends Curbs on Feeding of Needy: 9-Month Dispute Has Quiet Ending," ibid., April 28, 1998, p. A1.

17. See, e.g., Julia Duin, "Faith, Justice, Culture and the American Way," *Washington Times*, May 6, 2004, p. A2; Miriam Rozen, "Liberty Legal Succeeds in Triggering DOJ Investigations Statewide," *Texas Lawyer*, April 25, 2005, p. 11.

18. "Feeding a Solution," *Richmond Times Dispatch*, Nov. 21, 1996, p. A28.

19. Daniel Wakin, "Suit Claims Group's Staff Is Pressured on Religion," *New York Times*, Feb. 25, 2004, p. B6.

20. Richard B. Schmitt, "Justice Unit Puts Its Focus on Faith," *Los Angeles Times*, March 7, 2005, p. A1.

21. Sherbert v. Verner, 374 U.S. 398, 403 (1963).

22. Ibid. at 406.

23. Ibid. at 410 (quoting Everson v. Board of Education, 330 U.S. 1, 16 [1947]).

24. Kate Stone Lombardi, "Faith That Reaches Out," *New York Times*, Sept. 14, 2003, p. WC10 (Westchester Weekly Desk).

25. Iver Peterson, "Faith, Public Dollars, and Charity: Religion and Government Intertwine in Some Programs," *New York Times*, July 5, 2001, p. B1.

26. See, e.g., Kyle Johnson, "Reforming Convicts through Scripture," *Christian Science Monitor*, Dec. 30, 1998, p. 3; Laurie Goodstein, "Group Sues Christian Program at Iowa Prison," *New York Times*, Feb. 13, 2003, p. A39; William Petroski, "Challenge of Prison Ministry Should Go to Trial, Judge Says," *Des Moines Register*, April 30, 2005, p. 4.

I. Separation and Its Cousins

1. Philip Hamburger, *Separation of Church and State* 1 (2002).
2. Rectors, Wardens, and Members of the Vestry of St. Bartholomew's Church v. City of New York, 914 F.2d 348, 351–354 (2d Cir. 1990).
3. See, e.g., East Bay Asian Local Dev. Corp. v. State of California, 24 Cal. 4th 693 (2000); Alger v. City of Chicago, 748 F. Supp. 617 (N.D. Ill. 1990); see also Laura S. Nelson, "Remove Not the Ancient Landmark: Legal Protection for Historic Religious Properties in an Age of Religious Freedom," 21 *Cardozo Law Review* 721, 764–766 (1999).
4. Douglas Laycock, "Formal, Substantive, and Disaggregated Neutrality toward Religion," 39 *DePaul Law Review* 993, 1002 (1990).
5. Michael W. McConnell, "Religious Freedom at a Crossroads," 59 *University of Chicago Law Review* 115, 169 (1992).
6. Douglas Laycock, "The Underlying Unity of Separation and Neutrality," 46 *Emory Law Journal* 43 (1997).
7. Thomas Hobbes, *Leviathan* (1651) 185–186 (Penguin 1985).
8. Everson v. Board of Education, 330 U.S. 1 (1947). As a technical matter, *Everson* was a Fourteenth Amendment case, not a First Amendment (Establishment Clause) case. *Everson* dealt with a New Jersey statute. By its express terms, the Establishment Clause applies to the national government, and the Supreme Court long ago held that neither it nor anything else in the Bill of Rights applies directly to the state governments. See Barron v. Baltimore, 32 U.S. (7 Pet.) 243 (1833); see also Permoli v. Municipality No. 1 of City of New Orleans, 44 U.S. 589, 609 (1845). The Supreme Court has, however, held that the important provisions of the Bill of Rights bind the states through the effects of the Fourteenth Amendment, and in *Everson* it made clear that this doctrine, called the "incorporation" doctrine (because the Fourteenth Amendment "incorporates" the Bill of Rights), held true with regard to the Establishment Clause.
9. Everson, 330 U.S. at 3 and n. 1.
10. Ibid. at 3; ibid. at 30 n. 7 (Rutledge, J., dissenting).
11. Ibid. at 3–4.
12. Hamburger, *Separation of Church and State* 454–478; Robert Wuthnow, *The Restructuring of American Religion: Society and Faith since World War II* 73–76 (1988).
13. Everson, 330 U.S. at 8–16.
14. Ibid. at 16–18 (citing Pierce v. Society of Sisters, 268 U.S. 510 [1925]).
15. Ibid. at 17–18.
16. Board of Education v. Allen, 392 U.S. 236, 248 (1968); Wolman v. Walter, 433

U.S. 229, 250–251 (1977). For Moynihan's comment, see 124 *Cong. Rec.* 25661 (1978).

17. Committee for Public Education & Religious Liberty v. Nyquist, 413 U.S. 756, 789–794 (1973).

18. Mueller v. Allen, 463 U.S. 388, 396–403 and n. 6 (1983).

19. Walz v. Tax Commission, 397 U.S. 664, 675–676 (1970).

20. Aguilar v. Felton, 473 U.S. 402 (1985).

21. This principle is part of the Court's "public forum" doctrine. See, e.g., Boos v. Barry, 485 U.S. 312 (1988); Heffron v. International Society for Krishna Consciousness, Inc., 452 U.S. 640 (1981); Southeastern Promotions Ltd. v. Conrad, 420 U.S. 546 (1976).

22. Widmar v. Vincent, 454 U.S. 263 (1981).

23. Lamb's Chapel v. Center Moriches Union Free School District, 508 U.S. 384 (1993).

24. Rosenberger v. Rector and Visitors of the University of Virginia, 515 U.S. 819 (1995).

25. Ibid. at 825 (brackets in original).

26. Ibid. at 832.

27. Ibid. at 828–831.

28. Ibid. at 868 (Souter, J., with whom Stevens, J., Ginsburg, J., and Breyer, J., join, dissenting).

29. Zobrest v. Catalina Foothills School District, 509 U.S. 1 (1993); Witters v. Washington Department of Services for the Blind, 474 U.S. 481 (1986).

30. Aguilar, 473 U.S. at 412–413; ibid. at 421 (O'Connor, J., dissenting); see also Wolman v. Walter, 433 U.S. at 244–248 (approving provision of remedial services at "mobile units" that function as "neutral sites").

31. Agostini v. Felton, 521 U.S. 203, 231, 240 (1997); ibid. at 240–254 (Souter, J., with whom Stevens, J., and Ginsburg, J., join, and with whom Breyer, J., joins in part, dissenting).

32. Zelman v. Simmons-Harris, 536 U.S. 639 (2002). *Rosenberger* and *Agostini* left open the possibility that voucher programs were unconstitutional. The majorities in both cases had taken care to point out that neither *Rosenberger* nor *Agostini* involved a direct transfer of state funds to religious institutions. In *Rosenberger,* the university delivered its support by paying the creditors of student groups rather than by making disbursements directly to the groups. 515 U.S. at 841. In *Agostini,* New York sent teachers, not dollars, into private religious schools. 521 U.S. at 228–229. It is hard to understand how these details could provide a principled basis for distinguishing vouchers from the policies approved in *Rosenberger* and *Agostini*—but, as we have seen, the Court had

drawn many arbitrary lines in its Establishment Clause jurisprudence. Opponents of vouchers were hopeful that the Court might do so once again.

33. *Lamb's Chapel* was a unanimous opinion. *Widmar*, the Missouri case, was eight to one. Justice White dissented, but he did so on the ground that the state should be free to exercise discretion about whether to allow religious groups to use rooms at the university for worship services. He did not contend that the Establishment Clause prohibited Missouri from allowing religious groups to use its classrooms. Widmar, 454 U.S. at 282. Indeed, White was a vocal critic of *Everson's* "no aid" rule. See, e.g., Lemon v. Kurtzman, 403 U.S. 602, 661–671 (1971) (opinion of White, J.).

34. Sherbert v. Verner, 374 U.S. 398, 399–401 (1963).

35. Ibid. at 406.

36. Gerald Gunther, "Foreword: In Search of Evolving Doctrine on a Changing Court: A Model for a Newer Equal Protection," 86 *Harvard Law Review* 1, 9 (1972).

37. Adarand Constructors v. Pena, 515 U.S. 200, 237 (1995); Grutter v. Bollinger, 539 U.S. 306, 326–327 (2003).

38. See, e.g., Quaring v. Peterson, 728 F.2d 1121 (8th Cir. 1984), aff'd by an equally divided Court, 472 U.S. 478 (driver's license photo); "No Veils on Driver ID, Court Rules," *New York Times*, Sept. 8, 2005, p. A20; Tony and Susan Alamo Foundation v. Secretary of Labor, 471 U.S. 290, 303 (1985) (minimum wage); and Hunt v. Hunt, 162 Vt. 423 (1994) (child support).

39. United States v. Lee, 455 U.S. 252, 255 (1982) (footnote omitted).

40. Ibid. at 262 (concurring opinion).

41. Tony and Susan Alamo Foundation, 471 U.S. at 303–305.

42. Goldman v. Weinberger, 475 U.S. 503 (1986); Lyng v. Northwest Indian Cemetery Protective Association, 485 U.S. 439 (1988); and O'Lone v. Estate of Shabazz, 482 U.S. 342 (1987).

43. Frazee v. Illinois Department of Employment Security, 489 U.S. 829 (1989); Hobbie v. Unemployment Appeals Commission, 480 U.S. 136 (1987); Thomas v. Review Board of the Indiana Employment Security Division, 450 U.S. 707 (1981).

44. Wisconsin v. Yoder, 406 U.S. 205 (1972).

45. See James E. Ryan, "*Smith* and the Religious Freedom Restoration Act: An Iconoclastic Assessment," 78 *Virginia Law Review* 1407, 1417 (1992).

46. Texas Monthly v. Bullock, 489 U.S. 1, 14–17 (1989) (Brennan, J., joined by Marshall and Stevens, JJ.) (plurality opinion); ibid. at 26 (White, J., concurring); ibid. at 28–29 (Blackmun and O'Connor, JJ., concurring). Five justices (Brennan, Marshall, Stevens, Blackmun, and O'Connor) characterized the

Texas law as an unconstitutional establishment of religion; one, White, characterized it as a violation of the Free Speech Clause.

47. Employment Division v. Smith, 494 U.S. 872 (1990).

48. Ibid. at 879–885.

49. Church of the Lukumi Babalu Aye, Inc. v. City of Hialeah, 508 U.S. 520 (1993).

50. See, e.g., Robert Wuthnow, The Struggle for America's Soul: Evangelicals, Liberals, and Secularism 51–54 (1989).

51. See, e.g., ibid. at 19–38; Wuthnow, The Restructuring of American Religion 218–222.

52. 42 U.S.C. §§ 2000bb–2000bb-4 (2000).

53. City of Boerne v. Flores, 521 U.S. 507 (1997).

54. See, e.g., Gonzales v. O Centro Esperita Beneficente Uniao do Vegetal, 126 S. Ct. 1211 (2006); Worldwide Church of God v. Philadelphia Church of God, Inc., 227 F.3d 1110, 1120–21 (9th Cir. 2000).

55. U.S. Senate Committee on the Judiciary, The Religious Freedom Restoration Act: Hearings on S. 2969, 102d Cong., 2d sess., 1992, S. Hearing 102–1076, p. 42 (statement of Oliver S. Thomas, General Counsel, Baptist Joint Committee on Public Affairs), referring to Scott v. Sandford, 60 U.S. 393 (1857).

56. Douglas Laycock, a scholarly proponent of RFRA, reports that Alabama, Arizona, Connecticut, Florida, Idaho, Illinois, Missouri, New Mexico, Oklahoma, Pennsylvania, Rhode Island, South Carolina, and Texas have all adopted statutes or constitutional provisions in response to Smith and Boerne. Douglas Laycock, "Theology Scholarships, the Pledge of Allegiance, and Religious Liberty: Avoiding the Extremes but Missing the Liberty," 118 Harvard Law Review 155, 211–212 and n. 368 (2004). See also idem, "State RFRAs and Land Use Regulation," 32 University of California at Davis Law Review 755 (1999).

57. 42 U.S.C. §§2000cc (2000).

58. Antonin Scalia, "God's Justice and Ours," 123 First Things 17–21 (May 2002).

59. Tom Baxter, "Alabama's Governor Fights to Save Tax Plan," Atlanta Journal and Constitution, Sept. 8, 2003, p. A5. Alabama voters rejected Riley's proposal at the polls. Tom Baxter, "Alabama Voters Turn Back Record $1.2 Billion Tax Plan," ibid., Sept. 10, 2003, p. A1.

60. For example: "Fondly do we hope—fervently do we pray—that this mighty scourge of war may speedily pass away. Yet, if God wills that it continue, until all the wealth piled by the bond-man's two hundred and fifty years of unrequited toil shall be sunk, and until every drop of blood drawn with the lash, shall be paid by another drawn with the sword, as was said three thousand years ago, so still it must be said 'the judgments of the Lord, are true and righteous altogether.'" Abraham Lincoln, "Second Inaugural Address," March

4, 1865, in Roy P. Basler, ed., *The Collected Works of Abraham Lincoln* 332, 333 (8th ed. 1953).

II. Equal Liberty

1. We have developed this model in a series of articles over the last decade, including Christopher L. Eisgruber and Lawrence G. Sager, "The Vulnerability of Conscience: The Constitutional Basis for Protecting Religious Conduct," 61 *University of Chicago Law Review* 1245 (1994); idem, "Unthinking Religious Freedom," 74 *Texas Law Review* 577 (1996); and idem, "Equal Regard," in Stephen M. Feldman, ed., *Law and Religion: A Critical Anthology* 200–225 (2000).

2. Philip Hamburger, *Separation of Church and State* 89–100 (2002); see especially 96–97 and n. 14.

3. Equality-based arguments have become increasingly prominent in Supreme Court religious freedom jurisprudence and among constitutional scholars. See, e.g., Ira C. Lupu, "The Lingering Death of Separationism," 62 *George Washington Law Review* 230 (1994); William P. Marshall, "What Is the Matter with Equality? An Assessment of the Equal Treatment of Religion and Non-Religion in First Amendment Jurisprudence," 75 *Indiana Law Journal* 193 (2000); Eugene Volokh, "Equal Treatment Is Not Establishment," 13 *Notre Dame Journal of Law, Ethics and Public Policy* 341 (1999); Alan Brownstein, "Harmonizing the Heavenly and Earthly Spheres: The Fragmentation and Synthesis of Religion, Equality, and Speech in the Constitution," 51 *Ohio State Law Journal* 89 (1990); and Michael Stokes Paulsen, "Religion, Equality, and the Constitution: An Equal Protection Approach to Establishment Clause Adjudication," 61 *Notre Dame Law Review* 311 (1986).

4. Church of the Lukumi Babalu Aye v. City of Hialeah, 508 U.S. 520 (1993) (holding that a law prohibiting the "ritual slaughter" of animals violated the Free Exercise Clause).

5. Witters v. Washington Dept. of Services for the Blind, 474 U.S. 481 (1986) (holding that the Establishment Clause did not prevent states from allowing recipients of state-subsidized scholarships to use the scholarships to pursue religious training).

6. Lamb's Chapel v. Center Moriches Union Free School Dist., 508 U.S. 384 (1993) (holding that the Free Speech Clause required that religious groups have equal access to school facilities that were available to other, nonreligious groups for evening meetings).

7. See Grutter v. Bollinger, 539 U.S. 306, 326–327 (2003) (race); United States v. Virginia, 518 U.S. 515, 532–534 (1996) (gender).

8. See, e.g., 42 U.S.C. §§ 2000e–2000e-3 (employment); ibid., §§ 3601–07 (housing).

9. Michael McConnell discusses such a possibility briefly in an article devoted in significant part to criticizing our theory: Michael McConnell, "The Problem of Singling Out Religion," 50 *DePaul Law Review* 1, 45 (2000). In his hypothetical, McConnell assumes that the NER would select projects on the basis of their "religious merit"; he correctly assumes that this institution would be unconstitutional.

10. In McClure v. Salvation Army, 460 F.2d 553, 560–561 (5th Cir. 1972), a federal appellate court concluded that "Congress did not intend, through the nonspecific wording of the applicable provisions of Title VII, to regulate the employment relationship between church and minister." Commentators usually assume that the exemption must rest on constitutional grounds. See, e.g., Douglas Laycock, "Towards a General Theory of the Religion Clauses: The Case of Church Labor Relations and the Right to Church Autonomy," 81 *Columbia Law Review* 1373, 1375–76 (1981). For criticism of the right recognized in *McClure*, see generally Ira C. Lupu, "Free Exercise Exemptions and Religious Institutions," 67 *Boston University Law Review* 391, 395–399 (1987).

11. See Pierce v. Society of Sisters, 268 U.S. 510 (1925) (attending private schools); Meyers v. Nebraska, 262 U.S. 390 (1923) (teaching German).

12. Carey v. Population Services International, 431 U.S. 678 (1977); Griswold v. Connecticut, 381 U.S. 479 (1965).

13. Planned Parenthood v. Casey, 505 U.S. 833 (1992); Roe v. Wade, 410 U.S. 113 (1973).

14. Moore v. City of East Cleveland, 431 U.S. 494 (1977).

15. Lawrence v. Texas, 539 U.S. 558 (2003).

16. See, e.g., Griswold, 381 U.S. at 486. See generally David J. Garrow, *Liberty and Sexuality: The Right to Privacy and the Making of* Roe v. Wade (1998).

17. Boy Scouts of America v. Dale, 530 U.S. 640 (2000).

18. See, e.g., ibid. at 678–685 (Stevens dissenting).

19. McConnell notes the analogy between the religious and secular cases. McConnell, "Singling Out Religion" 45–46. He conceives of the free exercise right and the secular associational right as distinct, but recommends that courts broaden the latter to match his conception of the former.

20. Lupu, "Free Exercise Exemptions" 435–438.

21. This argument requires no reinterpretation of Lupu's view; like us, he regards the debate as one about broader principles of associational autonomy, such as those involved in the Boy Scouts case, rather than about principles specific to religious freedom. Ibid. at 431–435.

22. On arguing from the inside out, see Ronald M. Dworkin, *Life's Dominion* 28–29 (1993).

23. "'When I use a word,' Humpty Dumpty said, in a rather scornful tone, 'it

means just what I choose it to mean, neither more nor less.'" Lewis Carroll, *Alice in Wonderland* (1872) 163 (Donald J. Gray, ed., 1971).

24. Douglas Laycock, "The Remnants of Free Exercise," 1990 *Supreme Court Review* 1, 5 (1990); Stephen Pepper, "Conflicting Paradigms of Religious Liberty," 1993 *Brigham Young University Law Review* 7, 12–13 (1993).

25. Laycock offers a substantive, rather than textual, argument for distinguishing equality and liberty rights in Douglas Laycock, "Free Exercise and the Religious Freedom Restoration Act," 62 *Fordham Law Review* 883, 885–886 (1994).

26. William P. Marshall makes arguments to the same effect in "The Case against the Constitutionally Compelled Free Exercise Exemption," 40 *Case Western Reserve Law Review* 357, 374–375 (1990).

27. As one of us has written elsewhere, "we dishonor neither the Constitution nor the framers if we regard some of its provisions as clumsy, vague, regrettable or redundant." Christopher L. Eisgruber, *Constitutional Self-Government* 114 (2001).

28. Donald Drakeman, *Church-State Constitutional Issues* 72 (1991): "No matter what the Supreme Court and modern commentators have found in the way of 'proof texts,' there is no clear mandate and hardly any useful guidance to be found in the records of the adoption of the Establishment Clause."

29. Michael McConnell, "The Origins and Historical Understanding of the Free Exercise of Religion," 103 *Harvard Law Review* 1409, 1516 (1990).

30. Ibid. at 1455.

31. Ibid. at 1452, 1453.

32. Ibid. at 1455.

33. Stephen D. Smith, *Foreordained Failure: The Quest for a Constitutional Principle of Religious Freedom* (1995). More recently Smith has argued that mutual respect among people of different religions can be based on the theological idea of "justification by faith" emphasized by Protestantism and Martin Luther. Stephen D. Smith, *Getting Over Equality: A Critical Diagnosis of Religious Freedom in America* 163–184 (2001).

34. Stanley Fish, *The Trouble With Principle* 162–242 (1999).

35. For example, the 1979 Constitution of Iran, in Articles 12–14, spells out the scope of rights of religious dissenters. Article 13 provides that "Zoroastrian, Jewish, and Christian Iranians are the only recognized religious minorities, who, within the limits of the law, are free to perform their religious rites and ceremonies . . ." Excerpted and translated in Henry Steiner and Philip Alston, *International Human Rights in Context* 460–461 (2000).

36. For a thoughtful view, with which we disagree, about the obligations of liberal states to theocrats, see Lucas Swaine, "A Liberalism of Conscience," 11 *Journal of Political Philosophy* 369–391 (2003).

37. Smith, for example, says that "a theory that privileges [some religious] positions and rejects others a priori is not truly a theory of religious freedom at all—or, at least, it is not the sort of theory that modern proponents of religious freedom have sought to develop." Smith, *Foreordained Failure* 63.

38. In Dworkinian terminology, the argument would take the form of internal, rather than external, skepticism. Ronald M. Dworkin, *Law's Empire* 78–85 (1986).

III. The Exemptions Puzzle

1. Since 1967 federal drug law has exempted the use of peyote in Native American Church religious ceremonies. 21 C.F.R. § 1307.31 (2004) ("The listing of peyote as a controlled substance in Schedule I does not apply to the nondrug use of peyote in bona fide religious ceremonies of the Native American Church, and members of the Native American Church so using peyote are exempt from registration"). At the time of Smith's case, many state laws had similar exceptions, but Oregon had none.

2. Employment Division v. Smith, 494 U.S. 872 (1990). On the *Smith* litigation, see Garrett Epps, *To an Unknown God: Religious Freedom on Trial* (2001).

3. An Act Relating to Peyote, 1991 Or. Laws c. 329, § 1 (codified at Or. Rev. Stat. § 475.992[5], [6] [2003]); American Indian Religious Freedom Act Amendments of 1994, Pub. L. No. 103–344, § 2, 108 Stat. 3125 (codified at 42 U.S.C. § 1996a [2000]).

4. Marci A. Hamilton, *God vs. the Gavel: Religion and the Rule of Law* (2005).

5. Goldman v. Weinberger, 475 U.S. 503 (1986).

6. Mitchell v. McCall, 273 Ala. 604, 143 So. 2d 629 (Ala. 1962). Public schools typically find ways to accommodate families whose religious convictions prohibit their daughters from wearing shorts; as a result, litigated cases are relatively rare. See, e.g., Peter Schworm, "Mastering Shyness and a New Language," *Boston Globe*, July 25, 2004, p. C1. A related case is Moody v. Cronin, 484 F. Supp. 270, 272 (C.D. Ill. 1979), in which the plaintiffs complained about coed gym classes in which their children had to "view and interact with members of the opposite sex who are wearing 'immodest attire.'"

7. Fraternal Order of Police Newark Lodge No. 12 v. City of Newark, 170 F.3d 359 (3d Cir. 1999).

8. Examples include Hale O Kaula Church v. The Maui Planning Commission, 229 F. Supp. 2d 1056 (D. Haw. 2002) (church seeks to build in agricultural district); North Pacific Union Conference Association of the Seventh Day Adventists v. Clark County, 74 P.3d 140, 146 (Wash. App. 2003) (same); Rector, Wardens, and Members of Vestry of St. Bartholomew's Church v. City of New York, 914 F. 2d 348 (2d Cir. 1990) (church wants to construct of-

fice building); Macedonian Orthodox Church v. Planning Board of Township of Randolph, 269 N.J. Super. 562, 636 A. 2d 96 (N.J. Super. A.D. 1994) (church seeks to double its size and obtain exemption from wetlands regulations); and Burlington Assembly of God Church v. Zoning Board of Adjustment Township of Florence, 238 N.J. Super. 634, 570 A.2d 495 (N.J. Super. L. 1989) (requiring town to allow church to construct and operate a radio station on its property). Marci Hamilton collects a number of other cases in *God vs. the Gavel* 78–110.

9. An example of such a controversy is Walker v. Superior Court, 763 P.2d 852, 869–871 (Calif. 1988). The topic receives an extended, if somewhat polemical, treatment in Hamilton, *God vs. the Gavel* 12–49.

10. Kahane v. Carlson, 527 F.2d 492 (2d Cir. 1975) (affirming order that federal prison authorities provide Orthodox Jewish prisoner with food that comports with his religious dietary obligations).

11. Stephen Gey created a stir by asserting in an article that not only did the state have no constitutional obligation to accommodate a student who refused for religious reasons to wear shorts, but that a school would violate the Establishment Clause if it allowed her to wear long pants without permitting other students to do so. Stephen Gey, "Why Is Religion Special? Reconsidering the Accommodation of Religion under the Religion Clauses of the First Amendment," 52 *University of Pittsburgh Law Review* 75, 182–183 (1990). Gey's extreme view provoked criticism in law reviews and, indeed, in congressional hearings after the *Peyote Case*. Gey's view is, however, highly idiosyncratic. He based his example on a 1962 case from Alabama, Mitchell v. McCall, 273 Ala. 604; even in that old case, school authorities were willing to accommodate the religiously based needs of the student by making an exception to their dress code. Anecdotal evidence, plus the absence of reported cases, suggests that school officials do so today—even when the religious beliefs of the family are highly unusual. See, e.g., Christopher B. Gilbert, "Harry Potter and the Curse of the First Amendment: Schools, Esoteric Religions, and the Christian Backlash," 198 *Education Law Reporter* 399, 417–418 (July 28, 2005), reporting that a school district excused a girl from outdoor gym class because she and her family were practicing witches who believed themselves obliged to avoid suntans.

12. Sherbert v. Verner, 374 U.S. 398 (1963).

13. The Peyote Case, 494 U.S. at 886 (footnote omitted).

14. Michael McConnell, "Free Exercise Revisionism," 57 *University Chicago Law Review* 1109, 1127 (1990).

15. Ibid.

16. Ibid. at 1128.

17. Fraternal Order of Police Newark Lodge No. 12 v. City of Newark, 170 F.3d 359 (3d Cir. 1999).

18. Menora v. Illinois High School Association, 683 F.2d 1030, 1031 (7th Cir. 1982).

19. Ibid. at 1035.

20. See, e.g., Liz Szabo, "Yarmulkes Firmly in Place, Jewish Boys Back in Game," *Virginia Pilot,* Feb. 26, 2000, p. B1. The National Federation of High Schools has permitted yarmulkes on basketball courts since 1983, though some referees still cause problems for Jewish players who cover their heads. Peter Barrington, "Yarmulkes Made for Rough Year," *USA Today,* Jan. 12, 1995, p. 11C.

21. Lyng v. Northwestern Indian Cemetery Protective Association, 485 U.S. 439 (1988). The Court said that the "Free Exercise Clause . . . does not afford an individual a right to dictate the conduct of the government's internal procedures," a category that, in the Court's view, included the government's use of its own land holdings. Ibid. at 448, 453.

22. House Committee on Appropriations, Department of the Interior and Related Agencies Appropriations Bill, 1989, H.R. Rep. No. 713, 100th Cong., 2d sess., 72 (1988).

23. Or. Rev. Stat. § 471.510 (2003) (local option law); ibid., § 471.430(2) (underage drinking). See also ibid., § 471.404(1)(b) (exception from regulations governing importation of wine into Oregon); ibid., § 471.405(2) (same).

24. The Peyote Case, 494 U.S. at 890.

25. McConnell, "Free Exercise Revisionism" 1129.

26. See above, notes 1 and 3.

27. Rader v. Johnston, 924 F. Supp. 1540 (D. Neb. 1996).

28. Keeler v. Mayor and City Council of Cumberland, 940 F. Supp. 879 (D. Md. 1996).

29. See Hobbie v. Unemployment Appeals Commission, 480 U.S. 136 (1987); Thomas v. Review Board of the Indiana Employment Security Division, 450 U.S. 707 (1981); Sherbert v. Verner, 374 U.S. 398 (1963).

30. Thomas, 450 U.S. at 709–712.

31. Bowen v. Roy, 476 U.S. 393, 708 (1986) (plurality opinion).

32. United States v. Lee, 455 U.S. 252, 263–264 n. 3 (1982) (Stevens, J., concurring). See also Hobbie, 480 U.S. at 148 (Stevens, J., concurring).

33. Douglas Laycock, "Conceptual Gulfs in *City of Boerne v. Flores,*" 39 *William and Mary Law Review* 743, 774 (1998). Laycock himself was among the most prominent and able academic critics of the *Peyote Case.* He, too, testified before Congress. In a retrospective article, Laycock says that he "avoided the worst of [the] rhetoric" directed against the decision, but admits that he "did not contradict the general impression." Ibid.

34. James E. Ryan, Note, "*Smith* and the Religious Freedom Restoration Act: An Iconoclastic Assessment," 78 *Virginia Law Review* 1407, 1417 (1992).

35. Amy Adamczyk, John Wybraniec, and Roger Finke sought to compare the success rate of free exercise claims before and after the *Peyote Case*. Amy Adamczyk, John Wybraniec, and Roger Finke, "Religious Regulation and the Courts: Documenting the Effects of Smith and RFRA," 46 *Journal of Church and State* 237 (2004). They reported that 39.5 percent of such claims prevailed in the period 1980–1990 (when the *Peyote Case* was decided), and that the success rate dropped to 28.4 percent in the period May 1990–November 1993 (when RFRA became law). They found that in the four years after RFRA's enactment, the rate rose to 45.2 percent. Ibid. at 250, table 1. These findings are intriguing, but we believe that it would be a mistake to attach much weight to them. To measure the impact of the *Peyote Case* without the effects of RFRA, Adamczyk and her coauthors looked only at cases before 1993; as a result the article ignores the impact of the Supreme Court decision in Church of the Lukumi Babalu Aye, Inc. v. City of Hialeah, 508 U.S. 520 (1993), in which a unanimous Supreme Court reversed the U.S. Court of Appeals for the Eleventh Circuit and upheld a free exercise claim. *Lukumi* clarified for lower courts that the Free Exercise Clause retained real protective content after the *Peyote Case*; not surprisingly, the post–*Peyote Case* decisions that we have praised in the text—such as the decision in the case about the Newark police officers—postdate *Lukumi*.

There are other features of the data collected by Adamczyk, Wybraniec, and Finke that would require further analysis before one could draw any conclusions from it. For example, the research team did not control for changes in the receptivity of the courts to civil rights claims in general over the periods that they analyzed. Nor did they attempt to describe variations in the patterns of cases being litigated. Finally, even if one takes their data at face value, it has an especially provocative feature that is consistent with our argument: they found that, both before and after the *Peyote* decision (but before RFRA), free exercise claims were *less* likely to succeed when courts invoked the compelling state interest test than when they did not. Adamczyk, Wybraniec, and Finke, "Religious Regulation and the Courts" 252, table 2. For other efforts to gauge the impact of the *Peyote Case* on free exercise claims, see James C. Brent, "An Agent and Two Principals: U.S. Court of Appeals Responses to Employment Division, Department of Human Resources v. Smith and the Religious Freedom Restoration Act," 27 *American Politics Quarterly* 236, 250 (1999); Gregory C. Sisk, Michael Heise, and Andrew P. Morriss, "Searching for the Soul of Judicial Decisionmaking: An Empirical Study of Religious Freedom Decisions," 65 *Ohio State Law Journal* 491, 567 (2004).

36. Douglas Laycock, "The Remnants of Free Exercise," 1990 *Supreme Court Review* 1, 16 (1990).

37. McConnell correctly observes that the concept of equal regard depends upon which secular interests are roughly comparable to religious ones, but then wrongly contends that equal regard must be incoherent because secular interests vary widely in their weight. "To treat religious claims as equal to the strongest [secular] claims is to privilege them over the weak [secular] claims; while treating religious claims as equal to the weaker claims is to disadvantage them compared to the strong," says McConnell. Michael W. McConnell, "The Problem of Singling Out Religion," 50 *DePaul Law Review* 1, 35 (2000). That observation is true, but it is not a problem for our theory, which clearly recognizes that religious interests or commitments are often serious, and identity-defining, just as are *some* secular interests and commitments, like maintaining one's health, coping with handicaps, or caring for loved ones.

McConnell, however, maintains that there "is nothing in 'equal regard' theory that guides the choice of [secular] comparisons [for religious claims], and in principle, such a guide cannot exist." Ibid. at 32–33. We are puzzled by this claim. McConnell's own critique of our theory assumes the intelligibility of the distinction between strong and weak secular interests, and he himself has elsewhere suggested that analogies between the needs of the handicapped and the needs of religious believers can illuminate the government's obligations. Michael W. McConnell, "Free Exercise Revisionism" 1140 and n. 133. Perhaps he means that it will be difficult to develop a metric that closely matches religious interests (which themselves vary in intensity) with strong secular needs and concerns (which also vary in intensity). But implausibly fine-grained comparisons are not required by equal regard, since what is being inquired after is the stance or attitude of the rulemaking body that fashioned the disparity in accommodation that is being contested. (This inquiry may sometimes be a close and difficult one, but all legal tests encounter hard cases.)

We undoubtedly bear some responsibility for McConnell's confusion. He mentions our treatment, in the 1994 article that introduced the concept of equal regard, of an example involving unemployment benefit claimants who turn down available work because they refused, as a matter of secular moral principle, to cross a picket line. Christopher L. Eisgruber and Lawrence G. Sager, "The Vulnerability of Conscience: The Constitutional Basis for Protecting Religious Conduct," 61 *University of Chicago Law Review* 1245, 1293 (1994). McConnell correctly reports that we analyzed this case by proposing that secular obligations had different "epistemic foundations" from religious ones, and that courts were accordingly free to second-guess the reasonableness of secular moral commitments with which they disagreed. Ibid.; see also McConnell, "The Problem of Singling Out Religion" 34. McConnell points out that this argument lands us in trouble if we compare the case of the secular union sympathizers to that of other union sympathizers who hold exactly the same beliefs for religious reasons. He is correct about that; the claim we made in 1994 about the differing "epistemic foundations" of secular and religious obligations is inconsistent with our general argument, and we have abandoned it.

38. Andrew Koppelman, "Is It Fair to Give Religion Special Treatment?" *University of Illinois Law Review* 571 (2006). In an effort to remedy what he sees as a failure of our view, Koppelman formulates and endorses a theory of secular and religious interests, derived from the philosophical arguments of Charles Taylor.

39. McConnell, for example, has suggested that "the free exercise clause accords a special, protected status to religious conscience not because religious judgments are better, truer, or more likely to be moral than nonreligious judgments, but because the obligations entailed by religion transcend the individual and are outside the individual's control." Michael W. McConnell, "The Origins and Historical Understanding of the Free Exercise of Religion," 103 *Harvard Law Review* 1409, 1497 (1990). As we say in the text, we think it unnecessary, for purposes of defending Equal Liberty, to decide whether the metaphysical underpinnings of McConnell's claim are true or false. But two things are worth noting: first, it is inconceivable that the Constitution should be understood to align itself with or against a specific theological claim like the one McConnell makes; and second, if construed as a purported distinction between the subjective experience of religious and secular commitments, McConnell's claim is plainly false. Secular moral requirements, too, are experienced as duties that "transcend the individual and are outside the individual's control." Persons who recognize such obligations are not at all likely to believe, for example, that their duties to care for their children, or to refrain from harming others, or to aid the weak are optional: they can and do experience these as binding moral strictures, albeit strictures that do not emanate from a mystical spirit or being.

40. See, e.g., Christopher G. Lund, "A Matter of Constitutional Luck: The General Applicability Requirement in Free Exercise Jurisprudence," 26 *Harvard Journal of Law and Public Policy* 627, 648–649 (2003).

41. See Americans with Disabilities Act of 1990, Pub. L. No. 101–336, §§ 101–103, 104 Stat. 327, 330–333 (codified at 42 U.S.C. §§ 12111–13).

42. The Peyote Case, 494 U.S. at 901–902 (O'Connor, J., concurring in the judgment).

43. See Church of the Lukumi Babalu Aye, 508 U.S. 520.

44. Board of Airport Commissioners v. Jews for Jesus, Inc., 482 U.S. 569 (1987).

45. United States v. Seeger, 380 U.S. 163, 176 (1965).

IV. Ten Commandments, Three Plastic Reindeer, and One Nation . . . Indivisible

1. Lynch v. Donnelly, 465 U.S. 668 (1984).

2. Ibid. at 688 (O'Connor, J., concurring).

3. For an early critique, see Steven D. Smith, "Symbols, Perceptions, and Doctrinal Illusions: Establishment Neutrality and the 'No Endorsement' Test," 86 *Michigan Law Review* 266 (1987).

4. Lee v. Weisman, 505 U.S. 577, 631, 640–644 (1992) (Scalia, J., dissenting). See also the milder dissent by Justice Kennedy in County of Allegheny v. American Civil Liberties Union, 492 U.S. 573, 655 (1989) (concurring in the judgment in part and dissenting in part), the first case in which the Supreme Court required a town to take down its Christmas display; the Supreme Court eventually upheld the Pawtucket display at issue in *Lynch* on the ground that it was sufficiently secular to pass the relevant tests, including, in Justice O'Connor's opinion, the endorsement test.

5. Lee, 505 U.S. at 642.

6. According to the *Lynch* Court, the crèche originally "cost the City $1365; it now is valued at $200. The erection and dismantling of the crèche costs the City about $20 per year; nominal expenses are incurred in lighting the crèche. No money has been expended on its maintenance for the past 10 years." 465 U.S. at 671.

7. Myron Stoller, a Jewish retail merchant who ran a store in Pawtucket, testified at trial that the city's holiday display was important to his business, though from a commercial standpoint he did not think that it mattered whether the display included a nativity scene alongside its Santa Claus. Donnelly v. Lynch, 525 F. Supp. 1150, 1159 (Dist. R.I. 1981).

8. Will Herberg, *Protestant-Catholic-Jew: An Essay in American Religious Sociology* 36 (2d ed. 1960). Herberg observed that "to have a name and identity, one must belong somewhere; and more and more one 'belongs' in America by belonging to a religious community, which tells one *what* he *is*." Ibid. at 40.

9. Plessy v. Ferguson, 163 U.S. 537, 551 (1896).

10. Ibid. at 560 (Harlan, J., dissenting).

11. The concept of social meaning also figured prominently in one of the most powerful justifications for Brown v. Board of Education, 347 U.S. 483, 494 (1954), the case in which the Supreme Court repudiated *Plessy's* doctrine that "separate but equal" facilities could satisfy the demands of the Equal Protec-

tion Clause. At the time, critics of the decision suggested that segregated institutions might be constitutionally acceptable if they were in fact equally good. In a famous article, Charles L. Black Jr. replied that separate was not equal because "the social meaning of segregation is the putting of the Negro in a position of walled-off inferiority." Charles L. Black, "The Lawfulness of the Segregation Decisions," 69 *Yale Law Journal* 421, 427 (1960).

12. Justice O'Connor wrote that "the overall holiday setting changes what viewers may fairly understand to be the purpose of the display—as a typical museum setting, though not neutralizing the religious content of a religious painting, negates any message of endorsement of that content." Lynch, 465 U.S. at 692 (concurring opinion).

13. As Justice O'Connor herself has pointed out, "There is always *someone* who, with a particular quantum of knowledge, reasonably might perceive a particular action as an endorsement of religion. A State has not made religion relevant to standing in the political community simply because a particular viewer of a display might feel uncomfortable." Capitol Square Review and Advisory Board v. Pinette, 515 U.S. 753, 80 (1995) (O'Connor, J., with whom Breyer, J. and Souter, J., join, concurring in part and concurring in the judgment).

14. See Glassroth v. Moore, 229 F. Supp. 2d 1290, 1294–1295 (M.D. Ala. 2002).

15. Though Paulson had prevailed over the city in several court rulings, San Diego continues to look for ways to keep the cross in place. Kelly Wheeler, "Judge Refuses Hearing on Motion to Vacate Mount Soledad Cross Ruling," *City News Service,* Oct. 31, 2005 (available on Lexis/Nexis); Randal C. Archibold, "High on a Hill above San Diego, a Church-State Fight Plays Out," *New York Times,* Oct. 1, 2005, p. A9.

16. Stone v. Graham, 449 U.S. 39 (1981); ibid. at 39 n. 1 (quoting Ky. Rev. Stat. § 158.178[2]).

17. See McCreary County v. American Civil Liberties Union, 125 S. Ct. 2722, 2728–31 (2005). *McCreary* dealt only with the courthouse displays. In a related case, the Supreme Court refused to review the appellate court's finding that the schoolhouse display was unconstitutional under the clear precedent in *Stone.* Harlan Co. v. ACLU, 125 S. Ct. 2988 (2005).

18. See, e.g., Isaac Kramnick and R. Laurence Moore, *The Godless Constitution: A Moral Defense of the Secular State* 195 (2d ed. 2005).

19. McCreary County, 125 S. Ct. at 2729–30.

20. Ibid. at 2730–31.

21. County of Allegheny v. American Civil Liberties Union, 492 U.S. at 652–653 (Stevens, J., concurring in part and dissenting in part).

22. McCreary County, 125 S. Ct. at 2741.

23. Ibid. at 2761 (Scalia, J., with whom Thomas, J., Rehnquist, C.J., and Kennedy, J., join, dissenting); ibid. at 2748–57 (Scalia, J., with whom Thomas, J., Rehnquist, C.J., join, dissenting).

24. Van Orden v. Perry, 125 S. Ct. 2854, 2858, 2877 (2005). The Utah, Colorado, and Indiana cases are Anderson v. Salt Lake City Corp., 475 F.2d 29 (10th Cir. 1973); State v. Freedom from Religion Foundation, Inc., 898 P.2d 1013 (Colo. 1995); and Books v. City of Elkhart, 235 F.3d 292 (7th Cir. 2000), respectively.

25. Tex. H. Con Res. 38, 77th Leg.(2001).

26. Van Orden v. Perry, 351 F.3d 173, 180–181 (5th Cir. 2003).

27. Van Orden, 125 S. Ct. at 2871 (Breyer, J., concurring in the judgment).

28. Newdow v. United States Congress, 328 F.3d 466 (9th Cir. 2003); Engel v. Vitale, 370 U.S. 421 (1962).

29. Elk Grove United School District v. Newdow, 542 U.S. 1 (2004).

30. See, e.g., Myers v. Loudon Co. Schools, 418 F.3d 395 (4th Cir. 2005) (pledge does not violate Establishment Clause).

31. Justice O'Connor's observations on this point are apt: "I know of no religion that incorporates the Pledge into its canon, nor one that would count the Pledge as a meaningful expression of religious faith. Even if taken literally, the phrase is merely descriptive; it purports only to identify the United States as a Nation subject to divine authority. That cannot be seen as a serious invocation of God or as an expression of individual submission to divine authority . . . A reasonable observer would note that petitioner school district's policy of Pledge recitation appears under the heading of 'Patriotic Exercises,' and the California law which it implements refers to 'appropriate patriotic exercises.'" Newdow, 124 S. Ct. at 2325 (O'Connor, J., concurring in the judgment).

32. West Virginia State Board of Education v. Barnette, 319 U.S. 624 (1943). On the context, see Vincent Blasi and Seana Shiffrin, "The Story of *West Virginia State Bd. of Education v. Barnette:* The Pledge of Allegiance and the Freedom of Thought," in Michael C. Dorf, ed., *Constitutional Law Stories* 433–475 (2004).

33. Act of June 14, 1954, chap. 297, 68 Stat. 249.

34. In Torcaso v. Watkins, 367 U.S. 488 (1961), a unanimous Supreme Court held unconstitutional a Maryland law that required officeholders in that state to declare their belief in God. The Court rested its decision on the Free Exercise and Establishment Clauses, holding that they (and the Fourteenth Amendment) had incorporated and extended the principle of the "no religious oaths" clause of Article VI. Ibid. at 491–493. It was common at the time of the founding for state laws to insist on such declarations, and the Constitution's pointed elimination of any such requirement was deliberate, widely noticed, and much discussed. Kramnick and Moore, *The Godless Constitution* 32–45.

35. *See* U.S. Const., art. I, § 1, cl. 8; ibid., art. VI, cl. 3.

36. U.S. Const., art. II, § 1, cl. 8.

37. See, e.g., Fed. R. Civ. P. 43(d) ("whenever under these rules an oath is required to be taken, a solemn affirmation may be accepted in lieu thereof"); and Fed. R. Evid. 603, advisory committee's note (explaining that the rule "is designed to afford the flexibility required in dealing with religious adults, atheists, conscientious objectors, mental defectives, and children"). See also Gordon v. Idaho, 778 F.2d 1397, 1400–01 (1985) (district court had a constitutional obligation to find alternative formula for witness who refused, on religious grounds, either to "swear" or to "affirm" that he would tell the truth); and Moore v. United States, 348 U.S. 966 (1955) (per curiam) (witness who declined on religious grounds to use the word "solemnly" in an affirmation to tell the truth could testify without using that word). For a summary of the historical trend allowing affirmations as substitutes for oaths, see Comment, "Religion-plus-Speech: The Constitutionality of Juror Oaths and Affirmations under the First Amendment," 34 *William and Mary Law Review* 287, 293–295 (1992).

38. Of course, no reference to God can be entirely neutral among religions, and the Pledge's reference is not: it refers to a singular "God," whereas some religions respect multiple deities, and others are "not based upon belief in a separate Supreme Being." 124 S. Ct. at 2326 (O'Connor, J., concurring). That is why we say the Pledge's reference to God is *relatively* (not completely) nonsectarian. We regard its theological content as sufficiently minimal to satisfy constitutional requirements, provided that it is coupled with an equally respected and nonreligious alternative.

39. We owe the suggestion to Robert K. Durkee, vice president and secretary of Princeton University. Durkee observed that Princeton has adopted an analogous practice with regard to its alma mater, "Old Nassau," which had referred to university alumni as "my boys" and "her sons." In 1987 the university (which coeducated beginning in 1969) substituted "we sing" and "our hearts" for these words (the change makes sense in context). Princeton's alumni, depending on their generation (and their sentiments), now sing both versions simultaneously, without disruption.

40. Van Orden, 125 S. Ct. at 2871 (concurring opinion).

41. David D. Kirkpatrick, "Conservatives to Seek Voters' Support for Commandments," *New York Times*, June 29, 2005, p. A18.

42. Ibid.

43. Van Orden, 125 S. Ct. at 2871.

44. Noah Feldman, *Divided by God: America's Church-State Problem—and What We Should Do about It* 16, 237 (2005).

45. Stephen D. Smith, *Foreordained Failure: The Quest for a Constitutional Principle of Religious Freedom* 116 (1995).

46. Ibid. at 117.

47. For further discussion, see Christopher L. Eisgruber, *Constitutional Self-Government* 100–101 (2001).

48. Robert Wuthnow, *The Restructuring of American Religion: Society and Faith since World War II* 73, 115 (1988).

49. Feldman, *Divided by God* 16.

50. Ibid. at 242 ("it is largely an interpretive choice to feel excluded by the fact of other people's religion"). Of course, what is at issue is not "the fact of other people's religion," but the fact of government sponsorship and support of it.

51. Ibid. at 240.

52. Plessy, 163 U.S. at 551.

V. God in the Classroom

1. Noah Feldman, *Divided by God: America's Church-State Problem—and What We Should Do about It* 135–148 (2005); Edward J. Larson, *Summer for the Gods: The Scopes Trial and America's Continuing Debate over Science and Religion* (1997); Jerome Lawrence and Robert E. Lee, *Inherit the Wind* (1969).

2. Laurie Goodstein, "Issuing Rebuke, a Judge Rejects Teaching of Intelligent Design," *New York Times*, Dec. 21, 2005, p. A1; idem, "Closing Arguments Made in Trial on Intelligent Design," ibid., Nov. 5, 2005, p. A14.

3. See, e.g., Jodi Wilgoren, "Kansas Board Approves Challenges to Evolution," *New York Times*, Nov. 8, 2005, p. A14; David Stout, "Frist Urges 2 Teachings on Life's Origin," ibid., Aug. 20, 2005, p. A10; Elisabeth Bumiller, "Bush Remarks Roil Debate over Teaching of Evolution," ibid., Aug. 3, 2005, p. A14; and Cornelia Dean, "Evolution Takes a Back Seat in U.S. Classes," ibid., Feb. 1, 2005, p. F1.

4. An excellent recent treatment of these topics is Kent Greenawalt, *Does God Belong in Public Schools?* (2005).

5. See, e.g., Michael W. McConnell, "The Problem of Singling Out Religion," 50 *DePaul Law Review* 1, 10 (2000); idem, "A Response to Professor Marshall," 58 *University of Chicago Law Review* 329, 329 (1991); and Abner Greene, "The Political Balance of the Religion Clauses," 102 *Yale Law Journal* 1611, 1638 (1993).

6. Engel v. Vitale, 370 U.S. 421 (1962).

7. "When the House Judiciary Committee finally held hearings in 1964 on a constitutional amendment to reverse the Court, most of the religious organizations testified in favor of the schoolprayer decision." Louis Fisher, "Nonjudicial Safeguards for Religious Liberty," 70 *University of Cincinnati Law Review* 31, 68 (2001). See also ibid. at 72. In 1992 "the [National Council of Churches] argued in *Lee v. Weisman* that prayers at graduation should be disallowed." John C. Jeffries Jr. and James E. Ryan, "A Political History of the Establishment Clause," 100 *Michigan Law Review* 279, 356 (2001).

8. In Santa Fe Independent School District v. Doe, 530 U.S. 290 (2000), the plaintiffs were Mormon and Catholic. Ibid. at 294. In Lee v. Weisman, 505 U.S. 577 (1992), the plaintiffs were Jewish. Marshall Ingwerson, "High Court's School Prayer Ruling Puts Bush's Voucher Plan in Doubt," *Christian Science Monitor,* June 26, 1992, p. 1; see also Fox Butterfield, "Plaintiffs Are 'Thrilled' by Supreme Court Ruling," *New York Times,* June 25, 1992, p. B11.

9. West Virginia State Board of Education v. Barnette, 319 U.S. 624, 642 (1943).

10. 505 U.S. 577; 530 U.S. 290.

11. See, e.g., Nadine Strossen, "How Much God in the Schools? A Discussion of Religion's Role in the Classroom," 4 *William and Mary Bill of Rights Law Journal* 607, 611–616 (1995); Geoffrey Stone, "In Opposition to the School Prayer Amendment," 50 *University of Chicago Law Review* 823, 835–839 (1983). Walter Dellinger, who served as solicitor general of the United States in the Clinton administration, has vividly described the pressure he felt when obliged to opt out from school-run religious ceremonies while growing up. Walter Dellinger, "Say Amen, or Else: Piety and the Law: The Court Revisits the School Prayer Decision," *Washington Post,* Nov. 3, 1991, p. C1.

12. As Kenneth L. Karst has observed, "officially sponsored prayer . . . tells school children who do not share the dominant religious faiths represented by the prayer that they are outsiders, that they do not belong as full members of the community . . . The school board's message to the religious outsider is clear: 'This is our town.'" Kenneth L. Karst, "Paths to Belonging: The Constitution and Cultural Identity," 64 *North Carolina Law Review* 303, 358–359 (1986).

13. See, e.g., Good News Club v. Milford Central School, 533 U.S. 98 (2001); Board of Education v. Mergens, 496 U.S. 226 (1990); see also Douglas Laycock, "The Meaning of Separation," 70 *University of Chicago Law Review* 1667, 1692 (2003) ("not once has the Court held that separation requires or even permits limits on religious speech that has not been sponsored or preferred by government. The school prayer cases reflect the view that government should not support or sponsor religion, not the view that government should restrict religion or keep it out of public view").

14. McConnell, "A Response to Professor Marshall" 329.

15. Tinker v. Des Moines Independent School District, 393 U.S. 503, 506 (1969).

16. Hedges v. Wauconda Community Unit High School District No. 118, 807 F. Supp. 444, 463 (N.D. Ill. 1992). In the end, this conclusion proved irrelevant twice over: the district court granted relief on other grounds, and the U.S. Court of Appeals for the Seventh Circuit rightly held that religious publications were entitled to the same free speech protections as were secular ones. Hedges v. Wauconda Community Unit High School District No. 118, 9 F.3d 1295 (7th Cir. 1993).

17. Good News Club, 533 U.S. 98; Laycock, "The Meaning of Separation" 1692. Teachers, too, have free speech rights, but theirs are limited by the requirements of their job. See, e.g., R. West Donehower, "Boring Lessons: Defining the Limits of a Teacher's First Amendment Right to Speak through the Curriculum," 102 *Michigan Law Review* 517 (2003). These requirements include the constitutional duty to respect the limits imposed by the Establishment Clause; public school teachers, unlike their students, are agents of the state.

18. Applying this principle may in practice require some subtle distinctions; for a discussion, see Kathleen A. Brady, "The Push to Privatize Religious Expression: Are We Missing Something?" 70 *Fordham Law Review* 1147 (2002).

19. 319 U.S. 624.

20. Ibid. at 642.

21. Nick Madigan, "Snub of Creationists Prompts U.S. Inquiry," *New York Times,* Feb. 3, 2003, p. A11.

22. Kris Axtman, "Texas Wrangles over Bias in School Textbooks," *Christian Science Monitor,* July 22, 2002, p. 3; Hilary DeVries, "Book Banning: Saving Morals or Giving Up Key Freedoms?" ibid., Nov. 27, 1981, p. B14.

23. 505 U.S. at 580.

24. 530 U.S. at 297–298, 302–303.

25. Wallace v. Jaffree, 472 U.S. 38 (1985).

26. Ibid. at 60.

27. Ibid. at 69 (concurring opinion), quoting Lynch v. Donnelly, 465 U.S. 668, 688 (O'Connor, J., concurring).

28. Andrew Koppelman, following the lead of the *Jaffree* dissenters, suggests that there was indeed a possible secular purpose for the Alabama amendment's prayer-focused text, namely, eliminating "considerable confusion" about whether the Court's own decisions prohibited silent, student-initiated prayer in schools. Andrew Koppelman, "Secular Purpose," 88 *Virginia Law Review* 87, 148 (2002). If this were a plausible explanation for Alabama's enactment of the statute, it would indeed answer the majority's argument. According to the *Jaffree* majority, however, "In this case, it is undisputed that at the time of the [statute's] enactment . . . there was no governmental practice impeding students from silently praying." 472 U.S. at 57 and n. 45.

29. Debbie Kaminer, "Bringing Organized Prayer In through the Back Door: How Moment-of-Silence Legislation for the Public Schools Violates the Establishment Clause," 13 *Stanford Law and Public Policy Review* 267, 300 and n. 296 (2002).

30. Christopher L. Eisgruber, "Madison's Wager: Religious Liberty in the Constitutional Order," 89 *Northwestern University Law Review* 347, 395–396 (1995).

31. On prophylactic rules in general, see David Strauss, "The Ubiquity of Pro-

phylactic Rules," 55 *University of Chicago Law Review* 190 (1988). We examine the topic in greater detail in Chapter 6.

32. School District of Abington Township v. Schempp, 374 U.S. 203 (1963).

33. Ibid. at 225.

34. See, e.g., Paul C. Vitz, *Religion and Traditional Values in Public School Textbooks: An Empirical Study* (1985); Jay D. Wexler, "Preparing for a Clothed Public Square: Teaching about Religion, Civic Education, and the Constitution," 43 *William and Mary Law Review* 1159, 1172–1191 (2002). In parts of the country, on the other hand, the Bible remains a much-used textbook. Craig Timberg, "Bible's Second Coming: Scriptures Returning to the Schools as a Text for History and Literature," *Washington Post,* June 4, 2000, p. A1.

35. Mozert v. Hawkins, 827 F.2d 1058 (6th Cir. 1987). The case has generated a considerable secondary literature. See, e.g., Nomi May Stolzenberg, "'He Drew a Circle That Shut Me Out': Assimilation, Indoctrination, and the Paradox of a Liberal Education," 106 *Harvard Law Review* 581 (1993); Stephen Bates, *Battleground: One Mother's Crusade, the Religious Right, and the Struggle for Control of Our Classrooms* (1993); Stephen Macedo, "Liberal Civic Education and Religious Fundamentalism: The Case of God v. John Rawls," 105 *Ethics* 468 (1995); Christopher L. Eisgruber, "How Do Liberal Democracies Teach Values?" in Stephen Macedo and Yale Tamir, eds., *Nomos XLIII: Moral and Political Education* 58–86 (2002).

36. Bates, *Battleground* 16, 21–22, 29, 81, 204.

37. Ibid. at 32.

38. Pierce v. Society of Sisters, 268 U.S. 510 (1925).

39. Eisgruber, "How Do Liberal Democracies Teach Values?" 67–69, 82.

40. George Gallup Jr. and D. Michael Lindsay, *Surveying the Religious Landscape* 38 (1999).

41. Ibid.

42. Laurie Goodstein, "Teaching of Creationism Is Endorsed in New Survey," *New York Times,* Aug. 31, 2005, p. A9.

43. Epperson v. Arkansas, 393 U.S. 97 (1968).

44. Ibid. at 103 (emphasis added).

45. Edwards v. Aguillard, 482 U.S. 578 (1987).

46. Laurence Tribe, *American Constitutional Law* 1208–1209 (2d ed. 1988).

47. Our understanding of the topic owes much to Greenawalt, *Does God Belong in Public Schools?* 101–115 and "Establishing Religious Ideas: Evolution, Creationism, and Intelligent Design," 17 *Notre Dame Journal of Law, Ethics, and Public Policy* 321 (2003).

48. Greenawalt, "Establishing Religious Ideas" 358.

49. Ibid. at 356–358.

50. Ibid. at 374; William Paley, *Natural Theology; or Evidences of the Existence and Attributes of the Deity, Collected from the Appearances of Nature* 9–10 (1809).

51. For leading treatments of the positions for and against intelligent design, see Michael Behe, *Darwin's Black Box: The Biochemical Challenge to Evolution* (1998); and Richard Dawkins, *Blind Watchmaker: Why Evidence of Evolution Reveals a Universe without Design* (1996).

52. Stephen Carter, *The Culture of Disbelief* 168–169 (1993).

53. See, e.g., David Kinney, "DiFancesco Signs Sex Ed Abstinence, Nurse Overtime Bills," *Newark Star-Ledger,* Jan. 3, 2002, p. 20.

54. Greenawalt, "Establishing Religious Ideas" 327–328.

55. Ibid. at 367–368.

56. This conclusion is consistent with the ruling of Judge John E. Jones III, the trial court judge in the Dover, Pennsylvania, intelligent design case. Judge Jones correctly observed that "the fact that a scientific theory cannot yet render an explanation on every point should not be used as a pretext to thrust an untestable alternative hypothesis grounded in religion into the scientific classroom." Kitzmiller v. Dover Area School District, 2005 U.S. Dist. LEXIS 33647 (2005).

57. Epperson, 393 U.S. at 99 and n. 3.

58. Ibid. at 107–109 and n. 16.

59. For an argument of this kind, see Michael A. Berg, "The Religious Right, Constitutional Values, and the Lemon Test," 1995 *Annual Survey of American Law* 37, 74–76 (1995) (recommending that courts examine the "political context" of a statute in order to determine whether it has the effect of advancing religion).

60. Meyer v. Nebraska, 262 U.S. 390 (1923); Bartels v. Iowa, 262 U.S. 404 (1923). The bans in these cases applied even to private teaching, and so raised more general questions of personal liberty.

61. Quoted in Epperson, 393 U.S. at 100 and n. 5.

62. Ibid. at 104–105.

63. Board of Education, Island Trees Union Free School District v. Pico, 457 U.S. 853 (1982); Meyer, 262 U.S. 390.

64. Freiler v. Tangipahoa Parish Board of Education, 185 F.3d 337 (5th Cir. 1999).

65. Ibid. at 341.

66. Catherine Prentke has argued that the Tangipahoa Parish disclaimer is impermissibly sectarian because it specifically references one creation story—namely, the biblical one. Catherine O. Prentke, "The Establishment Clause and the Constitutionality of Teaching Human Origins in Public Schools" 69–70 (Senior thesis, Princeton University, 2003). Prentke's objection is reason-

able, and one might insist that school districts draft more neutral disclaimers. But the needed modifications would be very modest.

67. See Behe, *Darwin's Black Box*.

VI. Public Dollars, Religious Programs

1. See U.S. Const., amend. I (*"Congress* shall make no law respecting an establishment of religion . . .") (emphasis added); Permoli v. Municipality No. 1 of City of New Orleans, 44 U.S. 589, 609 (1845).

2. See Everson v. Board of Education, 330 U.S. 1, 15 (1947); ibid. at 22 (Jackson, J., dissenting); ibid. at 29 (Rutledge, J., with whom Frankfurter, J., Jackson, J., and Burton, J., join, dissenting).

3. See ibid. at 15–16; ibid. at 31 (Rutledge, J., with whom Frankfurter, J., Jackson, J., and Burton, J., join, dissenting).

4. Ibid. at 18.

5. Ibid. at 16.

6. See ibid. at 17–18.

7. Ibid. at 18.

8. Ibid. at 19.

9. Thomas Hobbes, *Leviathan* (1651) 185–186 (Penguin 1985).

10. Justice Black seems to have been an Equal Liberty sheep in separationist clothing. His *Everson* opinion abruptly swerves from its separationist line to include the following famous dictum: "New Jersey cannot consistently with the 'establishment of religion' clause of the First Amendment contribute tax-raised funds to the support of an institution which teaches the tenets and faith of any church. On the other hand . . . New Jersey cannot hamper its citizens in the free exercise of their own religion. . . . [I]t cannot exclude individual Catholics, Lutherans, Mohammedans, Baptists, Jews, Methodists, Non-believers, Presbyterians, or the members of any other faith, *because of their faith, or lack of it*, from receiving the benefits of public welfare legislation . . . we must be careful, in protecting the citizens of New Jersey against state-established churches, to be sure that we do not inadvertently prohibit New Jersey from extending its general state law benefits to all its citizens without regard to their religious belief . . . Th[e First] Amendment requires the state to be a neutral in its relations with groups of religious believers and non-believers; it does not require the state to be their adversary. State power is no more to be used so as to handicap religions than it is to favor them." 330 U.S. at 16–18.

11. The "meaningful secular alternative" and "nonpreferentialism" requirements dovetail closely with existing law. See, e.g., Zelman v. Simmons-Harris, 536 U.S. 639, 669 (2002) (O'Connor, J., concurring) ("Courts are instructed to con-

sider two factors: first, whether the program administers aid in a neutral fashion, without differentiation based on the religious status of beneficiaries or providers of services; second . . . whether beneficiaries of indirect aid have a genuine choice among religious and nonreligious organizations when determining the organization to which they will direct that aid"). Likewise, the Personal Responsibility and Work Opportunity Reconciliation Act of 1996, Pub. L. No. 104–193, § 104, 110 Stat. 2105, 2161 (codified at 42 U.S.C. § 604a [2004]), allows states to provide services through faith-based organizations, but only if organizations are selected on the basis of neutral criteria; only if the organizations themselves do not discriminate on the basis of religion; and only if the state provides alternative, timely, and convenient secular services to beneficiaries who want it.

12. An extensive and balanced discussion appears in Stephen Macedo, *Diversity and Distrust: Civic Education in a Multicultural Democracy* 41–147 (2000).

13. See, e.g., Joseph Viteritti, "Blaine's Wake: School Choice, the First Amendment, and State Constitutional Law," 21 *Harvard Journal of Law and Public Policy* 657, 665–679 (1998). See also Diane Ravitch, *The Great School Wars: New York City, 1805–1973* (1974); Stephen K. Green, "The Blaine Amendment Reconsidered," 36 *American Journal of Legal History* 38 (1992).

14. Macedo, *Diversity and Distrust* 54–87; John C. Jeffries and James E. Ryan, "A Political History of the Establishment Clause," 100 *Michigan Law Review* 279, 297–306, 312–318 (2001).

15. Jeffries and Ryan, "Political History of Establishment Clause" 306–307.

16. Robert Wuthnow, *The Restructuring of American Religion: Society and Faith since World War II* 93–95 (1988).

17. Ibid. at 198; Jeffries and Ryan, "Political History of Establishment Clause" 328–338.

18. See, e.g., James E. Ryan and Michael Heise, "The Political Economy of School Choice," 111 *Yale Law Journal* 2043, 2082, and n. 209 (2002); Terry M. Moe, *Schools, Vouchers, and the American Public* (2001); David A. Bositis, "School Vouchers along the Color Line," *New York Times*, Aug. 15, 2001, p. A23.

19. Jeffries and Ryan, "Political History of Establishment Clause" 360–361.

20. Macedo, *Diversity and Distrust* 98–99. David B. Tyack, "The Perils of Pluralism: The Background of the *Pierce* Case," 74 *American Historical Review* 74 (1968).

21. Pierce v. Society of Sisters, 268 U.S. 510 (1925).

22. Ibid. at 534–535.

23. Ibid. at 535.

24. See, e.g., Barbara Woodhouse, "Who Owns the Child? *Meyer, Pierce* and the Child as Property," 33 *William and Mary Law Review* 995 (1992).

25. Christopher L. Eisgruber, "How Do Liberal Democracies Teach Values?" in

Stephen Macedo and Yael Tamir, eds., *Nomos XLIII: Moral and Political Education* 65 (2002).

26. The egalitarian benefits of vouchers are touted in, for example, John E. Coons and Stephen D. Sugarman, *Making School Choice Work for All Families* (1999).

27. Discrimination against groups that practice animal sacrifice was at the heart of Church of the Lukumi Babalu Aye, Inc. v. City of Hialeah, 508 U.S. 520 (1993), which we discussed in Chapters 1 and 3.

28. Of course, most public school systems depend upon contributions from corporations, businesses, and individuals without children, so it is entirely possible that the tax savings to Christian parents would not suffice to pay for private schooling. But we put that possibility to one side in order to analyze the underlying issue of principle.

29. San Antonio Independent School District v. Rodriguez, 411 U.S. 1, 35–37 (1973).

30. Palmer v. Thompson, 403 U.S. 217, 220 (1971).

31. Lawrence G. Sager, "Fair Measure: The Legal Status of Underenforced Constitutional Norms," 91 *Harvard Law Review* 1212 (1978).

32. "Secularism" is ambiguous in a way that invites confusion. "Secular" means "of or relating to the worldly or temporal" or "not overtly or specifically religious." At one time dictionaries distinguished sharply (and some still do) between "secularity" and "secularism." "Secularity" meant "something secular" or "the quality or state of being secular." "Secularism," by contrast, meant "indifference to or rejection or exclusion of religion and religious considerations." See, e.g., *Webster's Seventh New Collegiate Dictionary* (1972). The word "secularity," however, now seems rarely used, and people employ "secularism" to refer both to the idea of "something secular" and to a doctrine that rejects or excludes religion. The two meanings are different, and insofar as we defend secularism in this book, we have in mind the meaning that coincides with "secularity"—that is, we are defending the idea that institutions should not be overtly or specifically religious, not the quite different idea that they should reject or exclude religion.

33. Lemon v. Kurtzman, 403 U.S. 602 (1971).

34. Ibid. at 608, 610.

35. 536 U.S. 639.

36. See ibid. at 647.

37. Ibid. at 655.

38. Ibid. at 703 (Souter J., with whom Stevens, J., Ginsburg, J., and Breyer, J., join, dissenting).

39. Ibid. at 705.

40. Ibid. at 663 (O'Connor, J., concurring).

41. We do not mean to claim that all the justices agreed with us about this point. Though Souter and the other dissenters challenged the majority's claim that the voucher program allowed parents real choices, this question was ultimately immaterial to them. They endorsed a separation theory, pursuant to which the voucher program was unconstitutional because it subsidized religious education, even if it did so as a result of true parental choice.

42. Ira C. Lupu and Robert Tuttle, "Sites of Redemption: A Wide-Angle Look at Government Vouchers and Sectarian Service Providers," 18 *Journal of Law and Politics* 539, 586 (2002).

43. See Zelman, 536 U.S. at 704 and n. 11.

44. For example, the Supreme Court has ruled that the National Labor Relations Act does not authorize the National Labor Relations Board to regulate church-operated secondary schools. National Labor Relations Board v. Catholic Bishop, 440 U.S. 490 (1979). Such schools may nevertheless be subject to state regulation. See, e.g., Catholic High School Association v. Culvert, 753 F.2d 1161 (2d Cir. 1985).

45. See Martha Minow, "Reforming School Reform," 68 *Fordham Law Review* 257, 262 (1999).

46. Lupu and Tuttle, "Sites of Redemption" 577.

47. Ibid.

48. Ibid. at 598.

49. Ibid.

50. Ibid. at 599.

51. Ibid. at 600.

52. Ibid. at 605.

53. William A. Galston, *Liberal Pluralism: The Implications of Value Pluralism for Political Theory and Practice* 18–20, 102, 108–109 (2002); Stephen G. Gilles, "On Educating Children: A Parentalist Manifesto," 63 *University of Chicago Law Review* 937 (1996); Michael W. McConnell, "Education Disestablishment: Why Democratic Values Are Ill-Served by Democratic Control of Schooling," in Macedo and Tamir, *Moral and Political Education* 87; idem, "Multiculturalism, Majoritarianism, and Educational Choice: What Does Our Constitutional Tradition Have to Say?" 1991 *University of Chicago Legal Forum* 123 (1991).

54. See, e.g., Gilles, "On Educating Children" 1024–25; McConnell, "Education Disestablishment" 120.

55. Macedo, *Diversity and Distrust* 270–271; Stephen Macedo, "Constituting Civil Society: School Vouchers, Religious Nonprofits, and Liberal Public Values," 75 *Chicago-Kent Law Review* 417, 418 (2000).

56. Macedo makes this point well. See, e.g., Macedo, *Diversity and Distrust* 70–71, 120, 237.

57. Ibid. at 271.

58. During the 1960s and 1970s some school districts promoted private parental choice–through subsidies for private schools, options within the public school system, or, in one case, simply by closing the public schools entirely–in an effort to circumvent the constitutional prohibition on racially segregated schools. The Supreme Court ruled these plans unconstitutional. Griffin v. Prince Edward County School Bd., 377 U.S. 218 (1964) (closure of public schools); Green v. New Kent County School Bd., 391 U.S. 430 (1968) (parental choice plan within public schools); Norwood v. Harrison, 413 U.S. 455 (1973) (subsidies for textbooks).

59. Martha Minow nicely summarizes the competing factors in Minow, "Public and Private Partnerships: Accounting for the New Religion," 116 *Harvard Law Review* 1229, 1242–55 (2003). See also Joseph Viteritti, "Reading *Zelman:* The Triumph of Pluralism, and Its Effects on Liberty, Equality, and Choice," 76 *Southern California Law Review* 1105, 1175–82 (2003).

60. Locke v. Davey, 540 U.S. 712 (2004).

61. Ibid. at 715–717.

62. Ibid. at 716; see also Wash. Const., art. I, § 11 ("No public money or property shall be appropriated for or applied to any religious worship, exercise or instruction, or the support of any religious establishment").

63. Locke, 540 U.S. at 726–727 (Scalia, J., dissenting).

64. Ibid. at 722.

65. See ibid. at 719.

66. Ibid. at 722–723.

67. The real puzzle is about only three justices: Rehnquist, Kennedy, and O'Connor. The other four in the majority—Stevens, Souter, Breyer, and Ginsburg—dissented in *Zelman,* and it is easier to understand why they might have thought that the use of state money would raise Establishment Clause concerns.

68. Locke, 540 U.S. at 718.

69. See ibid. at 728 (Scalia, J., dissenting).

70. See Rust v. Sullivan, 500 U.S. 173 (1991); South Dakota v. Dole, 483 U.S. 203 (1987); Harris v. McRae, 448 U.S. 297 (1980); Maher v. Roe, 432 U.S. 464 (1977). Michael W. McConnell explored the problem in an oft-cited article, "The Selective Funding Problem: Abortion and Religious Schools," 104 *Harvard Law Review* 989 (1991).

71. Locke, 540 U.S. at 729 (Scalia, J., dissenting).

72. Miranda v. Arizona, 384 U.S. 436, 446 (1966); see also Dickerson v. United States, 530 U.S. 428 (2000).

73. David Strauss, "The Ubiquity of Prophylactic Rules," 55 *University of Chicago Law Review* 190 (1988).

74. On the relevance of strategic judgment to constitutional adjudication, see,

e.g., Lawrence G. Sager, "Foreword: State Courts and the Strategic Space between the Norms and Rules of Constitutional Law," 63 *Texas Law Review* 190 (1988); Richard H. Fallon Jr., *Implementing the Constitution* (2000); and Christopher L. Eisgruber, *Constitutional Self-Government* 136–140, 168–175 (2001).

75. Michael Seidman has suggested that the costs of the *Miranda* rule to law enforcement are low because it is ineffective: officers, he suggests, are free to use unfair interrogation techniques provided only that they give the necessary warnings. L. Michael Seidman, *Unsettled Constitution: A New Defense of Constitutionalism and Judicial Review* 100–101 (2001).

76. On the politics of the Bush initiative, see, e.g., Amy E. Black, Douglas L. Koopman, and David K. Ryden, *Of Little Faith: The Politics of George W. Bush's Faith-Based Proposals* (2004).

77. See, for example, Charles L. Glenn, *The Ambiguous Embrace: Government and Faith-Based Schools and Social Agencies* (2002); see also Marvin Olasky, *The Tragedy of American Compassion* (1992).

78. A thoughtful, qualified endorsement of such partnerships is Martha Minow, *Partners, Not Rivals: Privatization and the Public Good* (2002).

79. Stephen Monsma, *When Sacred and Secular Mix: Religious Nonprofit Organizations and Public Money* (1996); see also Elbert Lin et al., "Faith in the Courts? The Legal and Political Future of Federally Funded Faith-Based Initiatives," 20 *Yale Law and Policy Review* 183, 186–190 (2002); and Minow, "Public and Private Partnerships" 1237–42. Clinton administration statutes allowing for "charitable choice" include the Personal Responsibility and Work Opportunity Reconciliation Act of 1996, codified at 42 U.S.C. 604a (2004); the Community Services Block Grant of 1998, codified at 42 U.S.C. 9920 (2004); and the Children's Health Act of 2000, codified at 42 U.S.C. 300x-65 (2004).

80. White House adviser John DiIulio, who ran the president's office of faith-based services during the first six months of the administration, claims that the president's legislative efforts foundered because the president's aides were too eager to please right-wing evangelicals and beltway libertarians. Ron Suskind, "Why Are These Men Laughing?" *Esquire,* Jan. 1, 2003, pp. 96–105.

81. Ira C. Lupu and Robert W. Tuttle, "The Faith-Based Initiative and the Constitution," 55 *DePaul Law Review* 1, 8–12 (2005); Mary Leonard, "Bush Pressed Funding for Faith Groups," *Boston Globe,* Nov. 30, 2003, p. A1.

82. Lupu and Tuttle, "The Faith-Based Initiative and the Constitution" 13–14.

83. Mark Chaves, *Congregations in America* 78 (2004).

84. Ibid. at 93.

85. Robert Wuthnow, *Saving America? Faith-Based Services and the Future of Civil Society* 148–149, 172–174 (2004).

86. Martha Minow, "Choice or Commonality: Welfare and Schooling after the End of Welfare as We Knew It," 49 *Duke Law Journal* 493, 535 (1999).

87. Lupu and Tuttle, "Sites of Redemption" 561–562, 581; see also Minow, "Choice or Commonality" 532–533.
88. Chaves, *Congregations in America* 58–67, 75–78; Wuthnow, *Saving America?* 158–161.
89. Wuthnow, *Saving America?* 161.
90. We thus agree with the outcome in Freedom from Religion Foundation v. MacCallum, 214 F. Supp. 2d 905, 915 (W.D. Wisc. 2002), aff'd, 324 F.3d 880 (7th Cir. 2003), which upheld Wisconsin's subsidies of a religiously based alcohol and drug treatment program; the Court emphasized that Wisconsin provided a secular alternative and took steps to ensure that participants were aware that a secular option was available.
91. Not all such exemptions are constitutional. We discuss the permissible scope of legislatively crafted exemptions in Chapter 7.
92. An eye-opening account of the difficulties prison officials face when choosing Muslim chaplains is Paul M. Barrett, "Captive Audience: How a Chaplain Spread Extremism to an Inmate Flock," *Wall Street Journal,* Feb. 5, 2003, p. A1. See also Lisa Miller, "Religion: Inside the Competitive New World of Prison Ministries," *Wall Street Journal,* Sept. 7, 1999, p. B1; Eric Lichtblau, "Report Warns of Infiltration by Al Qaeda in U.S. Prisons," *New York Times,* May 5, 2004, p. A24.

VII. Legislative Responsibility for Religious Freedom

1. Goldman v. Weinberger, 475 U.S. 503 (1986).
2. Ibid. at 508–510; ibid. at 512–513 (Stevens, J., with whom Powell and White, JJ., join, concurring).
3. National Defense Authorization Act for Fiscal Years 1988 and 1989, Pub. L. No. 100–180, § 508(a)(2), 101 Stat. 1019, 1086 (1987) (codified at 10 U.S.C. § 774 [2004]). In particular, Congress provided that "a member of the armed forces may wear an item of religious apparel while wearing the uniform of the member's armed force" (10 U.S.C. § 774[a]), except in circumstances in which the military determines that "the wearing of the item would interfere with the performance of the member's military duties" (ibid., § 774[b][1]), or if the military determines by regulation that "the item of apparel is not neat and conservative" (ibid., § 774[b][2]). For the legislative history of this provision, see Dwight H. Sullivan, "The Congressional Response to *Goldman v. Weinberger,*" 121 *Military Law Review* 125 (1988).
4. Employment Division v. Smith, 494 U.S. 872 (1990).
5. Lyng v. Northwest Indian Cemetery Protective Association, 485 U.S. 439 (1988).
6. American Indian Religious Freedom Act Amendments of 1994, Pub. L. No. 103–344, § 2, 108 Stat. 3125 (codified at 42 U.S.C. § 1996a [2004]). Congress also responded to the Court's decision in the *Peyote Case* with a far more dramatic,

sweeping, and problematic piece of legislation, the Religious Freedom Restoration Act (RFRA). We take up the tangled tale of RFRA later in this chapter.

7. U.S. House Committee on Appropriations, *Department of the Interior and Related Agencies Appropriations Bill,* 100th Cong., 2d sess., 1988, H.R. Rep. 100–713, p. 72.

8. 10 U.S.C. § 774 (2004).

9. Robert A. Wuthnow, *The Restructuring of American Religion: Society and Faith since World War II* (1988).

10. For example, Congressman Stephen Solarz sought congressional support for the Santerians who were fighting a discriminatory prohibition on the ritual sacrifice of animals, but could not find a single representative willing to join him—"the Santeria religion was too unpopular to touch." Douglas Laycock, "Conceptual Gulfs in *City of Boerne v. Flores*," 39 *William and Mary Law Review* 743, 776 (1998). Whereas the Santerians could get only a single vote in Congress, they eventually won all nine in the Supreme Court. Church of the Lukumi Babalu Aye, Inc. v. City of Hialeah, 508 U.S. 520 (1993).

11. Hernandez v. Commissioner, 490 U.S. 680, 698–700 (1989).

12. Revenue Ruling 93-73 (Nov. 1, 1993); Elizabeth MacDonald, "Scientologists and IRS Settle for $12.5 Million," *Wall Street Journal,* Dec. 30, 1997, p. A12; Douglas Frantz, "Taxes and Tactics: Scientology's Puzzling Journey from Tax Rebel to Tax Exempt," *New York Times,* March 9, 1997, p. 1; *http://www.wsj.com.*

13. See, e.g., Alan Cowell, "Germany Will Place Scientology under Nationwide Surveillance," *New York Times,* June 7, 1997, p. 1.

14. See, e.g., Clay v. United States, 403 U.S. 698 (1971); see also Sicurella v. United States, 348 U.S. 385 (1955).

15. 42 U.S.C. § 2000e-1(a) (2004).

16. See, e.g., Ira C. Lupu, "Reconstructing the Establishment Clause: The Case against Discretionary Accommodation of Religion," 140 *University of Pennsylvania Law Review* 555 (1991).

17. 26 U.S.C. § 501(c)(3) (2004).

18. United States v. Seeger, 380 U.S. 163 (1965).

19. Cutter v. Wilkinson, 125 S. Ct. 2113, 2121, 2122, 2123 (2005).

20. Ibid. at 2119 n. 5.

21. Estate of Thornton v. Caldor, 472 U.S. 703 (1985).

22. Texas Monthly v. Bullock, 489 U.S. 1 (1989).

23. 472 U.S. at 710.

24. See Texas Monthly, 489 U.S. at 14–17 (plurality opinion of Brennan, J., in which Marshall, J., and Stevens, J., join); ibid. at 28–29 (Blackmun, J., with whom O'Connor, J., joins, concurring in the judgment); ibid. at 25–26 (White, J., concurring in the judgment).

25. Corporation of the Presiding Bishop of the Church of Jesus Christ of Latter-day Saints v. Amos, 483 U.S. 327 (1987).

26. U.S. Const., amend. XIV, § 5 ("The Congress shall have power to enforce, by appropriate legislation, the provisions of this article").

27. Lawrence G. Sager, "Fair Measure: The Legal Status of Underenforced Constitutional Norms," 91 *Harvard Law Review* 1212 (1978). For a full theoretical explanation of the idea, see idem, *Justice in Plainclothes: A Theory of American Constitutional Practice* 84–128 (2004).

28. U.S. Const., amend. XIV, § 5; see also amend. XIII, § 2 (authorizing Congress to enforce amendment prohibiting slavery); amend. XV, § 2 (same for amendment prohibiting racial discrimination in elections); amend. XIX (same for amendment granting women the right to vote); amend. XXIV, § 2 (same for amendment prohibiting poll taxes).

29. Plyler v. Doe, 457 U.S. 202 (1982).

30. San Antonio Independent School District v. Rodriguez, 411 U.S. 1, 37 (1973).

31. Our argument here is an abbreviated version of the account developed more fully in Sager, *Justice in Plainclothes* 95–97.

32. Religious Freedom Restoration Act of 1993, Pub. L. No. 103-141, 107 Stat. 1488 (codified as amended 42 U.S.C. §§ 2000bb—2000bb-4 [2004]).

33. U.S. Senate Committee on the Judiciary, *The Religious Freedom Restoration Act: Hearings on S. 2969*, 102d Cong., 2d sess., 1992, Senate Hearing 102–1076, p. 42 (statement of Mr. Thomas). *Scott* held that the Missouri Compromise was unconstitutional and that African-Americans were neither "persons" nor "citizens" within the meaning of the Constitution. For a brief study of the case, see Christopher L. Eisgruber, "The Story of *Dred Scott*: Originalism's Forgotten Past," in Michael C. Dorf, ed., *Constitutional Law Stories* (2004).

34. 42 U.S.C. § 2000bb(b)(1) (2004).

35. Laycock, "Conceptual Gulfs in *City of Boerne v. Flores*" 775.

36. Ibid. at 774.

37. Ibid.

38. Thomas C. Berg, "What Hath Congress Wrought? An Interpretive Guide to the Religious Freedom Restoration Act," 39 *Villanova Law Review* 1, 26, and n. 119 (1994).

39. Ira C. Lupu, "Why the Congress Was Wrong and the Court Was Right–Reflections on *City of Boerne v. Flores*," 39 *William and Mary Law Review* 793, 795 n. 10 (1997–98).

40. On the strength of the alliance and its impact on Congress, see ibid. at 795–802; Ira C. Lupu, "The Failure of RFRA," 20 *University of Arkansas at Little Rock Law Journal* 575, 577–585 (1998); Marci Hamilton, *God vs. the Gavel: Religion and the Rule of Law* 176–184 (2005).

41. RFRA provoked a spate of scholarly commentary. We criticized it before its enactment and again afterward. Christopher L. Eisgruber and Lawrence G. Sager, "Why the Religious Freedom Restoration Act Is Unconstitutional," 69 *New York University Law Review* 437 (1994). An early and especially good collection of articles by leading scholars appears in "The James R. Browning Symposium for 1994: The Religious Freedom Restoration Act," 56 *Montana Law Review* 1 (1995). For a more extensive though still not comprehensive list, see Daniel O. Conkle, "Congressional Alternatives in the Wake of *City of Boerne v. Flores:* The (Limited) Role of Congress in Protecting Religious Freedom from State and Local Infringement," 20 *University of Arkansas at Little Rock Law Journal* 633, 634 n. 8 (1998).

42. See generally Neil Devins, "How Not to Challenge the Court," 39 *William and Mary Law Review* 645 (1998). Clinton's comments are from "Remarks on Signing the Religious Freedom Restoration Act of 1993," 29 *Weekly Compilation of Presidential Documents* 2377 (Nov. 16, 1993) ("The power to reverse . . . by legislation, a decision of the United States Supreme Court, is a power that is rightly hesitantly and infrequently exercised by the United States Congress. But this is an issue in which that extraordinary measure was clearly called for").

43. "To say that a nondiscriminatory religious-practice exemption is . . . desirable . . . is not to say that . . . the appropriate occasions for its creation can be discerned by courts." 494 U.S. at 890. See also ibid. at 889 and n. 5 ("it is horrible to contemplate that federal judges will regularly balance against the importance of general laws the significance of religious practice").

44. Ibid. at 890.

45. 42 U.S.C. § 2000bb(a)(5) (2004) ("the compelling interest test as set forth in prior federal rulings is a workable test for striking sensible balances between religious liberty and competing prior governmental interests"). See also 42 U.S.C. § 2000bb(b)(1), which declared that one purpose of the act was to "restore the compelling interest test as set forth in Sherbert v. Verner . . . and Wisconsin v. Yoder . . . and to guarantee its application in all cases where religion is substantially burdened."

46. 42 U.S.C. § 2000bb-1 (2004).

47. City of Boerne v. Flores, 521 U.S. 507 (1997).

48. Ibid. at 529.

49. David Cole, "The Value of Seeing Things Differently," 1997 *Supreme Court Review* 31, 59–71; Michael W. McConnell, "Institutions and Interpretation: A Critique of *City of Boerne v. Flores,*" 111 *Harvard Law Review* 153, 184–189 (1997).

50. 521 U.S. at 536–537 (concurring opinion).

51. Ibid. at 533.

52. Ibid. at 535.

53. Ibid.

54. Gonzales v. O Centro Esperita Beneficente Uniao Do Vegetal, 126 S. Ct. 1211 (2006).

55. See, e.g., 21 C.F.R. § 1307.31 (1986); see also Native American Church of New York v. United States, 468 F. Supp. 1247 (S.D.N.Y. 1979).

56. 42 U.S.C. § 1996(b) (1).

57. 126 S. Ct. at 1222.

58. Oliver Thomas, who had previously compared *Smith* to the *Dred Scott* decision, now claimed that *Boerne* was "going to be remembered as the *Dred Scott* of church-state law." Laurie Goodstein, "Bitter over Ruling, Groups See Trouble for Minority Faiths," *Washington Post*, June 26, 1997, p. A1. The Religious Action Center of Reform Judaism invoked the same comparison. Frank J. Murray, "Justices Strike Down Law Used to Protect Faith," *Washington Times*, June 26, 1997, p. A1. Other overwrought statements about *Boerne* are collected in Lupu, "Why Congress Was Wrong and the Court Was Right" 793 n. 4.

59. Hamilton, *God vs. the Gavel* 181–182.

60. Pub. L. No. 106–274, 114 Stat. 803 (codified at 42 U.S.C. §§ 2000cc–2000cc-5 [2004]).

61. A Rhode Island district court had rejected a free exercise claim from a Hmong family in You Vang Yang v. Sturner, 750 F. Supp. 558, 560 (D.R.I. 1990). The case became a frequently discussed example in both press reports and congressional hearings. See, e.g., House Committee on the Judiciary, *Religious Liberty Protection Act of 1999*, 106th Cong., 1st sess., 1999, H.R. Report 106–219, pp. 12, 34 n. 5 (the "Religious Liberty Protection Act" died without a floor vote, but eventually evolved into RLUIPA).

62. Lupu, "The Failure of RFRA" 585–617.

63. See 42 U.S.C. §2000cc(2)(A) (2004) (Spending Clause) (providing that RLUIPA land-use provisions apply in any case in which "the substantial burden is imposed in a program or activity that receives Federal financial assistance, even if the burden results from a rule of general applicability"); ibid. at §2000cc(2)(B) (Commerce Clause invocation) (providing that RLUIPA land-use provisions apply in any case in which "the substantial burden affects, or removal of that substantial burden would affect, commerce with foreign nations, among the several States, or with Indian tribes, even if the burden results from a rule of general applicability").

64. Westchester Reform Temple v. Brown, 22 N.Y. 2d 488, 496–497 (1968) ("religious structures cannot be excluded, directly or indirectly, from residential zones. We have said that factors such as potential traffic hazards, effects on property values and noise and decreased enjoyment of neighboring proper-

ties cannot justify the exclusion of such structures"); see also Jewish Reconstructionist Synagogue, Inc. v. Roslyn Harbor, 38 N.Y. 2d 283 (1975) (holding that, under New York law, religious uses must be presumed to be beneficial).

65. As we saw in Chapter 3, these examples are real, not hypothetical. And there are many others; for a survey, see Hamilton, *God vs. the Gavel* 78–110.

66. The study appears as an appendix to Von G. Keetch and Matthew K. Richards, "The Need for Legislation to Enshrine Free Exercise in the Land Use Context," 32 *University of California at Davis Law Review* 725, 736–741 (1999).

67. Mark Chaves and William Tsitsos, "Are Congregations Constrained by Government? Empirical Results from the National Congregations Study," 42 *Journal of Church and State* 335, 341 (2000).

68. Douglas Laycock, "Theology Scholarships, the Pledge of Allegiance, and Religious Liberty: Avoiding the Extremes but Missing the Liberty," 118 *Harvard Law Review* 155, 211–212 (2004).

69. See, e.g., Bettina Krause et al., "Panel Discussion Reports," 32 *University of California at Davis Law Review* 811 (1999).

70. Eugene Volokh, "A Common-Law Model for Religious Exemptions," 46 *UCLA Law Review* 1465, 1492–1505 (1999).

71. Ibid. at 1487–88.

72. Volokh notes that he himself has some reservations about the way that "little RFRAs" have been drafted, precisely because they inappropriately prefer religious convictions over others. Ibid. at 1493.

Index